The Warning Carriers

1 *'High life at midnight', anon, circa 1765. In the middle of a street brawl, the assailant (who may have been defending himself from an earlier attempted robbery) has his pocket picked.*

The Warning Carriers

How messengers of The Goldsmiths' Company
warned the luxury trades of criminal activities
in eighteenth-century London

JUDY JOWETT

SILVER STUDIES
The Journal of the Silver Society
NUMBER 18

Editor: Vanessa Brett

A special issue of *Silver Studies*, the Journal of the Silver Society
Number 18

ISBN 0-9549144-1-4

Printed by Cromwell Press Ltd, Trowbridge, Wilts

Contents

2 Goldsmiths' Hall, circa 1692, by John Ward, watercolour on parchment.
The second Hall on this site, erected in 1634–36, was damaged in the Great Fire of 1666 and
again in 1681 when there was a fire in the Assay Office. It was pulled down in the late 1820s.
The route of each Walkman began here.

Acknowledgements

Firstly, my thanks must go to David Beasley, Librarian at Goldsmiths' Hall and his assistant, Jane Bradley, for their friendly co-operation in giving me access to the *Warning Carriers Walks* manuscript notebook and other ancient records of The Worshipful Company of Goldsmiths, and for generously providing images for this book.

We are lucky in London to have such diverse, in-depth and accessible resources for research and I am very grateful to the staff of several archive centres who have gone beyond the call of duty in helping me, particularly all three sections of Guildhall Library whose cheerful staff never failed to provide helpful suggestions and assistance. Ursula Carlyle (Archivist and Curator) at The Worshipful Company of Mercers and Dr Alex Buchanan at The Worshipful Company of Clothworkers granted me the privilege of searching their archives and Dr Tessa Murdoch's staff in the Victoria and Albert Museum Metalwork Department kept me cool while working there through a very hot summer. Hazel Forsyth (Curator, Post Medieval Studies) and Beverley Cook (Assistant Curator, Social and Working History Collections) at the Museum of London, both responded enthusiastically to my queries. Time spent investigating the 1749 Westminster Pollbook was more than halved by Peter Cameron's very generous gesture of letting me use his research and this is particularly acknowledged. I thank you all and the many others who listened to this story and contributed to it. I have discussed the project with many people whose advice and help in providing references has been invaluable, including Philippa Glanville, John Culme, Robert Barker, Eileen Goodway and Luke Schrager. Others, including Richard Edgcumbe at the Victoria and Albert Museum, David Thompson and Jeremy Evans at the British Museum, and Harry Williams-Bulkeley at Christie's, have kindly helped with illustrations.

It is the people behind the scenes who make the difference to the end result and in this respect I am extremely grateful to Grant Shipcott for painstakingly producing the maps and to Michael Sherratt for proof-reading. Simon Brett's artistry and attention to detail has resulted in the delightful Walkman image. However, it is the editor who bears the brunt of the work and the honours go to Vanessa Brett, whose tolerance and expertise have met every challenge with cheery determination.

Lastly, it is unlikely this investigation would have taken place without the support of the Silver Society research committee led by Philippa Glanville, and its benefactors. Philippa's enthusiastic encouragement has always been reassuringly present. I very much appreciate the opportunity I have had in undertaking this research, which has proved fascinating and entertaining, and will hopefully slot a tiny fragment into the jigsaw of London's history.

Judy Jowett

The Silver Society is grateful to The Worshipful Company of Goldsmiths for financial assistance towards the cost of this publication.

Illustration acknowledgements

British Museum 25 (Heal 67.156), 55–58, 60, 62
Christie's 28, 35–39, 41, 43, 45, 49–50, 53–54
The Worshipful Company of Goldsmiths 2, 4–17, 24, 26–27, 33, inside cover
Guildhall Library 1, 3, 19–21, 23, 29, 32
C. Hoare & Co 30
Sotheby's 34, 40, 42, 44, 46–48, 51–52
Victoria and Albert Museum 22, 26, 59
Private collection 18, 31

Illustrations on pp133–37

BM: British Museum; V&A: Victoria and Albert Museum; C: Christie's; S: Sotheby's (L: London; NY: New York)

33 The Worshipful Company of Goldsmiths	45 CNY, 11 April 2003 lot 305	57 BM, CAI-2352
34 SL	46 SL	58 BM, CAI-634
35 CL, July 1936 lot 134	47 SL, 28 Jan 1965 lot 163	59 V&A, M.61-1959, given by the family of
36 CL, 22 Nov 2000 lot 175	48 SL, 8 June 1999 lot 94	William Macdonald Matthews of
37 CNY, 14 April 2005 lot 259	49 CNY, 24 Oct 2002 lot 297	Tunbridge Wells
38 CL, 1 Dec 2004 lot 675	50 CL, 1 Dec 2004 lot 704	60 BM, CAI-631
39 CL, 12 June 2002 lot 106A	51 SL, 24 March 1960 lot 13	61 SL 9 June 1977 lot 227,
40 SL, 4 June 1998 lot 233	52 SL, 14 Oct 1954 lot 149	courtesy Richard Edgcumbe
41 CNY, 14 April 2005 lot 258	53 CL, 1 Dec 2004 lot 678	62 BM, 1912, 11-7.1
42 SL, 28 Jan 1965 lot 120	54 CL, 14 June 2005 lot 196	
43 CL, 14 June 2005 lot 218	55 BM, CAI-1867	
44 SL, 9 April 1959 lot 150	56 BM, CAI-1807	

The wood engraving on the cover is by Simon Brett, his © 2005. Whilst every effort has been made to portray the image of a Walkman as accurately as possible, no historical records survive to give a description of what the men would have worn, other than the fact that each wore a gown of murrey, with a badge of The Goldsmiths' Company.

Maps are reproduced from John Rocque's 1746 map of London, kindly provided by Motco Enterprises. The maps are available on CD rom (www.motco.com).

The maps have been adapted for this publication by Grant Shipcott.

Dates are written in the following styles:
- 1722/23   Assay year
- 1722/3   Calendar year : 1 January – 24 March, before 1752
- 1722–23   More than one calendar year

TEMPLE BARR   The West-Side

3 View of the West side of Temple Bar, engraving by Johannes de Ram, circa 1700.
Below: detail of maps on pp42 and 45.

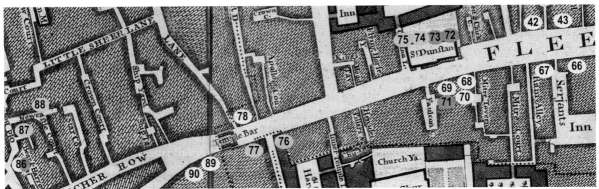

A useful Advertisement, for any Persons who shall have the misfortune of losing any Bank Notes, Sword Blade Notes, Goldsmiths or other Notes for Money, or any Diamonds, Jewels, Rings, Plate, Watches, & c.

Upon Application to the Beadle of the Goldsmiths Company at Goldsmiths Hall in Foster Lane, you may have Warnings printed and delivered, in three Hours time, at all the Goldsmiths, Jewellers, Brokers, and Watchmakers Shops, within the Bills of Mortality; to prevent and forbid the taking such Notes in payment, and desiring them to stop and detain such Goods. The Printer and Messengers always attending to dispatch the same. The Charge thereof if delivered to Goldsmiths only is 11s. 8d. if to Jewellers, Brokers, and Watchmakers is 1 l. 3s. 4d. It having been found by long Experience to be the readiest method for recovering Notes or Goods lost.

N.B. That all Goldsmiths, Watchmakers, Ec. are oblig'd to enter their Names and places of abode in the Assay Office at Goldsmiths Hall; whereby the Beadle and Messengers of that Company and no others can give so speedy notice as aforesaid.

Advertisement issued by the Goldsmiths' Company, 1722.

1

A notebook titled
1744 Warning Carriers Walks

*An explanation of what the notebook contains and the terms 'warning', 'carriers'
and 'walks'. The story of the Walks taken from The Goldsmiths' Company archives,
and their impact on the luxury goods trade, crime and criminals*

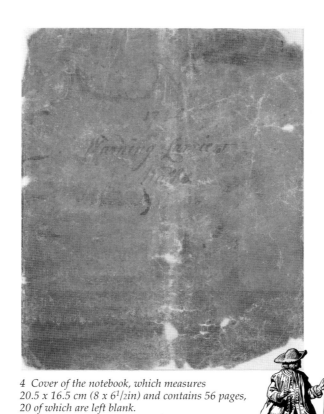

4 *Cover of the notebook, which measures
20.5 x 16.5 cm (8 x 6¹/₂in) and contains 56 pages,
20 of which are left blank.*

THIS IS AN INVESTIGATION into the contents of an eighteenth-century notebook. Similar in size and shape to an old school exercise book, it has *1744 Warning Carriers Walks* inscribed on its darkened marbled cover. The pages contain lists of names written in several hands which, on analysis, lead us to crime and punishment, luxury and poverty, pawn-broking, banking, retailing and advertising in eighteenth-century London.

What were the Walks? Who organised them and compiled the lists? What was their real purpose? Did they have any significance within the activities of the Goldsmiths' Company, in whose archives the book is kept? Research into the book's subject matter and the diverse personalities involved has proved very revealing.

The notebook seems to have been compiled by a newly appointed Beadle of the Goldsmiths' Company, initially as a means of administering the Walks, and was very probably used by a subsequent Beadle as an aide-memoire. The title indicates its principal contents: lists of those whose establishments were visited by Goldsmiths' Company Walkmen (messengers or carriers) who distributed warnings (Notices) of lost and stolen property. The lists were probably written in the early 1730s and the date 1744 on the cover is misleading, for the book was clearly in use before and after that date.[1]

5 *The Queen's fee for warning; extract from the 1559 Wardens Accounts and Court Minutes Book.*

There was a system for distributing warnings as early as the sixteenth century. Goldsmiths' Company records from 1559 describe 'the queens fee for warning'

> Also whereas of ancient custom there is yearly a rent fee paid by ye maistr. of ye Jewelhouse for ye king or queens warning to ye use of those of the poor officers of this Companie that take pains and travail about the same warning: that is to say, ye Clerk, ye Beadle and ye 2 brokers of this Companie.[2]

Records also exist which state that 'every sovereign from Henry VIII to Charles I paid an annual reward to the beadles of Goldsmiths' Hall for searching the shops of the London guildsmen for plate stolen from Court'.[3] At what stage the warnings ceased to be only for the King's Jewel House and entered the public arena is not known.[4]

On 11 June 1652 John Evelyn wrote in his diary that he had

> 500 tickets printed and dispers'd by an officer of Goldsmiths' Hall

in an endeavour to retrieve his stolen property, which in the main was successful.[5]

In 1728 Christopher Clark stated in court that, having been robbed of a quantity of silver tableware and furniture, together with a cloak and other goods, he

> went to Goldsmiths-hall, and caus'd his Plate to be advertis'd by Description, and the Advertisements distributed to the several Silver-Smiths and Pawn-brokers about Town…[6]

6 Flyleaf of the notebook (right: transcription).
See fig 54 on p134 for a tea caddy bearing the mark of Samuel Wood, London 1754/55.

The Box wich is usualy kept by the prime Warden
is lodg[d] in y[e] hands of Joseph Martin, Esq[r] Lom[d] street
by the order of Mr Sam[l] Wood y[e] now prime Warden
June y[e] 17th 1763

*Warning Carriers Walks containing the Names
and Places of abode of Bankers Refiners*

1. ~~Abodes of~~ Goldsmiths, jewellers Watchmakers Toymen
Salesmen and Pawnbrokers to whom warnings should be delivered
~~Pawnbrokers, Salesmen and Flatters in the different Walks~~
N.B. Single warnings for Bank notes etc. lost are delivered to
Bankers Goldsmiths and Jewellers only

Warning Carriers	1744	Double	Single
John Watts - late Gresham		380	190
John Waggett, late Ben: Gardner - late Bulstrode		160	80
John Burgis, late Weatherhead		240	120
Joseph Collins, late Jenkins, late Hopkins, late Holtom		220	110
A Double Warning		1000	500

Clearly this system of dispersing vital information was well established and widely known to be speedy and reliable. It drew together Goldsmiths' Hall, a wide variety of tradesmen and the general public, from nobility to rambunctious 'lower sorts'. How often the Walks were undertaken and how long they took to complete is uncertain, but some light is shed on this below.

1 Lodged with the *Warning Carriers Walk Book* is a folded, undated sheet written in yet another hand which is unrelated to the notebook. This requests payment of £2 for 'the extra duty perform'd (but not as demand) to the Gentlemen Wardens Consideration'. From Ed Toulman, the paper sets out names and addresses of approximately 20 widows he has visited on two occasions on Goldsmiths' Company business and delivered 'Sundry letters'. A freeman and 'gownsman' (almsman), in 1810, Toulman, aged 62, was elected to the office of Staffsman. It appears that the work performed took place after 1810 – there is no indication that he was paid. Goldsmiths' Company Court Minute Book (hereafter GCCB) vol 22, p53. In the early 1740s

payment for delivery of a letter / warning / 'carrying Gowns' was 1s (Clothworkers' Company, Wardens Chits or Wardens Receipted Bill 1740–41 to 1744–45) and 1s 6d by early 1790 (Corporation of London, Guildhall Library, (hereafter GL) MS 5859; Fishmongers' Company, *Beadles' Account Book*, 1793-4).

2 GCCB, vol 8 1557-77, K, Part 1, p117.

3 A.J. Collins, *The 1574 Inventory of the Jewels and Plate of Queen Elizabeth*, British Museum 1955, pp142-3, 153-4, 156. Between the accession of Elizabeth I (1558) and 1596, 15,600oz of plate had disappeared, mostly from 'the scullery', ie through royal household use, and as much as a quarter of this was written off as having been 'stollen and embeasled

by vntrewe [untrue] persons as well as gret Feastes and marriages, banquets and Progresses, as other ways'. The remainder was lost through 'the disorder and insecurity of the Tudor and Stuart palaces' and the Jewel House, which were a target for thieves. Losses also occurred through fire, pawning by the sovereign, removal abroad to ambassadorial residences and, because plate was often lent for prestigious events, retention by light-fingered borrowers. Although signed for, the value was often so great that little redress from the culprits was possible. Many of these items would have been advertised through the warnings and the annual rent fee paid by the Master of the Jewel House to the Goldsmiths' Company would have been very worthwhile when at

least some of the smaller, pilfered items were traced. The disbursement of this fee is authorised in numerous warrants for Jewel House payments. I am indebted to Philippa Glanville for this reference.

4 There is evidence that in the early seventeenth century the system was changing. Clearly by 1652 (see the Evelyn quotation below) the warning system was available to the general public. It was recorded in 1614 that no warnings for lost plate (except for the King's plate) be issued. This was followed in 1629, during the years when Charles I was plundering the Jewel House plate to try to offset his debts, by an order that 'no warnings to be in future signed by the Clerk or the Beadle, and no one to claim that office as a right, except the King'. Sir Walter S.

Prideaux, *Memorials of the Goldsmiths' Company being Gleanings from their Records Between the Years 1335 and 1815*, private circulation, vol 1 pp 125, 146; Collins (as note 3) pp175 (note i), 179.

5 M. Rickards, *Encyclopaedia of Ephemera*, 2000, p273, which also states that Notices were printed three or four to a sheet.

6 Old Bailey Proceedings June 2004 (www.oldbailey-online.co.uk) (hereafter OBP), December 1728, t17281204-33 (William Mathews accused).

7 Locations of the parish records used for this research can be found on p141 and an explanation of how the parish collectors seem to have operated on p82. It appears from the many Old Bailey trials and from my enquiries of other livery companies that the Goldsmiths' Walkman's dispersal system was not used elsewhere, except possibly by Hoare's Bank (see p106). Other 'Walks' for the collection of quarterages / rents can be found. These do not, however, trespass beyond the bounds of the livery company in question. The Worshipful Company of Clockmakers has five Walks dated 1733/34/35: City, North, East, South West and later New. Each Walk has several collectors. Familiar watch and clockmakers' names are listed but without addresses – GLMS 2715/4.

8 C. Spence, *London in the 1690s A Social Atlas*, 2000, p162, fig5.29.

9 Not the better-known Brick Lane in Spitalfields.

The lists detailing the Walks

The flyleaf of the book [6] is inscribed *Warning Carriers Walks containing the Names and Places of abode of Bankers Refiners ... Goldsmiths, Jewellers, Watchmakers, Toymen, Salesmen and Pawnbrokers to whom warnings should be delivered*. Following pages list three Walks undertaken by Mr Holtom, Mr Weatherhead and Mr Bulstrode. Their names, together with their successors and 'John Watts, late Gresham', also appear on the flyleaf. The Walks are set out in columns in eighteenth-century script, now faded, and entries are clean and without corrections. These pages are sandwiched between others bearing less formal, later annotations. The flyleaf and the Walk listings occupy the first 28 pages of the book.

The columns in the lists tell us
♦ A number for each property on the three routes (or Walks) undertaken by the messengers, who were called Walkmen (or carriers)
♦ The names and addresses of the businesses visited
♦ The trade of each establishment visited
♦ A breakdown of the type of trades in order that the Beadle might administer the Walks efficiently.

Column 1

The premises visited were allocated consecutive numbers by the lists' compiler so the route of each Walk can be followed.[9] It is not unusual to find set routes to guide messengers through the metropolis – indeed those collecting parish taxes used a similar system.[7] Goldsmiths' Walkmen did not trespass into each other's territory nor did they follow the same routes as the parish collectors. Taking into account the fact that premises were crowded together, without street numbering (which began hesitatingly in the mid-1760s), and connected by notoriously unpleasant alleyways, it can be assumed that the Walkmen, and possibly an authoritarian Beadle, were keen to keep their journeys concise.

By superimposing the Walkmen's itineraries onto John Rocque's 1746 map of London (see pp38–79) and with the aid of the parish records, it is possible to see where tradesmen were located, even if not precisely. The maps indicate an approximate position in a street and confirm how trades, nationalities and different levels of society clustered or scattered themselves across London at the time.[8]

The Walks are an average of five miles long, with Holtom having 202 calls to make, Weatherhead 201 and Bulstrode, with the longest Walk of nearly eight miles, having 146 premises – 549 addresses in all. The Walks started at Goldsmiths' Hall. Holtom (pp40–51) went along the side roads and passages of Fleet Street and the Strand to Charing Cross and Westminster. Weatherhead (pp52–67) wended his way through Smithfield, Holborn, Seven Dials, Soho, Leicester Fields (now Leicester Square) and Mayfair to Tyburn (now Marble Arch) and finally south to St James's. Bulstrode (pp68–79) walked east through the Barbican, Bishopsgate, Spitalfields, Ratcliffe Highway as far as Shadwell and back through Wapping past the Tower, Houndsditch, Moorfields, eventually reaching Brick Lane just north of Old Street.[9]

Parish records show that once the Walkmen had left Goldsmiths' Hall only a handful of addresses in Holtom's Walk and one tradesman in Bulstrode's Walk came within the old City boundary of wall and gates, leaving the heart of the City unaccounted for. This poses the question: were the rest of the City and Southwark not part of this scheme? In support of the assumption that there must have been another Walk covering the remainder of the City, an Old Bailey trial report of 1730

7 Notice no11773 dated 1729.
Richard Gines, in Lombard Street, was in the City and so would not have been visited by any of the three Walkmen in the notebook.

states that a Jasper Robins

> went to Mr. Langton's, a Goldsmith, in Lombard-Street, and desired him to let him see his File of Advertisements, … then he went to Mr. Barker's, a Goldsmith, to whom the Advertisement directed, … Mr. Barker depos'd, That the Prosecutor having desired him to get an Advertisement printed, according to the Custom of the Trade, he did, …[10]

Lombard Street is between the Royal Exchange and Mansion House – well inside the City. Notices dated around 1727-30 (slightly before the period of the Walks listed in the book) reveal the names of four (rather than three) previous Walkmen: Joseph Boucher, J. [Jacob] Ray, [John] Hoseman, Tho. Wright – this also suggests a missing Walk (see p33).[11] If the City and Southwark were included in the scheme, why do they not appear in the book? If they were the Beadle's territory, perhaps he did not need to note down his own circuit.

Elizabethan records also tell us that the Goldsmiths' Company Beadle was

> to warn his circuit himself … unless he be otherwise lett, then he to appoint an almsman in his stead[12]

At the time of Jasper Robins' advertisement (above) Benjamin Pyne Snr, the Goldsmiths' Beadle, was approximately 75 years old and in poor health. The fact that none of the four names on the Notices above is the Beadle's must mean that Pyne had appointed an almsman to walk his circuit for him.[13] Figures compiled in 1720 indicated that 'in the City' there was a total of 954 traders in gold and silver wares, including watchmakers, toymen and pawnbrokers.[14] The flyleaf of the notebook [6] suggests that a fourth Walk covering the City was undertaken by Gresham and then Watts.

Columns 2 and 4

The second and fourth columns give tradesmen's names and addresses visited. Many of those listed would have been known to the Goldsmiths' Company not only through their craft but also for the part they played as senior officers of the Company. Some of these businesses would have been household names at the time, such as Parkes & King, watchmakers of Newgate Street; Mr Wildy at his 'Great Toy-Shop, the Corner of Ludgate-Street' with his wife, who 'died very rich' and who were neighbours of Henry Hurt at the Golden Salmon, St Paul's Churchyard; 'honest Geo. Graham – Tompion Graham' on Fleet Bridge; William Hart 'at a Fan Shop' at the Grasshopper in Fleet Street; members of the Pinchbeck family. Denis Cherack[Chirac] of York Buildings, Strand, in 1736 made and fashioned 'a Coronet for her Royal Highness the Princess of Wales' and lent the 'Brilliant Diamonds set therein' all for the sum of £120.[15] Several establishments were owned by men who diversified their wealth into property – both in town and country and these, together with bankers (Hoare, Child and Drummond) linked the City to Westminster. Calls were made to offices, for example to 'The Charitable Corporations, Spring Gardens' and the 'Tellers Office, Westminster Hall', emphasising the association between Goldsmiths' Company and The Exchequer.[16] Whereas this area of town was of a retail nature, further north and west were craftsmen who actually supplied the goods. Here were the second generation Huguenots – Paul Crispin [sic] of Compton Street, Soho, the jeweller Dupain of Lombard Street [presumably Court] Seven Dials, Paul Delamerie [sic] of Windmill Street, Peter Archambo in Hemmings Row and many

10 OBP, April 1730, t17300408-63 (George Downing, William Downing accused).

11 All four men were recipients of a variety of Goldsmiths' Company charities and Hoseman was an unsuccessful applicant to become Beadle in 1728. GCCB, vol 1726–36 13 p78.

12 As note 2.

13 In 1746 and 1748 respectively, James Burgess and David Nash state in Old Bailey trials that they are Goldsmiths' Company Beadles. Presumably they were standing in for the ageing Beadle, Robert Jenkes. OBP, May 1746, t17460515-10 (Jane King accused), December 1748, t17481207-25 (William Thomson accused). Similarly John Watts, late Gresham, is listed on the flyleaf of the notebook [6]; both these names appear in the Goldsmiths' records from around 1755 (see note 84). The three named Walks were being undertaken by

other almsmen at this time, so that Watts, making a fourth walkman, could have been covering the City Walk for Samuel Cawthorn (the current Beadle) who, it is recorded, 'is afflicted with Body Flux and violent Rheumatic Pains'. Cawthorn resigned in 1770 due to ill health and with 'weakened … sight and hearing'. GCCB vol 17 1767–77 p115. See the panel on p33.

14 J.S. Forbes, *Hallmark*, London 1998, p210.

15 National Archives (formerly PRO), E.404/246, f82, 14 September 1736.

16 'The Charitable Corporations' is listed as a banker/broker; the 'Tellers Office' is not designated. It is presumed that these two important premises were included in the itinerary to receive routine Goldsmiths' Company business notices and communications regarding their charities as well as any applicable Warning Notices.

Joseph Boucher

Numb. 11778.   **Oct. 6. 1729.**

LOST on Wednesday Oct. 1. 1729, a large sized Gold Repeating Watch, Name *William King*, in a chased Case plain Bottom, with a Gold Chain, three Seals set in Gold, one of them a Cornelian, with a Head in a Heart, one with the Stone out, the other Fancy forgot; as also a Gold Ring with a small square Diamond in the Middle, with three others at each Side. Whoever brings the said Watch, Chain, and Ring, to Baker's Coffee-House in Exchange-Alley, shall have *Five Guineas* Reward, and no Questions ask'd; or proportionable for any Part.
BENJAMIN PYNE, Beadle, at Goldsmiths-Hall.

8 Notice no11778 dated 1729. Joseph Boucher was a Walkman in the years before the notebook.

others. In Clerkenwell, London's watchmaking centre, were listed several watchmakers who appear to have had adjacent premises given as 'broker'.[17] Whereas Holtom's Walk covered a smart and wealthy area, Weatherhead's territory seems to have been a close-knit, mutually sustaining community within crowded alleys, sometimes offering only a precarious existence. The easterly Walk had craftsmen clinging to the periphery of town, with only a clutch of goldsmiths and watchmakers further out in Wapping and Shadwell, where generally pawnbrokers flourished in this fluid area of shipping and trade.

There are several names listed, mainly from allied trades, which are difficult to identify, such as Flippo [?Phelipeau]; Leopard [?Le Parr/Leaper]; Oman [?Osman/Homan/Orme]; Shoppo [?Shapeau] and Wessea [?Wellesey/Wellington/Welles]; and improbable names such as Mr Highstreet and [Imacer] Mr Eyemaker. Phonetic spellings also raise problems, such as Jeroet/Jaroet which translate as Gerrard; Wyatt for White. However 'by the Sheep Pens' is a legitimate address and pinpoints Hartley precisely.

Each surname is suffixed with the title Mr or Mrs although at times it is difficult to distinguish between the two. In places research has confirmed which gender is indicated because some are known today to have been important women silversmith/retailers. Few women are mentioned in Holtom and Weatherhead's Walks but records confirm that wives or servant girls were often left to mind the shop. On her husband's death a widow might register a mark in order to continue his business, so safeguarding her livelihood.[18] In a trial in 1768 a silversmith's wife states

> My husband has been very ill for twelve months: I have attended the business more than he latterly: and there are marks upon many of the things of my making.[19]

Pawnbrokers predominate in Bulstrode's Walk, which covered the notoriously poor areas of Spitalfields, Ratcliffe Highway and Wapping wharves, and this may account for the higher percentage of female proprietors, pawnbroking being an easily established and acceptable occupation for women at the time.[20]

It has not yet been established whether those taking part in the warnings scheme applied for their premises to be included, whether they had a particular connection with the Hall, or if a subscription was paid for the service. Those listed in the Walks do not comprise a comprehensive list of craftsmen working at the time. It is curious that some known silversmiths, who entered their marks at Goldsmiths' Hall, do not feature in the notebook.

The list on pp81–129 enables the reader to check the names that appear in the Walks against entries in Grimwade and Heal.[21] A separate list has not been made of those who do appear in the Walks but not in these publications, or vice versa.

Column 3

The abbreviations for the trades set out in the third column are:

- (B) Brokers[22] or Pawnbrokers
- (G) Goldsmiths (Also G/J and G/TM: Goldsmiths/Jewellery makers and Goldsmiths/Toymen – counted as goldsmiths)
- (J) Jewellers
- (TM) Toymen
- (W) Watchmakers

One of the lists was subsequently amended by the addition of other

17 Weatherhead's Walk nos44-45 (White); nos74-76 (Clark); nos90-91 (Harrison); nos101-103 (Ganderoon); nos119-120 (Wright); nos121-122 (Butterfield).

18 Mrs Elizabeth Blisset (Bisset) [BULSTRODE NO117] of Wapping, having taken over from her husband, Isaac, on his death in 1729, appears in the Walks. Listed as a goldsmith, her establishment in the midst of the tough, bustling docks was significant enough to be marked on Rocque's map. Not only did she pay 5s Land Tax but in 1734 contributed a further lump sum of £100. Her business acumen and the strength of character required to continue operating in such an area can only be imagined. For women in the goldsmith's trade see P. Glanville and J.F. Goldsborough, *Women Silversmiths 1685-1845, Works from the Collection of The National Museum of Women in the Arts*, Washington, D.C, 1990, pp13-28.

19 OBP, 7 December 1768 t17681207–9, John Andrew Martin accused. The reference to marks does not necessarily refer to hallmarks as many small items were exempt. She may have scratched the items in order to identify them.

20 There are 31 addresses in Ratcliffe Highway, Shadwell and Wapping, 19 are pawnbrokers (13 registered for Land Tax).

21 A.G. Grimwade, *London Goldsmiths 1697-1830, their marks and lives*, 3rd edn, London 1990, is the standard reference work for marks of the period covered; Ambrose Heal, *The London Goldsmiths 1200-1800*, Cambridge 1935, lists trade cards, names, addresses and dates. Both works give biographical material of goldsmiths.

22 This implies a negotiator/intermediary's role between the Goldsmiths' Company and craftsmen. (see note 23). Definitions alter over the years but the term 'broker' in respect of the Walks should be understood as a person who handled second-hand goods, either as pledges or for sale, usually pawnbrokers/auctioneers. They were not 'Sworn Brokers' who were freemen, licensed by the Corporation of London, acting as middlemen between merchants dealing in commodities (*Sworn Brokers' Archives* leaflet, Corporation of London Record Office (hereafter CLRO)). A late fourteenth-century Goldsmiths' Company record, when a goldsmith was expelled from the Company, mentions that 'the company's brokers [may not] display to him or sell any thing whatsoever that pertains to the said mystery on pain of losing their job for ever'. See L. Jefferson, *Wardens' Accounts and Court Minute Books of the Goldsmiths' Mystery of London, 1334-1446*, The Boydell Press, Woodbridge 2003, p393.

9 Page from the notebook showing the start of Weatherhead's Walk.

Column 1	Column 2	Column 3	Column 4	Column 5	
1	Mr Hutton	G	Goswell Street	1	[first goldsmith to receive a Notice]
2	Mr Makin	B	Do	1	[first broker to receive a Notice]
3	Mr Harrison	B	Do	2	[second broker to receive a Notice]
4	Mr Freeman	W	Charterhouse Square	1	[first watchmaker to receive a Notice]
5	Mr Bowman	B	Do Street	3	[third broker to receive a Notice]
6	Mr Cole	B	Long Lane	4	[fourth broker to receive a Notice]
7	Mr Cartwright	G	Do	2	[second goldsmith to receive a Notice]
8	Mr Cragg	G	Duck Lane	3	[third goldsmith to receive a Notice]
9	Mr Marquai	J	Do	1	[first jeweller to receive a Notice]
10	Mr Lilley	G	Do	4	[fourth goldsmith to receive a notice]

10 Extract from the notebook showing the totals of each trade in Weatherhead's walk. The fourth total is dated 1744, the year that is shown on the cover of the notebook.

trades, namely flatters, refiners and salesmen (see below). It is clear that by 1740 establishments such as Child, Hoare and Drummond classified themselves as bankers although the Walkmen's lists refer to them as goldsmiths. Trades at the time were still intertwined, and goldsmiths and silversmiths incorporated pawnbroking into their business.[23]

Column 5

The final column gives a real clue as to the purpose of the Walks – the issuing of printed information called Warnings or Notices.[24] Each address was given a consecutive number according to its trade so that it is possible to see how many Notices were required for delivery to each trade.

To clarify this, the start of Weatherhead's Walk is analysed on p17, with an added column on the right to assist the reader.[9]

Individual Walks are totalled to show the number of premises to be visited, followed by a breakdown of trades, each of which has inscribed against it the number of Notices required to be sent out to that trade. Only Weatherhead's is totalled more than once.[10] Of his four totals, the first relates to the premises set out in the book, ie 201 addresses. It is suggested that the second, third and fourth totals refer to subsequent phases of the Walks as they include flatters, refiners or salesmen, trades that are not mentioned originally. The added information does not include names and addresses. It is the fourth of Weatherhead's totals that is dated 1744. His four totals, 201 (original Walk), 254 (including pawnbrokers and salesmen), 244 (including flatters and salesmen) and finally 196 in 1744 (including salesmen), record an arc of activity the cause of which is suggested later in this introduction. It is important to note where '1744' appears since there are other pointers that suggest an earlier origin of the book.

It was easy, therefore, for the Beadle to consult the end of each Walk to see how many Notices to have printed for each trade category. For example for Weatherhead's Walk the Beadle would have printed 61 identical Notices relating, perhaps, to stolen plate or a missing bank note, one for each of the 61 goldsmiths (including bankers) to be visited by Weatherhead. Lost or 'dropt' items such as watches, jewellery, snuff boxes, gems, etc, all came within the scope of the remaining trades so he would print 140 identical Notices for delivery to each appropriate address, ie 22 for jewellers, 41 for watchmakers and 77 for brokers/pawnbrokers – total 140. The Company could therefore operate a two-tier system for circulating Notices: for distribution to goldsmiths only, designated 'single', the fee was 11s 8d, but if the Notice was to go to every address listed (goldsmiths, bankers, jewellers, toymen, watchmakers and brokers/pawnbrokers) the cost would be 'double' at £1 3s 4d. The Beadle wrote 'double' or 'single' on the Notices to indicate to the Walkman what he was to do and what payment was due. [12–14] If each of the tradesmen on the three Walks was to be notified then the Beadle needed 549 Notices all bearing the same information. Jotted calculations relating to 'double' and 'single' Notices are also written on the flyleaf of the book but it is unclear how these high, rounded figures fit into the scheme of things. The considerable charges probably precluded use of the system for all except valuable items.[25]

In 1722 the Goldsmiths' Company took steps to promote the Warning Carriers system by having printed on the back of an official trial summary of the Old Bailey Proceedings a 'useful Advertisement'. It clearly sets out who can benefit, what action to take, the range of items and area covered, speed, reliability and cost.[26][p10]

11 Extract from the notebook recording the print run required for Summons cards (invitations) to officers to attend functions at Goldsmiths' Hall.

Other information in the book

A further seven pages of the notebook (the final 20 pages are left blank) seem unrelated to the Walks but appear to confirm that this is a record put together for reference. Four pages detail the print run for Summons cards (invitations) to officers to attend functions at Goldsmiths' Hall.[11] These were ordered from printers with areas left blank for completion by the Beadle – as the administrative staff at Goldsmiths' Hall do today. The inducement of the Hall's hearty hospitality did not always produce an instant response, necessitating repeat summonses. The record, covering the period May 1747 to April 1753, shows the amount of stationery required for the summoning of routine meetings of Courts of Assistants and Wardens, other committees and the issuing of rent receipts. In 1750 Sir John Blachford (Goldsmith), took over from the elected Lord Mayor, Sir Samuel Pennant, who had died as a result of gaol fever (a type of typhoid), resulting in only a six-month term of office. Sir John completed Pennant's term without the normal ceremony, an event which would have produced considerably greater stationery requirements.[27]

Lists of Wardens and committee members required to attend 'ye Trial of ye Diett' on 28 May 1763, 1765 and 1770 are written in different handwriting on the following three pages and are signed by Samuel Cawthorn, Beadle. As expected, the names appearing here are those of well-documented senior officers of the Goldsmiths' Company whose

23 It is recorded from the fourteenth century that 'The Goldsmiths Company and its members, even in this early period appear to have acted as bankers and pawnbrokers. They received pledges not only of plate, but of other articles, such as cloth of gold and pieces of napery'. Prideaux, (as note 4), Introduction, p xviii.

24 Collins *Concise Dictionary of the English Language*, 2nd edn 1988 , gives 'Warning' as an archaic word for 'Notice' and carries no implication of threat.

25 A 2004 value for £1 in

1720 is £83.37, *Bank of England's Retail Price Index*, August 2004 (excluding property and wages).

26 It may be that by selecting a route including jewellers, watchmakers, toymen and brokers only (ie excluding goldsmiths and bankers), distributions were also made at the 'single' rate of 11s 8d. See **[13, 24]**. GL, Proceedings of the Old Bailey, September 1722, (OBP, a17220907-1). I am indebted to Robert Barker for this reference.

27 CLRO, Lord Mayors' biographies.

Numb. 11746. *Hoseman Double*

May 13. 1729.

WHereas a Porter did laſt Night about Ten o' Clock, by Miſtake, deliver two Bundles and a Band-Box, containing the things following, viz. a Ground Bruſſels Laced Head with four Lappets, a Handkerchief and Ruffles of the ſame; as alſo another Suit of Dreſs'd Night Cloaths, with a Scollop Macklin Edging about half an Inch deep, a plain Cambrick Handkerchief, three Shirts mark'd, viz. two with a P. M. and the other with an L. five Gulgee Handkerchiefs mark'd, viz. four with P. M. and the other with an L. a Green Italian Luteſtring Gown and Petticoat, a Brocaded Luteſtring Night Gown ſtriped and flowered upon a white Ground, a white Sattin Quilted Petticoat, a white Callico Quilted Petticoat, a white Cambrick Apron, three Stocks, one Turnover, a Diaper Table-Cloth mark'd P. M. and a Fan with the Story of the Sacrifice of Iphigenia, painted on a Leather Mount, with ſeveral other things. Whoever brings them to Mr. Stephen Wiggin, at Baker's Coffee-houſe in Exchange-Alley, ſhall have Five Guineas Reward, or proportionable for any Part, and no Queſtions ask'd; and alſo the like Reward to any Perſon who can give any Information thereof.

BENJAMIN PYNE, Beadle, at Goldſmiths-Hall.

Numb. 11711. *Tho: Wright Single*

December 6. 1728.

DRopt out of a Lady's Ear, on Wedneſday or Thurſday, in the Hay Market or thereabout, a Night Ear Ring, ſet with three Brilliants weighing about three Grains, the Corner of the Bottom Stone a little broke. Whoever will bring it to Mr. Jacob Levy, jun. Jeweller at the Upper End of the Hay Market; or, at Chadwell's Coffee houſe behind the Royal Exchange, ſhall have Two Guineas Reward. If offer'd to be pawn'd, ſold, or valued, you are deſired to ſtop it, and give Notice as above, and you ſhall have the ſame Reward.

BENJAMIN PYNE, Beadle, at Goldſmiths-Hall.

Numb. 11736. *J. Ray Double*

March 14. 1728.

STole this Morning being the 14th of March, out of the Houſe of Mr. Chriſtopher Randel, a Gardener living near the Blue Anchor in S. Mary Magdalen's Pariſh Bermondſey, a full Quart Silver Tankard, mark'd on the Handle C. M. Value about Ten Pounds, with three Silver Spoons with different Marks. If offer'd to be pawn'd, ſold, or valued, you are deſired to ſtop them and the Party, and give Notice to Mr. Randel as above, and you ſhall have Two Guineas Reward for the Whole, or for the Tankard alone.

NB. To be Lett, An old and well-accuſtom'd Goldſmiths Shop, ſituate in Holborn, next Door to the Croſs Keys Tavern, over againſt Hatton Garden. Enquire at the aforeſaid Shop and know farther.

BENJAMIN PYNE, Beadle, at Goldſmiths-Hall.

12 (above) Notice no11746 dated 1729. 'Double' indicates that the notice would have gone to all the trades (see p18). Hoseman, like Wright and Boucher was a Walkman before the period covered by the notebook.
13 (above right) Notice no11711 dated 1728. Thomas Wright (see p33) would have distributed this notice to goldsmiths and bankers.
14 (below right) Notice no11736 dated 1728 also advertises a shop to let.

28 Forbes, (as note 14) pp40-1.

29 Ibid, pp305–8.

30 See p29 for an example involving marks; however many newspaper advertisements which have a description such as 'marked with' may actually refer to engraved ownership initials. See p31.

31 Original Indentures held at the CLRO (accessed through Alphabet of Freedoms Records) show similar holes where they have been filed.

32 The exception is Notice no12610 (see inside cover and [63]) issued in 1737. To establish the system's age, if 87 (average number of Notices per year in the late 1720s) is divided into the lowest serial number available, ie, 11563, a period of 133 years has elapsed since inauguration; that takes it as far back as 1591. It must be presumed that 87 Notices per year is high in view of disruptions to the service over the years.

33 (OBP, t17880507-36 (Michael Hoy accused). There were several reasons for this. For a time, after 1775, the percentage of craftsmen who were Goldsmiths' Company officers dropped and the Company's finances had improved. This is reflected in the Company archives which deal with weightier matters from this time. (S.M. Hare, *The History of the Goldsmiths' Company from their Records*, 1982, p6). www.thegoldsmiths.co.uk/history. These new officers may have felt the Walks had outgrown their usefulness. By this time, better control was kept of the royal plate and early forms of policing were beginning to take effect. Chelsea, Bloomsbury, Islington and Bethnal Green were developed between 1750 and 1800 making it difficult to send Walkmen across this greater area. Newspapers were more effective and a cheaper way of advertising for lost or stolen property.

duty it was to test the scrapings taken by individual assayers from items sent in for marking in order to ensure that sub-standard goods were not being passed overall.[28] This annual event ceased only with the enactment of the 1973 Hallmarking Act in 1975.[29]

The Notices

The Notices carried by Goldsmiths' Hall messengers were small printed squares of paper (normally approximately 5x7.5cm (2x3ins)). They described the scene and date of the crime, details of an object, including any distinguishing marks,[30] the address(es) for return of the items and frequently offered a reward. Also printed were the Notice date and name of the current Beadle, and each had a serial number. Close examination of original Notices suggests they were cut from a larger sheet and each has a hole – as if it had been threaded on to a string for filing.[31] To date few have come to light – the majority that have fall between November 1726 (the end of John Bodington's term as Beadle) to June 1731 (Benjamin Pyne Snr's death). During this time about 390 Notices were issued – on average 87 per year.[32] A similar calculation results in an increased average of about 109 Notices per year between 1731 and 1737. No reference to the Walks has been found after 1788 and it is believed that they ceased around that time.[33]

Although the principal purpose of the Notices was to circulate details of lost and stolen items, the Walks scheme had other uses, for example to advertise that 'An Old and well-accustom'd Goldsmiths Shop' was to be let.[14]

Numb. 11874.   *Sept.* 7. 1730.

WHereas the Shop of Mr. Benjamin Bentley was broke open laſt Night, and the following things taken away; about 50 or 60 Gold Rings, moſt of them mark'd W. E. about 24 Cryſtal and Seven Stone Rings; 12 Pair of Gold Ear-rings, 6 Gold Lockets, mark'd S. W. Two Seven-Rows Gold Chains and Lockets, about two Ounces each, and one Five-Row Gold-Chain and Locket, about one Ounce Two Penny Weight; 8 Gold Necklaces, one of them very large, weighing one Ounce Ten Penny Weight: Some Cornelian Seals ſet in Gold; ſome Poliſh'd and wrought Buckles, Mark'd J. A.

If any of the above things are offer'd to be ſold, pawn'd or valu'd, pray ſtop them and the Party, and give Notice to Mr. Benjamin Bentley, Goldſmith at the Ring on London-Bridge, and you ſhall have *Ten Guineas* Reward for the whole, or proportionable for any Part.
       BENJAMIN PYNE, Beadle,
         at Goldſmith's-Hall.

Numb. 11585.
         Auguſt 28. 1727.

STole yeſterday Morning the 27th inſtant, 2 ſilver Snuff-Boxes, coſt 1 *l.* 8 *s.* 2 Gold Chains 4 Links apiece, 1 Chain leſs thon the other, the leſſer Chain the Hook as the ſtring goes thro' is broke, and turn'd up a-French for a ſtring to go thro', 2 Gold Necklaces of a Middle Beed, 1 Chain 2 Holes for the ſtring to go thro', 1 Gold Mourning Ring with a ſtone, with *John Rich* Eſq; *ob.* 14 *Jan.* 1718. aged 90. 1 Mourning Ring, the Poſie of it is, *I do Rejoice in thee my Choice,* 1 Mourning Ring with a Cypher, the Poſie is, *Mary Sarſon died ſuch a time,* 1 ſmall Gold Ring, the Poſie, *The God above, encreaſe our Love,* 1 ſmall Ring with a Red ſtone, and 3 ſmall ſtones on each ſide, 1 ſmall Gold Ring, the Poſie, *Content has no Want,* 1 ſmall Gold Ring with a fine white ſtone ſquare, and ſeveral Nobs riſing up on each ſide of the ſtone, enamel'd with Green, 1 Gold Bob, 1 Old Faſhion Chace work'd Tea ſpoons gilt, flat Handles, 2 Tea ſtrainers and Tea Tongs, and 1 Tea ſpoon with *A. G.* the Tongs open like Ciſers, 12 Gold Beads, a little ſilver ſpoon for Salt mark'd *K. T.* Whoever gives Notice to Mr. *William Twyford,* Blackſmith, at the Blackſmiths Arms in the *Upper Ground* in *Chriſt-church, Surrey;* or, to Mr. *Barnet,* Goldſmith in *Tooly-ſtreet, Southwark,* ſhall have Two Guineas Reward for the whole, or proportionable for any Part.
       JOHN-BODINGTON, Beadle,
         at *Goldſmiths-Hall.*

15 (left) Notice no11874 issued by Benjamin Pyne in 1730.
16 (above) Notice no11585 issued by John Bodington in 1727.

Beadles and almsmen of the Goldsmiths' Company

It can be seen that the book was a useful reference for Beadles. The Company continually tightened procedures and there are two job descriptions for Beadles relating to the period. One is dated 1714, on the appointment of John Bodington as Beadle. The other, entitled 'Chief Business of the Beadle, etc. of the Worshipful Company of Goldsmiths, London' is from 1732, when Bodington's successor, Benjamin Pyne Snr, who had been Beadle for five years, died. Immediately before Bodington's appointment a review of the Beadle's remuneration took place.[34] It was decided that

> the Clerk might have one Moiety of the profits arising by warnings; & the Beadle the other moiety

calculated at £15 each man, ie £30 per year. Approximately £7 from freemen and apprentices' fees and £5 'By Legacies Summons for Defaulters & other perquisites' was added to the Beadle's moiety. It was also agreed that his salary be increased from £16 13s 4d to £20. This made a total of £47 which the Company would raise to £50 per year 'if by his care & diligence in collecting thereof [meaning the Quarterage and debts due to the Company] he should deserve the same'. The Wardens were of the opinion that this figure, together with 'a Dwelling House would be sufficient maintenance for any Beadle hereafter to be elected'.

However because of his advanced age, by 1730 Pyne was having difficulty with collecting the part of his salary not guaranteed by the Company, so the Wardens agreed to pay him a set annual salary of £50.[35] This meant that future Beadles would no longer have to depend on uncertain funds (ie revenue from the Walks) to supplement their income. In 1742 the guaranteed quarterly salary of £12 10s 0d was still being paid to the Beadle though there is no indication whether he was

34 GCCB, vol 11,1708-19, pp250-1.

35 GCCB, vol 13 1726-36, pp195-6, 200. The appointment of Benjamin Pyne Snr and his retention when he was obviously infirm must have been a dispensation; Beadles had to be under 50 years of age on appointment (see GCCB, vol 13, 1726-36, pp253-4).

17 Extract from the Goldsmiths' Company Court of Assistants' Minutes of February 1714 setting out the revised salary payments to the Beadle and Clerk.

also receiving surplus income, if any, from the Walks.[36] Records of other livery companies reveal that their Beadles received a similar level of remuneration, either as salary or salary plus their expenses.[37]

By 1732 the new Beadle's duties included

> That he Endeavour to get an Account of the places of Abode and Trades of all the Members of the Company and keep a regular Alphabetical List according to their Seniority of freedom and that he Write the same fair from time to time in Order that it may be the better known who are fit to be called Officer.[38]

It is therefore reasonable to assume that the new, younger and zealous Beadle, Robert Jenkes, responsible for a new set of Walkmen, would have drawn up the lists, as they appear in the *Warning Carriers Walks* book, in 1732.

Another significant duty was 'That he … regulate the Almsmen according to their orders …'. John Holtom (Holton/Holtam), James Weatherhead (Wethered), William Bulstrode, the men listed in the book as Walkmen, and their successors, were almsmen and therefore under the authority of the Beadle of the day, who in turn was answerable to the Court of Wardens.

Poor freemen, preferably of the Goldsmiths' Company ('no Wiredrawers need apply'[39]) were elected by the Court of Assistants to receive benefits from Sir Hugh Middleton's Charity, which was funded

36 GC Standing Order Book no2, 1740-54, p26.

37 Examples of other Beadles' remuneration follow: Clothworkers' Company Beadle (also acting as Butler), wife (and maid) received a total of £8 10s pa + considerable expenses – The Clothworkers' Company, *Quarter Wardens Bills & Receipts 1740-1760*, p17; Fishmongers' 'Clk & Beadle Salary' - £33 15 0d pa + expenses - GLMS 5842 1-9, Fishmongers' Company, *Prime Warden's Accounts, Midsumer 1740 to Midsumer 1742*; 'John Clark Beadle' at Mercers' Hall received £12 3s 4d, wages for cleaning the Hall and 'looking after

the Stuff', plus £5 for his 'Trouble for enquiring after the Health of Subscribers' and a further £25 'as a Gratuity for his Pains taken the Year past' – Mercers' Company, Acts of Court Book, 1735-42, pp74, 159.

38 GC, E.III I(iii). There is another list of Beadle's duties dated 1753, perhaps to coincide with the appointment of Samuel Cawthorn as the new Beadle on Robert Jenkes's death earlier that year. See note 13.

39 GCCB vol 15 1743-53, p198. The Gold and Silver Wyre Drawers was a separate livery company (Forbes as note 14) pp106-8.

by dividends from one share in the New River Company.[40] The three Walkmen qualified for this desirable grant and in due course became one of 26 elected almsmen who received increased assistance. In their decline they could be considered for a place in Mr Morrell's almshouse in Hackney, as vacancies occurred.[41] At the Court of Wardens' first meeting of the incoming Prime Warden, each May, new gowns were distributed (they may 'dispose of [their] old Gowns as they think fit' but it was recommended that they convert them to warm winter garments) and pensioners who had proceeded through the charitable system were elected to the almshouse. All were 'admonished' to behave themselves and a box-keeper was appointed to keep account 'of all the ffines [and] particular Breaches of their order for which such ffines' were received and 'to lay the same before Mess Wardens to be perused at their next private Court before they go out of office'.[42] Selected pensioners were expected to attend Hall events in their gowns and wait at table during dinners, a task which earned them the remains of the feast afterwards and perhaps a small payment. In all probability the Walkmen received additional *ad hoc* payments out of the Walks' income for undertaking the Walks, since the Wardens agreed at a meeting in November 1559 that

> 2 almsmen that shall warn their circuit shall have viii[d] a-piece The Beadle to warn his circuit himself the whole fee of xx[d] to himself, unless he be otherwise lett, then he to appoint an almsman in his stead and to give him viii[d].[43]

Undoubtedly these almsmen were in good enough health to undertake the Walks but it seems unlikely that Holtom and Weatherhead continued the Walks once resident in the Hackney almshouse. Their successors, also freemen who had fallen on hard times and who in most cases were already pensionable, are listed on the flyleaf of the notebook [6] – confirmation that the Walks continued at least until the late 1760s.[44]

The three Walkmen in the 1732 lists

William Bulstrode

William Bulstrode is a shadowy figure. Although a freeman of the Goldsmiths' Company,[45] he does not appear in their apprenticeship and freedom index though he was recipient of Sir Hugh Middleton's Charity in 1731 and elected one of 26 almsmen in 1738.[46] In 1739 he applied, with another father and son, to the Court of Assistants for financial help in placing his son, Thomas, aged 14, with a master 'to be Apprentices to ffreemen of London for the Term of Seven Years'. On submission of a 'Certificate of the Boys Ages' their petitions were granted.

Bulstrode died in 1743 aged approximately 49 years, without attaining a place in Mr Morrell's almshouse. It seems that Ben Gardner took over his Walk duties.[47]

John Holtom

John Holtom first received a small pension in 1729 and shortly afterwards was a recipient of Sir Hugh Middleton's Charity.[48] In 1737, unusually, it was recorded he was

> unanimously elected ... to enjoy the said [Morrell's] almshouse and pension with the additional pension ... [and] was called in & acquainted therewith & was very thankfull for the same ... [and] promised obedience to all the orders of this Court relating to Mr. Morrell's Almesmen.[49]

40 Sir Hugh Middleton (Midleton/Myddleton), a London goldsmith, took over the City's licence to bring water from Hertfordshire to Clerkenwell in 1609, success being assured by 1622 after near failure. Under the terms of his will the Goldsmiths' Company received one share of this New River Company to be used 'for the benefit of such poor men (or widows of such members) of his name, kindred, Country as shall be free of the said Company'. The first half-yearly payment of £12 12s 10d (£107 13s by 1745) (GCCB vol 15 1743–53 p139) was received in 1644 and from then on, despite fluctuations in Goldsmiths' Company revenues, increasing numbers of almsmen and women benefited, since the larger the dividend the greater number of poor freemen could be supported. Although there were other smaller charities supporting almsmen, Sir Hugh Middleton's Charity was the most significant and enabled the Goldsmiths' Company to guarantee payments into the late nineteenth century, when all their charities were put on a more formal footing. *A Prospect of the City from the North* (Guildhall Art Gallery) shows a distant detailed view of the City with the New River head in the foreground. Further information is available from the Guildhall Art Gallery. See also Sir W.S. Prideaux, *The Charities under the management of the Goldsmiths' Company being An Account of their Foundation and History*, 1899, pp45-6, 277.

41 GCCB vol 15 1743-53, pp42-3. An almsman's progression, called his seniority, began when he was elected to receive a charitable payment – this was not automatically repeated at the following distribution. The next step was to become one of 26 almsmen, who received a secure pension and additional benefits; this allowed for later election to one of the six places in the almshouse at Hackney, the gift of Mr Richard Morrell.

42 GCCB vol 14 1736-42, p135. In December 1741, '3 Storesmen's [sic] gowns & 23 other almsmen's gowns' cost £48, Standing Order Book no2, 1740-54, p24.

43 GCCB vol 8 1557-77 K part 1 p105.

44 OBP, December 1768, t17681207-9 (John Andrew Martin accused).

45 The entry in this record confirms his freedom and the almost illegible (standard) form of indenture shows '1718 Goldsmith, free by Service', CLRO Alphabet of Freedoms 1714-25.

46 GCCB vol 13 1726-36, p220; vol 14 1736-42, p164.

47 GCCB vol 14 1736-42, pp255-7. Bulstrode's death: GCCB, vol 15 1743-53, p52.

48 GCCB vol 13 1726-36, p155; vol.13, pp176-9.

49 GCCB vol 14 1736-42, p45.

50 Holtom was apprenticed to his father, Edward in 1699, free 1714 (Apprenticeship and Freedom Index 1578). A new incumbent took his place at the almshouse in 1750, indicating Holtom's death. (GCCB vol 15 1743-53, p295). In 1751 Johanna Holtom (his widow?), on application to the Court of Assistants, was granted a pension from Agas Harding Charity and continued to receive support from the Hall until her death in 1765 (GCCB, vol 15 1743-53, pp345-6; vol 16 1754–66 p344).

51 GCCB, vol 14 1736-42, p35.

52 Since Holtom was not one of these men and was living in Hackney by this date, his involvement with the Walks and his 'employment' at Goldsmiths' Hall had presumably ceased.

53 GCCB, vol 14 1736-42, pp178-80, 182-3. It is presumed that their links with the Goldsmiths' Company had to be cut in order for them to give unbiased evidence to the House of Lords Committee with regard to The Plate (Offences) Act 1738. The Bill was the result of agreed terms between the trade and Goldsmiths' Company in order to regulate the craft. The Act required craftsmen to re-register

their marks at Goldsmiths' Hall and these were to be punched on all gold and silver items, other than agreed categories of small articles. New charges for hallmarking (freemen and non-freemen were to pay the same rate) and fines for infringements were set out. No sub-standard metal or over-soldering was to be tolerated. Paper records were to be submitted with articles brought in for assaying and those records kept by the Goldsmiths' Company for inspection by an Excise Officer. For the trade, searching by Goldsmiths' Wardens of tradesmen's premises for malpractice was to cease. Although dated 1738, the Bill did not become law until 1739, a delay which resulted in the Act applying to all England (not Scotland and Ireland) rather than to the 50 miles round London. The Act, with only minor amendments, remained in force until 1975. Forbes (as note 14), pp200-5, 208, 220.

54 GCCB, vol 15 1743-53, p220; presumed dead 1748 (GCCB, vol 15, p247).

55 British Library Colindale, the Burney Collection of Early Newspapers (hereafter BL Col), Burney 331B; *Fog's Weekly Journal*, 5 April 1729; Holtom's Walk no99 lists Haydon, not Etherington, at the stated address.

18 Notice issued by Benjamin Pyne, 1729. It is interesting to note that this notice was re-issued a week later (see p30 centre right).

He lodged there until his death in 1750, aged approximately 60.[50] Holtom, who was singled out for his trustworthiness and reliability, was the appropriate person to undertake the prestigious route that involved calling at the bankers and goldsmiths of Fleet Street and the Strand, then going on to the Palace of Westminster.

James Weatherhead

Weatherhead comes across as a rather different character. In 1731 he received payment from Sir Hugh Middleton's Charity but in 1736 there was a complaint made against him for 'procuring several Charitys of this Company … to be given to his Brother Wm Wethered tho' he know that he is not a Freeman of the Company'; which he denied and 'prayed Ms Wardens therefore to forgive him', whereupon he was 'reproved'.[51]

In 1739, with William Bulstrode and five others[52] he agreed to

> surrender and yield up to this Company their several ffreedoms and all Rights of being ffreemen or Members of the Company … and their Rights Titles & interest in … all Liberties Priviledges & Advantages … to the Lands Possessions and Estates of this Company … the Company [being] advised to Disenfranchise such Members of the Company … willing to be Witnesses on the part of the Company before the Rt. Honble the House of Lords touching the Companys Bill.

(Mr. Joseph Ward, the Common Assayer, refused to surrender his freedom making 'some trifling excuses' which irritated the Court of Assistants.)[53]

Later in the year the Court restored their freedoms and rights 'according to their Seniorities before their surrenders'.

While he continued to receive support from Goldsmiths' charities, 1747 seems to have been an unruly year for Weatherhead. He appeared on three occasions before the Wardens concerning complaints about him and others for being drunk, frequently misbehaving and neglecting their duties. Suspension and removal of their gowns was the punishment. In all cases their 'good sober behaviour', albeit temporary, testified to by 'a credible person', resulted in their suspension being lifted and their gowns restored to them. Without their gowns they were unable to perform their duties, which suggests that some additional remuneration was forthcoming. This may explain why in 1748, shortly before his death aged approximately 63 years, Weatherhead applied for money rather than a new gown – upon which he was reprimanded again.[54]

Almost certainly a familiar figure on his rounds, it is unclear whether a Walkman would have been regarded by the trade as servant, spy or officer, though in Weatherhead's case he may well have been greeted as a comrade, ready for a gossip and a jug or two of ale.

Old Bailey trials: evidence for dating the notebook

It had been assumed before this research was undertaken that 1744 was the date when the lists were drawn up. However there is strong evidence from various sources, including advertisements, trial reports and parish records, for an earlier date. A few examples will suffice:

In 1728 'Thomas Hayden, Workman and Finisher' advertised that he had taken over the business of Mr George Etherington, an Eminent Watchmaker, against the New Church in the Strand (HOLTOM NO 99).[55]

On 11 September 1735, John Holton [sic] stood in Court at the Old Bailey:

19 Built in 1539, the Old Bailey Sessions House stood beside Newgate prison and took its name from a street nearby. Replaced in 1774 it became the Central Criminal Court in 1834.

> I am a Messenger to the Goldsmith's Company. On Monday, June 30 between three and four in the Afternoon, I left a Printed Advertisement of the same Tenour as this in my Hand at Barthelemi's Shop, … . It contains a Description of the two Tankards, the Marks, Weight, and Size. Then he read the Advertisement in Court …

Regrettably the advertisement is not included in the trial report. Holtom was giving evidence, as was Lewis Laroch, silversmith (WEATHERHEAD NO99), at the trial of Patrick Gaffney and James Barthelemi 'a Goldsmith at Charing-cross' (HOLTOM NO187 as 'Bartleme, Whitehall'). The former stood accused of pick-pocketing and theft and Barthelemi was indicted for receiving stolen goods on 5 July, knowing them to be stolen. Barthelemi's involvement with known criminals, his reputed attempt to bribe the magistrate and his changing story during the proceedings resulted in a sentence of 14 years' transportation, probably to the West Indies or America.[56] This may seem a harsh sentence for a doubtful crime but

> To turn his booty into money, the successful thief required as partner an unsuspecting or dishonest goldsmith. The craft was accordingly subject to narrow scrutiny …[57]

This trial determines a 1735 or earlier date for the Walks and Holtom's involvement in the case supports this.

The address for Paul de Lamerie in the lists is given as Windmill Street (WEATHERHEAD NO141). Although he did not relinquish these premises, the business moved to Gerrard Street in 1738. The same year, Thomas Hawksworth, a pawnbroker of St Martin's Court who does not appear in the Walks, states in Court that he had a Notice delivered to him from Goldsmiths' Hall.[58] If the three Walks were entered into the book in 1732, when Jenkes was appointed Beadle, the addresses must

56 OBP, September 1735, t17350911-14 (Patrick Gaffney, James Barthelemi accused). Gaffney, sentenced to death, either had his sentence reduced to transportation or escaped custody, for in 1744 he 'otherwise Casey of St James's, Westminster' was found guilty at the Old Bailey of stealing clothes, total value 9s 4d, and sentenced to transportation (OBP, January 1744, t17440113-1 (Patrick Gaffney accused)). There is no further news of Barthelemi (Bartelmi/ Barthelmi). It was relatively common for criminals to give evidence against one another to gain a lighter sentence or to receive the reward. This led to serious, bitter accusations and disturbances in Court. For details of sentences and pardons see J.M. Beattie, *Crime & the Courts in England, 1660-1800*, Clarendon Press, Oxford 1986 or, more concisely, www.oldbaileyonline.org.

57 A.J. Collins (as note 3) p156. I am indebted to Philippa Glanville for this reference.

58 OBP, December 1738, t17381206-2 (John Gardiner accused).

20 'Mode of punishment by Branding, or burning on the Hand, at the New Sessions House', engraving.

have been correct at that time. The cessation of a business, either through bankruptcy or death, and the incorporation of new ones, were perhaps reasons for the additional totals at the end of Weatherhead's Walk. The re-registration of marks in 1739,[59] coupled with the high number of elusive Huguenots and out-workers in Weatherhead's territory, might also have necessitated alterations as Jenkes tried to monitor the trade and keep his lists up-to-date.[60]

From 1725 there is a gradual increase in the number of Old Bailey trials mentioning those named in the Walks, the majority appearing between 1730 and 1740 and tailing off towards the 1750s. A peak of crime around the early 1740s can be explained by the huge increase in London's population, the very severe winter of 1739–40 which resulted in fuel and food being scarce and a doubling in the price of consumables during 1740–42.[61] It should also be remembered that the country was in a state of high alert due to the threat of Jacobite invasion – another reason perhaps for keeping an eye on 'strangers'. The majority of trial reports deal with petty and opportunist theft to alleviate hand-to-mouth existence, which resulted in draconian punishment for those convicted.[62]

Cases at the Old Bailey Sessions are reported in detail, describing the common methods of relieving a man of his valuable watch (a *de rigueur* possession of the period), the removal of silver tankards from taverns and the price of Old and New Sterling silver. Gold and silver items, along with clothing, roofing lead, cheese and animals, were popular objects to steal. They often had the added benefit of being small and easily hidden, able to be disposed of quickly or amateurishly melted down, though minute traces of metal could easily be discovered on melting utensils when searching a thief's lodging. A woman of the street, having enticed a man to buy her a drink, would take advantage of his 'fuddled' state, snatch his watch and slip it down the front of her dress, an area quite out of bounds to the confused owner. The stolen goods were swiftly pawned, disposed of at Rag Fair or to a passing sailor for enough coins to pay for the next drink or meal. More unfortunate was the naive man who, having been propositioned by a young lady and led to an upstairs tavern room, found himself robbed on waking, not only of his watch but his silver buttons, buckles or, worse still, all his clothes – valuable property of the time. As an unsympathetic judge who had heard it all before, commented: the knave 'had been tumbled in bed' by the prostitute!

Frequent impromptu crowds drew pickpockets working in pairs: while one seized a man's arm, holding it stretched high overhead, so lifting his coat's fashionably stiffened skirt, the victim felt the accomplice steal watch and chain 'out of my Fobb, for my Breeches were prodigious tight'. When accosted the assailant offered to be searched for the watch, while his accomplice made off into the crowd with the booty.[63] The audiences in the crush coming out of the Opera House in the Haymarket and the Playhouse in Drury-Lane were particularly vulnerable to pick-pocketing, causing jewellery and watches to be seized or 'dropt'; fashionable St James's Park also claimed many treasured possessions.

A common practice for an enterprising seller of silverware would be to open the lower sash of his front room window and place a shewglass just inside, or on the grating outside, in order to display his goods. Dexterous thieves were able to extract single items but some ran off with the complete case, chased by the shopkeeper shouting 'Stop Thief', whereupon it was the duty of any adjacent citizen to join in the

59 See note 53.

60 A reminder 'That all Goldsmiths, Watchmakers, Ec. are oblig'd to enter their Names and places of abode in the Assay Office at Goldsmiths Hall; whereby the Beadle and Messengers of that Company and no others can give so speedy notice' concluded the advertisement emphasising the Hall's constant endeavours to keep track of craftsmen (see p10).

61 Beattie, (as note 56) p206, pp181-92.

62 Mary Barrow, convicted of stealing a coral, value 4s, was sentenced to transportation OBP, June 1736, t17360610-17. Davenport (HOLTOM NO91) gave evidence.

63 OBP, September 1735, 17350911-14 (Patrick Gaffney, James Barthelemi accused) see note 56 above. *Fog's Weekly Journal* of Saturday, 23 November 1728 advertised publication of *Set a Thief to Catch a Thief*, showing an awareness of the problem (BL Burney, 331B).

pursuit and make a citizen's arrest. Once the miscreant was apprehended, the constable was called and he took the suspect to the local magistrate, who decided whether an indictable offence had occurred.[64]

It must be assumed that a considerable amount of theft took place which never reached court. The high costs of pressing charges and the waste of time and disruption to business for the self-employed that this involved, must have been a deterrent for many shopkeepers. To these obstacles would have been added a general mistrust of the law and the daunting responsibility of sending someone to their death or transportation for stealing a few shillings' worth of property – though it was difficult to drop a prosecution if witnesses were available and the criminal caught.[65]

Well-known gold- and silversmiths named in the Walks feature in Old Bailey trials, such as:

Peter Dutems (WEATHERHEAD NO191), jeweller and goldsmith, had been requested to repair a box for Lord Harvey, which he sent to Elisha Manisire, an engraver, for the work to be done, whereupon the box was 'lost'. After advertising it with a reward of £10, his apprentice came forward saying he could help. Isaac Dubois (HOLTOM NO87) accompanied Dutems to fields outside London where, after some bizarre incidents, the apprentice was tricked into confessing that his intention was to acquire the reward money.[66]

Paul Crispin [*sic*] (WEATHERHEAD NO151) had a silver dish stolen from his shop on 5 January 1733/4. His French accent, or maybe a lisp, is evident from the report:[67]

> *Paul Crispin.* What I have to tha ith thith, I lotht a thilver Dith belonging to Brigadier *Churchill*, out of my Grate in *Compton-Thtreet*, the Corner of *Greek-Thtreet*, but I can't tell when, becauth it ish impothible, and I never mitht it till the 3d of *January*, when it wath called for. I am a *Thilver-Thmith* by Trade, and the Dith wath left me to make a Cover to it. When *Baker* wath taken Prithoner, he akth me if I wath not rob'd of thuch a Dith, and I thaid, Yeth; but I never found it aga'n.

On 18 May 1738 Thomas Cross, 'a Person of a wicked and corrupt Mind, greedy of Lucre, &c. [was sentenced to death for] unlawfully contriving … to cheat and defraud Benjamin Hoare, Henry Hoare, Richard Hoare, and Christopher Arnold, of a great Sum of Money, viz. 75 l.' [£75] by forging a money order (HOLTOM NO68).[68]

In 1748, the trial of John Parkes found that he

> did cause and procure to be falsely made, forged and counterfeited, a certain paper writing, with the name of Paul de Lamerie subscribed thereto…for the delivery of two hundred ounces of sterling [silver] …

had he been successful it would have been a useful quantity of precious metal to be exchanged for currency (WEATHERHEAD NO141).[69] Lengthy trials concerning coining appear, but there is no indication that Goldsmiths' Hall took part.

64 'On Sunday Night, Mr Markham's Toy-Shop, The Seven Stars, adjoining to St Dunstan's Church in Fleetstreet, was robb'd to the Value of 200 l and upwards: The Villains found Means of sawing a round Hole in one of the Window Shutters, near that Part where the richest Goods were, then broke the Glass, gutted one of the Show-Glasses, and brought off all that was within reach, besides doing much Mischief otherwise by breaking and throwing down Glasses and Toys; and all this done within Sight of the Watchman's Stand …'. Mr Marcum (HOLTOM NO72), (GLMS: C42.03).

65 Beattie (as note 56) p202. The many pardons granted are set out in pp419-28.

66 OBP, April 1734, t17340424-13 (Daniel Cook accused).

67 OBP, May 1733, t17330628-30 (Alexander Watson, William Howard accused).

68 OBP, May 1738, t17380518-16, Thomas Cross, Richard Car accused).

69 OBP, February 1748, t17480224-40 (John Parkes accused).

21 (above left) Extract from a trial at which Paul Crespin gave evidence.
22 (above) Paul Crespin, 1694–1770, oil on canvas.

23 The Lady's Disaster. 'Drawn from the Fact. Occasion'd by a Lady carelessly tossing her Hoop to high in gooing to shun a littel Chimney sweepers Boy who fell down just at her Feet...' Beneath, a shopkeeper tries to rescue his shew-glass. These cases were easy prey for thieves and are frequently mentioned in trials. The verse beneath the engraving reads '... While from his stall the leering Jew / Would gladly have a better view...'.

There were complaints that a messenger sometimes arrived at a silversmith's or pawnbroker's shop too late and that the stolen item had already moved on or had been melted, leaving a question mark over the honesty of the tradesman. Pawnbrokers, victims of theft themselves, trod a fine line between accepting or rejecting goods (in which case the item had to be 'stopt'). There was a duty to enquire as to the origin of items brought in for pawning or sale, the object was examined for traces of erased coats of arms or marks and a fair price given in exchange. Pawnbrokers nearly always appeared as witnesses for the prosecution. Occasionally their honesty was praised by a court but there was the risk of being accused of receiving stolen goods, with the consequent stringent punishment, or a court reprimand for doubtful dealing. In 1731, pawnbrokers of the City of London and Westminster were threatened with total suppression if they did not act honourably[70] whilst counter-accusations were made that 'more Goldsmiths have been convicted of encouraging thieves than Pawnbrokers'.[71]

Despite this, and some questionable practices in other aspects of the gold- and silversmiths' craft, recipients of Notices must have been known and trusted by Goldsmiths' Hall. Their assistance and that of the general public surely helped in monitoring activities, not only of the 'lower sorts' and criminals, but also the less wealthy area of the trade, in return for which the Hall was ready to assist in identifying marks on stolen pieces. In 1748 David Nash, told the court

> I am beedle of Goldsmith's-hall, a constable came to me at Goldsmith's-hall, Oct. 14. to ask me who was the maker of two odd buckles he brought with him; I told him they were made by two different persons; I told him one was Mr. Smith's work of Fleet street, and the other a person in Swan-alley; and as I was going along Fleet-street, and knew Mr. Smith very well, I call'd on him to see if he had lost any thing ...

70 *Daily Advertiser*, 1 April 1731; GL Prints, Maps & Drawings dept, C64.24 .

71 *Gentleman's Magazine*, Weekly Essays in April 1731, p165; *The Daily Post-Boy*, Monday 26 April.

*Numb.*11503   *November. 3. 1726.*

ON Monday laft Mr. *Richard Hall's* Waggon, the Hertford Carrier was robb'd of the following Goods, viz. 7 Tankards, 3 Coffee Pots, 2 large scollop Waiters, one of them with Feet, 1 large Heart corner'd Waiter with 2 fmall ones all with Feet, 3 tea Pots, 1 ftand and lamp for a Tea Pot, 12 plain Cups of feveral fizes, 8 Nurld Cups of feveral fizes, 13 Bellied Mugs of feveral fizes, 5 Porrengers, 1 Wax Candleftick, 2 large faucepans, 1 large Tumbler gilt 5 Tumbers not gilt, 4 large falvers, 4 Hand falvers, 1 Pint Jug, all the above mentioned with *T.L.* for the Workman's Mark. 1 fugar Difh, 3 Orange ftrainers with 2 Ears, 1 ditto with a Wooden Handle and a Hook, 3 bellied Pepper Boxes, 2 ftrait ditto with Handles, 2 fetts of Cafters, 2 Pair of Oval falts, 3 foop Ladles, 2 of them Wooden Handles, 5 Punch Ladles, 3 Cream faucepans, 4 Cream Jugs, 2 fpoon Trays, 3 Panikins, 5 Nurld Dram Cups, thefe being mark'd with *I.S.* the Workman's Mark. 10 Pair of fquare falts, 4 Dozen and 2 Tea fpoons, 5 Pap fpoons, 38 Pair of Polifh'd and Burnifh'd Men's Buckles, 42 Pair of Women's ditto, 3 Girdle Buckles, 14 flock Buckles, 12 falt fpoons, 14 Pair of fhoo Clafps, 11 Watch Chains, 6 Tea ftrainers, 12 Cizar's Chains, thefe Goods being mark'd fome with *G.R.* and some with *I.G.* 27 fnuff-Boxes, 5 Heart Graters, 1 round one, 31 plain Rings, moft of them mark'd *R.C.* 10 Enamel'd Rings, 1 Gold Chain and Locket feven Rows, 1 ditto two Rows, 3 Gold Lockets, 4 Pair of Gold Ear Wires, 1 Pair of Gold Buttons, 1 Pair of Gold Earings, 1 Pair of Gold Necklace Rings, 5 Diamond Rings with Garnets in the Middle, 36 Cypher Rings, one Pair fet in Gold, 1 Pair of Buttons fet in Gold 1 feal fet with a Cornelian, 7 Corals, 1 Boatfwain Call, 1 Tea Canifter, 3 old falts, 1 Rattle, 1 heavy faffron Pot, 1 Quartern Pot, 1 Punch Cup two Ears, 4 fingle Dram Cups, 2 Children's Cups, 6 ftrings of Coat and Breaft Buttons, 1 ftring of plain and ftone Rings in filver, 1 ftring of Shields, 2 Tobacco Boxes, one with a Lyon-Rampant in a Camp, 2 Saucers, 4 filver Pach-Boxes, 6 fmall ditto with the King and Queen's Head, 1 ditto plain, 3 Equipages, 1 Metal Watch Chain and Hook, 4 foop fpoons, 4 Marrow fpoons, 5 Marrow fcoops, 3 Dozen and 10 large fpoons, the Mark, *H.G.* 7 Pair of Spurs, 2 Pair of them lined through with fteel, 32 Pair of Tea Tongs, fome Cizar Fafhion, 4 Watches, two of them named *Tawney*, 1 named *Crow*, 1 named *Lane*, 1 Card of Neck-Clafps, 1 of Collar Buttons and fhort Rings, 6 Cards of Coat Buttons, 2 Cards of Mens polifhed wrought Buckles, fteel Tongues and Chape fomewhat rufty, 2 Cards of Tortoifhel Snuff-Boxes, 1 Card of Cizar and Needle Cafes, 1 Card of Leg Tobacco-ftoppers, 1 Card with Coral Beads, 1 Card of Seals, fome fet with Cornelians, 1 Card of Lockets, 1 Card of Coat Clafps, 2 Cards of fleeve Buttons and Studs, 1 Pair of Mocho ftone Buttons fet in Gold Biffels, 1 Bundle of Ear Pickers and Bodkins, feveral fmall Cards of ftone buttons and ftuds, and a Bundle of fine Penknives; and feveral other Things not remember'd.

The above faid Marks are the Marks of the Makers of the Goods. If any of thefe Goods are offered to be fold, pawned, or valued, ftop them and the Party and give Notice to the abovefaid *Richard Hull* at the *Green Dragon* in *Bishopfgate* ftreet, and you fhall have Twenty Guineas for the Whole, and proportionable for any Part.

JOHN BODINGTON, Beadle,
at Goldsmiths-Hall.

Notices issued by John Bodington and Benjamin Pyne.
Above: no11503 dated 1726 (transcribed from a Notice in a private collection). It is remarkable for its detail, particularly the description of the 'Workman's Mark'. The remainder (right and overleaf), transcribed from Brian Lillywhite, London Coffee Houses. *Coffee houses and taverns provided anonymity and could be used rather like a Post Office Box today. Coffee Houses were not included in the list of premises visited by the Walkmen, however they may have featured in a City Walk, details of which have apparently not survived. No11790 (on p30) is a repeat advertisement of no11787* **[18]**.

---

*Numb.*11528   *February.7. 1726-7.*

LOST or miflaid laft Week, a Brilliant, weight nine Grains, and fixteen Square, Stone white and clean. If offer'd to be fold, pawn'd, or valued, pray ftop it, and give Notice to Mr. *Morris*, Mafter of *Robin's* Coffee-houfe, and you fhall have Ten Guineas Reward, and no Queftions ask'd; or if any body has found it, and give Notice as above, fhall have the fame Reward.

JOHN BODINGTON, Beadle,
at Goldsmiths-Hall.

---

*Numb.*11540   *March.8. 1726-7*

DROPT at Robin's Coffee-Houfe in *Exchange-Alley* in a Paper, a loofe, oval, very fine fpread Brilliant Diamond, weight about thirteen Grains and a half, with two or three little Specks in it. Whoever brings it to the Bar of the faid Coffee-House, fhall have Ten Guineas Reward, and no Queftions ask'd; if offer'd to be pawn'd, fold, or valued, pray ftop it and the Party, and give Notice at the above mentioned Place, and you fhall receive the fame Reward.

JOHN BODINGTON, Beadle,
at Goldsmiths-Hall.

---

*Numb.*11581   *Auguft. 7. 1727.*

LOST on *Saturday* the 5th infant, a Pocket-Book, containing a Bill of Exchange drawn from *Leghorn*, dated the 16th of *May* 1727, at Ufance, by Meff. *Benjamin Lambert Charron* and Comp. to the order of Mr. *Chriftian Colebrandt*, for Five hundred and forty Dollars, upon Sir *John Lambert* of *London*. 115 l.

The Perfon in whofe Poffeffion the fame is, upon delivering the faid Pocket Book with the above mention'd Bill to the Bar of *John Shipfton's* Coffee-houfe in *Swithen's* Alley by the *Royal Exchange*, fhall have one Guinea Reward, and no Queftions ask'd; or if offer'd in Payment, Difcount, or otherwife, you are defired to ftop it, and give Notice as above, and you fhall have the fame Reward.   *NB.* Payment is ftopt.

JOHN BODINGTON, Beadle,
at Goldsmiths-Hall.

---

*Numb.*11592   *September. 22. 1727.*

LOST or miflaid between the 13th and 14th of this infant *September*, one flat Chriftalline Diamond, weighing about five Grains and a half, round and clean, fit to fet the Hair under it. Whoever brings the faid Diamond to *Robin's* Coffee-houfe in *Exchange-Alley*; or, to Mr. *Abraham Telles*, or to Meffieurs *Richard* and *Thomas Woodwards*, Bankers in *Exchange-Alley*, fhall have Five Guineas Reward, and no Queftions ask'd.

N.B. If offer'd to be pawn'd or fold, pray ftop it, and give Notice to the Perfons above-mention'd.

JOHN BODINGTON, Beadle,
at Goldsmiths-Hall.

Numb.11582   *Auguft*. 10. 1727.

LOST Yefterday being the 9th of *Auguft*, a Note of Mr. *Nath. Braffey* and Comp. No 501. payable to *Dan. Ray*, 100 l. Whoever bring it to the Bar at *Baker's* Coffee-houfe in *Exchange - Alley*, fhall have Five Guineas Reward.

NB. Payment is ftopt.

J O H N B O D I N G T O N , Beadle,
at Goldsmiths-Hall.

Numb.11627   *December*. 21. 1727.

LOST between Twelve and One o'Clock this Morning, a Gold Watch, Thomas Wentworth, Sarum, in the Infide, a Sapphyr Ring, on each fide a Brilliant, a Sword of the Saxon Make with Silver Gripe, Steel Hilt gilt.

If offer'd to be fold, or pawn'd, pray ftop the Perfon and Things, and give Notice to Mr. *Brown* jun. at the Palfgrave Head Coffee-houfe without Temple-Bar, and you fhall have Three Guineas Reward.

J O H N B O D I N G T O N , Beadle,
at Goldsmiths-Hall.

Numb.11714   *December* 18. 1728.

LOST or miflaid, a Bank Note for 100 l. payable to Mr. *Sam. Betterefs* or Bearer, dated *Sept.* 7. 1728.

Whoever brings the faid Note to William Whitmore, at Jonathan's Coffee-houfe in Exchange-Alley; or, to Mr. William Pepys in Lombard-ftret, Banker, fhall have Five Guineas Reward, and no Queftions ask'd.

N.B. Payment is ftopt at the Bank..

B E N J A M I N P Y N E , Beadle,
at Goldsmiths-Hall.

Numb.11863   *July* 15. 1730.

LOST about Eleven of the Clock, between Temple-Bar and the Palfgrave Head Court, Two Bank Notes, one N°7 dated the 9th of July, 1730 payable to *Philip Hellier* for 30 l. and the other N° 79 dated the 13th of April 1730 payable to the Earl of *Cardigan* for 50 l. Payment of which Notes are ftop'd at the Bank: If the Perfon who hath found the faid Notes will bring them to Mr. *Brown's* at the Palfgrave's Head Coffee-Houfe at Temple-Bar, they fhall receive *Five Guineas* Reward, to be paid by the faid Mr. *Brown.* If offered in Payment or otherwife, you are defired to ftop it, and the Reward fhall be divided.

B E N J A M I N P Y N E , Beadle,
at Goldsmiths-Hall.

Numb.11639   *February*. 16. 1727.

SUppofed to be loft Yefterday, between the Hours of 5 and 6 in the Evening, in a Hackney Coach, that took up a Gentleman in *Conduit-ftreet, Hanover Square*; Two Brilliants weighing 39 Grains together, One being of a fquare Shape not very fpread, and of a yellowifh Water; the Other of an oval Shape and Brown. Whoever has found them, and will bring them to Mr. *Abraham Telles* at Robin's Coffee Houfe; Or, to Meffieurs *Woodwards* in Exchange Alley, fhall have Ten Guineas Reward, and no Queftions asked. If offered to be fold, pawn'd, or valued, pray ftop them and the Party, and give Notice as above, and you fhall have the fame Reward.

B E N J A M I N P Y N E , Beadle,
at Goldsmiths-Hall.

Numb.11790   *Nov*.24.1729.

Whereas there is lately mifs'd (and fuppofed to be ftolen) out of a Gentleman's House the following Parcels of Gold, viz
6 Doz. and eight Gold Waftcoat Buttons.
10 odd Pair of Gold Sleeve Buttons.
1 Large Pair for Breeches.
5 Pair of Shoo Buckles, fome plain and fome Wite.
1 gold Buckle for a Hat, on the upper Part is a Coronet.
2 Gold Toothpicks, with Earpickers, &c.
1 Gold Snuff Box. 3 Gold Wire Hatbands.
1 Bracelet for the Arm of Gold Wire. Being all Foreign Make
20 odd Gold Rings. 2 Seal rings, one engraved W.M. the other a Cypher. A Parcel of Gold Duft, and two large Pieces of Rock Gold, one wt. about 2oz. the other about 1oz. 14 Guineas of Will. & Mar. coin'd in the Years 1689 and 1690. If offer'd to be fold, pawn'd or vauled, pray ftop them and the Party, and give Notice to Mr. Wm Elliot, Goldfmith, near London-Stone, and they fhall receive 50 *l*. Reward, or in Proportion for any Part.

B E N J A M I N P Y N E , Beadle,
at Goldsmiths-Hall.

Numb.11953   *June* 24. 1731.

LOST in or about Exchange Alley this day, a Draught on the Bank of England, No 5437, N. for 530 l. drawn by Mr. John Edwards, payable to Mr. Benjamin Muftaphia or Bearer. Whoever has found it, and will bring it to the Bar at Baker's Coffee-houfe, and enquire for the faid Benjamin Muftaphia, upon the Delivery of the faid Draught to him, shall receive *Two Guineas* Reward, and no Queftions ask'd.

N.B. No farther Reward will be offer'd, Payment being ftop'd.

B E N J A M I N P Y N E , Beadle,
at Goldsmiths-Hall.

The constable confirmed this:

> ... the next day I went all over Leaden-hall-street and without Algate, to inquire what Goldsmith had lost any things; I went to Goldsmith's hall, and shew'd the buckles to Mr. Nash the beadle; he told me one was Mr. Smith's mark, and the other another name ...[72]

Co-operation on both sides must have consolidated relationships and to some extent helped to dispel the irritation felt by craftsmen caused by accusations of producing unmarked or sub-standard work.

The Walks, newspapers and the Bell-man: three methods of advertising

The procedures for advertising through the press and Goldsmiths' Warning Carriers (the Walkmen) reached those of the public who could read and targeted the trade without delay. In 1749, a Mr. Pain testified at a trial that he

> had notice sent me from Goldsmith's hall

and another witness claimed he

> carried the paper [listing the stolen goods] to be printed, and to be distributed from Goldsmith's-Hall, ...[73]

A victim could arrange printing of Notices himself and ask the Hall to distribute them, or he could ask the Hall to organise printing. It was also possible to go to the Hall to see copies of advertisements (maybe hanging on a string).[74] He could use either the Hall's system, newspaper advertisements or arrange for the Bell-man who proclaimed news of stolen items in the street to advertise the theft.[75] The competing services had different charges and targeted different audiences. The Walk lists do not include newspaper offices, constables' or magistrates' rooms, taverns or coffee houses – the latter popular places to read newspapers. The owner himself must have had to notify these establishments of missing property.

In order to deliver Notices to craftsmen within three hours (four hours by 1755), Walkmen would have had to be available to make a delivery. Holtom, Weatherhead and Bulstrode must have been waiting at Goldsmiths' Hall for Notices to come in.[76] In 1735 Goldsmiths' Wardens received a formal complaint from the Bank of England that Robert Jenkes, Goldsmiths' Beadle, was sending out Notices of lost bank notes before he had 'stopt' them at their Bank; perhaps he was trying to avoid the small fee they possibly charged for this service. He defended himself fiercely before the Court of Assistants stating that any hindrance would seriously affect the distribution of his Notices. The Court upheld the Beadle's actions.[77] The loss of bank notes was regularly advertised, for example Messrs Middleton & Co, Bankers in the Strand (HOLTOM NO175) inserted a Notice in *The Daily Advertiser* of 10 January 1744 seeking two bank notes for £20 each supposed 'dropt' between Portsmouth and Wimbledon Common.[78]

There is no doubt that the Goldsmiths' Hall warning system was reliable, efficient and detailed. In contrast, when a judge remarked on the delay in a newspaper advertisement being printed it was discovered that the printer had difficulty spelling names. *The Daily Post* of Tuesday, 5 January 1731 carried an advertisement for which an extended version appeared the following Saturday, detailing Warning Notice no11908 dated 'January 7. 1730'[79] which featured 'a Pair of Diamond Rose Ear-

[72] See note 30.

[73] OBP, October 1749, t17491011-45 (Elizabeth Killigrew accused)

[74] OBP, December 1733, t17331205-48 (Mary Gately accused) '... next Day I went to Goldsmith's-Hall, and found an Advertisement (on the File) with a Reward of seven Guineas, with a Direction to go to Mr. Stables, in Fountain-Court, in Cheapside...'.

[75] 'There is a great deal of Noise in this City, of publick Cries of things to be Sold, and great disturbance from Pamphlets and Hawkers The Gazetts come out twice a week, and a great many buy 'em. When a thing is lost, they do not as in Paris, put a Printed Paper on the Wall, but if it be of small value, the Bellman Cries it, and if it be a thing of greater moment as for Example, a Lapdog, &c. then they put it in the Advertisements. GL, A.2.2.No39, p11, Dr M. King, *Journey to London in the Year 1698 – After the Ingenuous Method of that made by Dr. Martin Lyster to Paris, in the same Year, &c, 1698*. I am indebted to Philippa Glanville for this reference.

[76] A senior almsman's day began with a good breakfast (5s was provided for this) prepared on a rota system by a fellow almsman. Once this was over, unless the men had been appointed to a special job, ie, manning the fire engine, cleaning the armour, etc, they were free until later in the day when they might be required to wait at table if a dinner was taking place. If they chose to wander away from the Hall there was no opportunity for them to take on occasional tasks such as 'delivering gowns' or letters, any payment for which would augment their income (see note 1).

[77] GCCB, vol 13 1726-36, p352. It is recognised today that goods are more likely to be recovered within the first 3-4 days of their theft.

[78] BL Col Burney, 387B; *The Daily Advertiser*, 10 January 1744

[79] BL Col Burney, 286B; *Daily Post*, 9 January 1731. Like many papers, the *Daily Post* used the Gregorian calendar (Jan-Dec) whilst the Goldsmiths' Beadle used the Julian calendar (which was abandoned in 1752).

24 Notice no11908 dated 1730. Information about the loss of this jewellery was advertised in the Daily Post and Daily Journal, *as well as being circulated by Goldsmiths' Hall.*

80 BL Col Burney, 689B; *Daily Advertiser*, 16 February 1743.

81 On one occasion 50gns was offered by a member of the Pinchbeck family for a large 'Oval Mocha Stone with three Sprigs' provided it was returned to his shop within three days, otherwise only two guineas would be forthcoming. BL Col Burney, 379B; *Daily Advertiser*, 19 March 1743.

82 OBP, December 1746, t17461205-4, — accused. Another reservation about advertising was the increasing threat of thief-takers. Through the 1730s and increasingly in 1740s, these people earned a living by tracing thieves on behalf of victims since at the time there was no police force to assist. From being a useful service to the general public, thief-takers gained a bad reputation for seeking out theft through newspaper advertisements, harassing victims and even arresting innocent people in order to obtain payment or the reward. Eventually the magistrate, Henry Fielding, took the matter in hand and formed a quasi-official group of the more reputable thief-takers, who became the nucleus of the Bow Street Runners. R. Shoemaker, *The London Mob, Violence and Disorder in Eighteenth Century England*, 2004, pp38-49.

83 Wakelin & Tayler's *Gentleman's Ledger* shows two entries of 3s and 8s being 'Cash p^d Advertising a Pocket Book' three times, the property of Samuel Hayes Esq in February 1778 – presumably a newspaper advertisement. In September 1778 'Cash [was] pd for Warning at Goldsmiths' Hall' for which Sir Alex Leith Bt was charged £1 4s 0d. It is interesting to see a firm such as Wakelin & Tayler using both systems and the cost. Only two such entries appear within the six-year span of the ledger. V&A, Garrard & Co Ltd, *John Wakelin & Willm Tayler's Gentleman's Ledger*, no1, VAM.11, VI 1776-1782, AAD/1995/7/11, pp1, 29. I am indebted to Luke Schrager for this reference. Sir Alex Leith appears in a rather intriguing trial in 1778, acquitted of 'Theft, simple Grand Larceny' (OBP, t17780715-5).

84 During the trial John Watts attested to the accused's good character though later he confessed he did not know him. The presiding Lord Mayor informed the Goldsmiths' Prime Warden of Watts's 'misbehaviour' before him in the proceedings, whereupon the wardens suspended Watts from being an almsman and from their charities for a period of three months despite his pleading that he was '69 years of Age and in no Business and in great Necessity'. In due course Watts, being 'heartily sorry', was reinstated and his gown restored to him. OBP, 24 February 1768, t17680224-66 (John Andrew Martin accused); GCCB vol 17 1767–77 pp27, 29–30. See also note 13.

rings'.[24] The details are the same but the layout different. From 1736 Notices increasingly appeared in news-sheets seeking the return of lost, mislaid or stolen items of all varieties. In 1743 *The Daily Advertiser* carried an advertisement which began

> To the Publick Advertisements having lately become the common Channel of Intelligence to Mankind, upon almost every given subject, that Method is pursued by this [advertiser][80]

With easier access to printers and increasing numbers of daily news-sheets, the same advertisement could be used for the Hall's Notices and newspapers.

Many advertisements offered rewards for the return of property. The size of the reward depended not only upon the value of the lost item but also the speed with which it was returned.[81] It was certainly a temptation for thieves hoping for leniency to return goods 'with no Questions ask'd', however to avoid bargaining and delay 'No greater Reward will be offer'd' was a further condition. As was seen in the Dutems case above, it was an accepted fact that petty criminals stole in order to claim the reward. Honest citizens returning recovered property could sometimes expect 'payment of expenses involved'. In order for stolen goods to be returned anonymously, arrangements were made with coffee houses and taverns.(pp29–30) No doubt enterprising keepers of these establishments, as well as goldsmiths, bankers and pawnbrokers, were quick to realise that featuring in advertisements gave them free publicity. However not all shopkeepers were keen to have their name in print. In 1746, John Neal of Leadenhall Street declared that he

> thought it was not prudent to advertise directly. I have often observed, when Watches are lost and advertised, with no Questions asked, they are seldom heard of, and I thought it would look like hiding Theft.[82]

By 1740 printers would accept advertisements delivered to one of several offices for inclusion in their news-sheet and were charging 2s for a medium-sized advertisement. Even if there had been no increase, Goldsmiths' Hall's 1722 rates (p10) were considerably more than those of newspapers in 1740.[83] Competition did not curtail the use of the Goldsmiths' Warnings, however, which played a significant role in catching and convicting criminals. Walkmen continued to be mentioned in trials as late as 1768, when John Watts (a later Walkman), 'a person that carried out notices from Goldsmiths' hall' was mentioned as an ineffective, inebriated witness in an Old Bailey trial.[84]

Summary

Research has revealed that almsmen undertook 'circuits' to retrieve stolen goods for several centuries. The listing of tradesmen and premises that is contained in this notebook was drawn up in the early 1730s, perhaps shortly after Benjamin Pyne's death. 'The Chief Duties of the Beadle …' were set out in 1732 and the appearance of Barthelemi and Holtom in Court in 1735, Paul de Lamerie's move from his Windmill Street address in 1738 and Thomas Hawksworth's statement in 1739 (see p25), are additional evidence that the lists were written before 1744. Parish records of 1728–34 also confirm names and addresses of those listed. Newspaper advertisements indicate that a number of tradesmen appearing in the Walks, particularly pawnbrokers, ceased trading between 1738 and 1744. In 1739, goldsmiths were required to attend

Goldsmiths' Hall to re-register their marks, which would have helped the Hall to have a better overall picture and control of the trade and clarified old addresses. Bulstrode was dead by 1743, Holtom and Weatherhead were quite elderly and their successors mentioned on the book's flyleaf appear in Goldsmiths' records in the 1740s and 1750s. There is therefore no reason to doubt that the date of 1744, on the cover and at the end of Weatherhead's Walk, was added later.

It is suggested that this notebook is not only a working document but an *aide mémoire* for a Beadle, which would explain the notes relating to stationery (1747–51), committee members for the Trial of the Diet (1763, 1765, 1770) and the first note on the flyleaf dated 1763, referring to 'The Box wich is usualy kept by the prime Warden …' – a reminder that the Beadle could find the Prime Warden's box, possibly required for Court of Wardens' meetings, at Joseph Martin's in Lombard Street.

Emanating from a requirement of the monarch, this ancient and obviously efficient dispersal of information from Goldsmiths' Hall shows how the Company's tentacles reached across London life unlike any other City livery company. The Old Bailey Sessions papers enable us to see the significant effect of the Notices' system on crime and reveal amusing, familiar and tragic stories of eighteenth-century life. Like Benjamin Pyne Snr, in his day one of London's foremost silversmiths, the Walkmen had seen better times and benefited from the support of the Goldsmiths' Company, whose benevolence and almshouses provided them with a dignified end to their lives. The *1744 Warning Carriers Walks* notebook is linked to the Beadle and his duties and in turn associates him with the Assay Office, the Courts of Wardens and Assistants and committee members of the Hall. Through the Walks these officers of the Goldsmiths' Company kept in touch with craftsmen, allied trades and the man in the street.

There is still plenty of information to be gleaned from the *Warning Carriers Walks* notebook. Many previously unknown names emerge from its pages, as well as those already familiar to us. Opening the pages of this manuscript is to look back over 250 years, not into a well-recorded élite but into everyday Hogarthian life. That this notebook survived when it could so easily have been dismissed in years gone by and discarded, is remarkable; however it is the information it contains that is so extraordinarily intriguing.

25 Trade card of Phillips Garden circa 1750–60. As Garden was in the City, he does not feature in any of the three Walks listed in the notebook. The card is a rare depiction of the interior of a goldsmith's shop.

Beadles		Acting Beadles	Walkmen
Ralphe Robinson	died 1649		
John Hastings	1649 – ?died 1665		
Peter White	?1665 – died 1713		
John Bodington	1714 – died 1727		
Benjamin Pyne	1727 – died 1732		Joseph Boucher
			John Hoseman
			Jacob Ray
			Thomas Wright
Robert Jenkes	1732 – died 1753	James Burgess (1746)	William Bulstrode
		David Nash (1748)	John Holtom
			James Weatherhead
Samuel Cawthorn	1753 – resigned 1770		*Names of the later*
Samuel Balston	1770 –		*Walkmen are listed on*
			the flyleaf of the note
			book. See p13.

*26 (above) Cup and cover, silver-gilt, John Bodington, London 1697,
with contemporary case.*

27 (opposite) Coffee pot, silver, Benjamin Pyne, London 1707.

John Bodington and Benjamin Pyne were leading silversmiths in London. Financial difficulties were presumably the reason for each of them to close their workshops and become Beadle of the Goldsmiths' Company. Bodington was Beadle from 1714 until his death in January 1727/28 and was followed by Pyne, who died in 1732. They were responsible for issuing the Warning Notices.

36

28 View of the City of London, taken from Southwark with London Bridge in the foreground, English school circa 1700. Goldsmiths' Hall lies a little to the north-east of (ie behind) St Paul's Cathedral.

2

The routes of the three Walks described in the notebook

Mr Holtom pp40–51
walked west from Goldsmiths' Hall, along the side roads and passages of Fleet
Street and the Strand to Charing Cross and Westminster. He had 202 calls to make.

Mr Weatherhead pp52–67
also went westwards, through Smithfield, Holborn, Seven Dials, Soho, Leicester
Fields and Mayfair, to Tyburn; then south to St James's. He visited 201 addresses.

Mr Bulstrode pp68–79
had the eastern circuit, through the Barbican, Bishopsgate, Spitalfields, Ratcliffe
Highway, to Shadwell; then south back through Wapping, past the Tower,
Houndsditch and Moorfields, to Old Street. He had the longest Walk, of nearly
eight miles, with 146 premises to visit.

Holtom and Weatherhead progressed in a logical fashion, making their calls only on the outward journey. Although at times it appears that they did not take a direct path, there is some underlying logic to the routes and there may have been shortcuts from one street to another that are not marked on John Rocque's map. Bulstrode, however, retraced his steps occasionally, which may have been the result of additional addresses being incorporated in the Walk or even businesses failing. Overall his Walk formed a loop and to help the reader trace where he walked, the men marking his route have been given a sequential number (circled in the image above).

Locations of premises indicated on the maps should be assumed to be approximate. It must be remembered that the lists were set down at a particular point in time and that over the years participants would have altered. By keeping within parish/ward boundaries and taking into account occasional specific addresses in 1734 parish records (when the notebook's addresses were current – see p82), it has been possible to verify some positions, but no attempt has been made to indicate which are precise and which are not. In addition, parish records suggest that occasionally addresses in the notebook are a loose description of the whereabouts of premises and may refer to a general area, eg Charing Cross, Smithfield and Ratcliffe Highway.

Map of London showing the routes

Pages 54–55

Pages 52–53

Pages 56–57

Pages 42–43

Pages 40–41

Pages 58–59

Pages 60–61

Pages 44–45

Pages 62–63

Pages 46–47

Pages 66–67

Pages 64–65

Pages 48–49

Pages 50–51

The Walks

1 *Holtom's Walk, pages 40–51*

2 *Weatherhead's Walk, pages 52–67*

3 *Bulstrode's Walk, pages 68–79*

 Goldsmiths' Hall

Locations of most premises are approximate

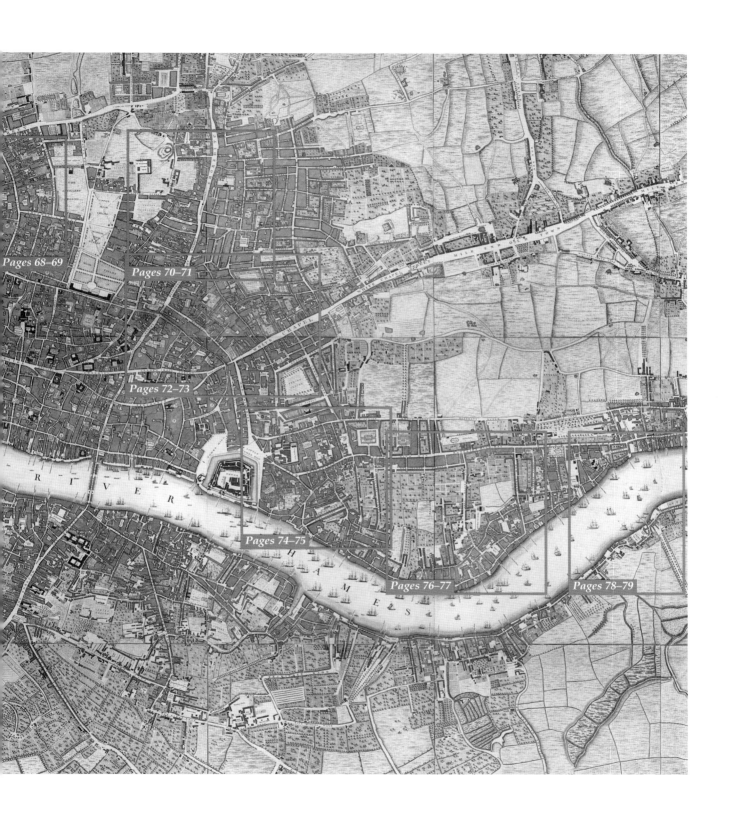

Pages 68–69

Pages 70–71

Pages 72–73

Pages 74–75

Pages 76–77

Pages 78–79

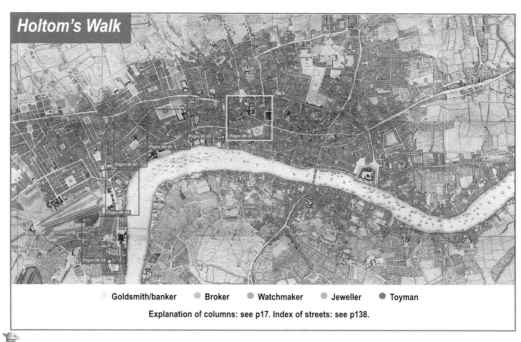

Holtom's Walk

○ Goldsmith/banker ● Broker ● Watchmaker ○ Jeweller ● Toyman

Explanation of columns: see p17. Index of streets: see p138.

Start

No.	Name	Address	Trades visited
1	Green	Angel St, St Martins Le Grand	J1
2	Peart	Crispin Court, Bagnio Passage, St Martins Le Grand	G1
3	Gibson	Round Court, St Martins Le Grand	W1
4	Parks & King	Rose St, Newgate St	W2
5	Pope	Rose St, Newgate St	G2
6	Pearce	Rose St, Newgate St	G3
7	Chad	Rose St, Newgate St	J2
8	Pattison	Warwick Court, Warwick Lane	J3
9	Robinson	Warwick Court, Warwick Lane	J4
10	Bagley	Oxford Arms Inn Yard, Warwick Ct, Warwick Lane	W3
11	Smith	Ye Wheat Sheaf, Warwick Ct, Warwick Lane	B1
12	Nelme	Amen Corner	G4
13	Grimstead	The Black Swan, St Paul's Churchyard	TM1
14	Hurt	The Fish, St Paul's Churchyard	TM2
15	Wildy	at the Corner of St Paul's Churchyard	TM3
16	Barnes	without Ludgate	G5
17	Keddin	Bell Savage Yard	W4
18	Edlin	Ye Old Bailey	G6
19	Wessea	Ye Old Bailey	J5
20	West	Ye Old Bailey	G7
21	Carpenter	Snow Hill	G8
22	Wildman	Snow Hill	G9

Locations of most premises are approximate

Holtom's Walk

Pages 42-43
Pages 44-45
Pages 46-47
Pages 48-49
Pages 50-51
Pages 40-41

○ Goldsmith/banker ● Broker ● Watchmaker ● Jeweller ● Toyman

Explanation of columns: see p17. Index of streets: see p138.

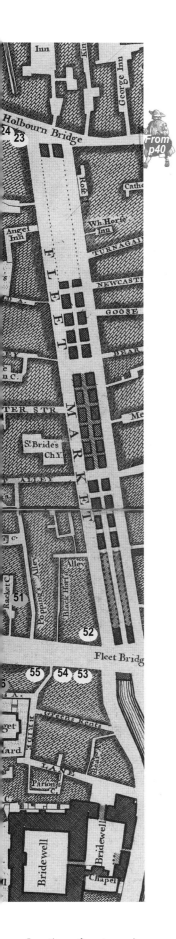

23	Warters	Holborn Bridge	G10
24	Farnel	Holborn Bridge	G11
25	Ray	Holborn Bridge	B2
26	Griffiths	Crabtree Court, Holborn Bridge	W5
27	Fowls	Crabtree Court, Holborn Bridge	B3
28	Brown	Crabtree Court, Holborn Bridge	W6
29	Cambden	Crabtree Court, Holborn Bridge	W7
30	Sidey	Crabtree Court, Holborn Bridge	W8
31	Croket	Shoe Lane	B4
32	Ray	Long Entry	B5
33	Sheldon	Long Entry	B6
34	Willson	New St	W9
35	Jarvis	New St	B7
36	Simmons	New St	W10
37	Luff	New St	G12
38	Rollins	Fetter Lane	B8
39	Thibauld	Fetter Lane	J6
40	Pack	Flower-de-Luces Court, Fleet St	G13
41	Price	Flower-de-Luces Court, Fleet St	G14
42	Wichcott	Corner of Flower-de-Luces Court, Fleet St	W11
43	Chambers	Fleet St	G15
44	Pinchbeck	Fleet St	W12
45	Colly	Fleet St	W13
46	Pinchbeck	Fleet St	W14
47	Pepys	Fleet St	W15
48	Grayham	Fleet St	W16
49	Robinson	Fleet St	W17
50	Martin	Fleet St	W18
51	Lefavor	Racket Court	J7
52	Paradise	by Fleet Bridge	G16
53	Hobkins	by Bride Lane	G17
54	Bristow	by Bride Lane	G18
55	Martin	Fleet St	G19
56	Molins	Bride's Alley	W19
57	Gun	Bride's Alley	B9
58	Grainger	Salisbury Court	B10
59	Robinson	Corner of Salisbury Court	G20
60	Almson	Perfumers' Shop, Corner of Salisbury Court	G21
61	Hallifax	at a Fan Shop,	W20
62	Wallis	at a Fan Shop	J8
63	Price	at a Fan Shop	J9
64	Hart	at a Fan Shop	G22
65	Jarvis	Water Lane	B11
66	Cranmore	Fleet St	G23
67	Seamor	Fleet St	G24
68	Hoare	Fleet St	G25
69	Curghey	Fleet St	G26
70	Houstown	Fleet St	G27
71	Deard	Fleet St	TM4
72	Marcum (Mrs)	Fleet St	TM5
73	Saunders (Mrs)	Fleet St	TM6
74	Benn	Fleet St	W21
75	Pearce	Fleet St	W22
76	Robinson	Middle Temple Gate	W23
77	Delander	Temple Barr	W24
78	Child, Sir F & Co	Temple Barr	G28

Locations of most premises are approximate

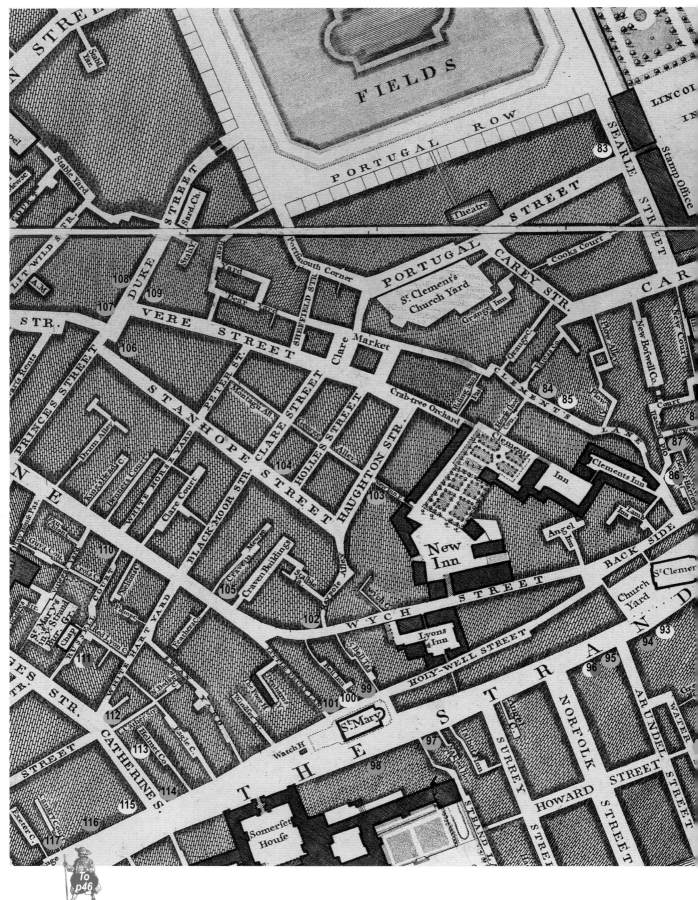

FIELDS

PORTUGAL ROW

LINCOI
IN

Stamp Office

SEARLE

83

PORTUGAL

STREET

Theatre

Cooks Court

St Clement's
Church Yard

CAREY STR.

CAR

Portsmouth Corner

Grange Inn

New Botwell Co.

New Court

DUKE

108

109

107

VERE

STREET

SHEFFIELD STR.

Clare Market

Grange C.

84

85

87

Plow Alley

STR.

106

PRINCES STREET

STANHOPE

PETER STR.

CLARE STREET

HOLLES STREET

Crab-tree Orchard

Riding Sun

Clement's

Inn

Clements Inn

86

104

HAUGHTON STR.

103

Lamb
Inn

N E

110

BLACK-MOOR STR.

STREET

Craven Mews

Craven Buildings

Stable

Angel Inn

New
Inn

BACK SIDE

St Clemer

105

102

WYCH

STREET

Church
Yard

93

Lyons
Inn

94

St Mary's
in ye Strand

111

HOLY-WELL STREET

96

95

CATHERINE S.

112

113

114

115

116

117

HART YARD

St Mary

Watch H

98

97

Angel C.

SURREY

NORFOLK

HOWARD

STREET

ARUNDEL

WATER

99
101 100

Somerset
House

T H E

S T R A N D

Locations of most premises are approximate

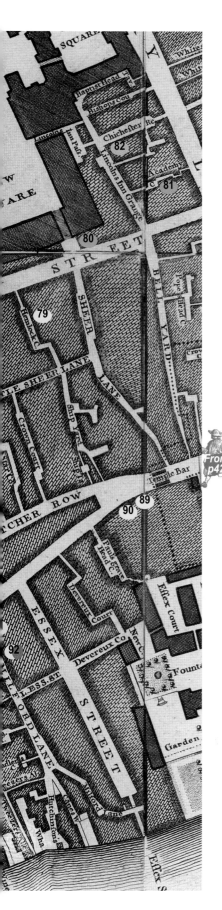

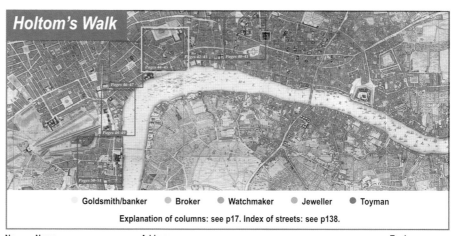

● Goldsmith/banker ● Broker ● Watchmaker ● Jeweller ● Toyman

Explanation of columns: see p17. Index of streets: see p138.

No.	Name	Address	Trades visited
79	Edwards (Mrs)	Hemlock Court	G29
80	King	Lincolns Inn Gateway	W25
81	Connier	Academy Court, Chancery Lane	W26
82	Stow	Chichester Rents, Chancery Lane	B12
83	Gilpin	Lincolns Inn Back gate	G30
84	Parr	St Clements Lane	B13
85	Brooks	St Clements Lane	G31
86	Brown	Clements Inn Gate	G&TM32
87	Du Bois	Boswell Court	J10
88	Salt	New Castle Court	J11
89	Boothby	without Temple Barr	G33
90	Snow	without Temple Barr	G34
91	Davenport	angle Temple Barr, Clements Church	G35
92	Radford	angle Temple Barr, Clements Church	G&TM36
93	Cooper	Arundel St end	G37
94	Bradshaw	Arundel St end	W27
95	Loyd	Arundel St end	J12
96	Loyd & Clark	corner of Arundel St	G&TM38
97	Hull	near ye new Church, Strand	J13
98	Everett	near ye new Church, Strand	W28
99	Haydon	near ye new Church, Strand	W29
100	Ashly	near ye new Church, Strand	G39
101	Clay	near ye new Church, Strand	W30
102	Johnson	Drury Lane	B14
103	Peters	Horton St, Clare Market	B15
104	Stone	Stanhope St, Clare Market	B16
105	Chambers	Drury Lane	B17
106	Kitchin	Stanhope St	B18
107	Hatton	Duke St, Lincolns Inn Fields	W31
108	Berrey	Duke St, Lincolns Inn Fields	W32
109	Pretty	Vere St	B19
110	Stringer	Drury Lane angle Russell Court	B20
111	Threlgale	in Russell Court	G&TM40
112	Cormal	Catherine Street	B21
113	Clifton	Catherine St	G41
114	Vick	angle Catherine St in the Strand	W33
115	Hadsel	in the Strand	G42
116	Harris	in the Strand	W34
117	Foot	in the Strand	W35

From p42

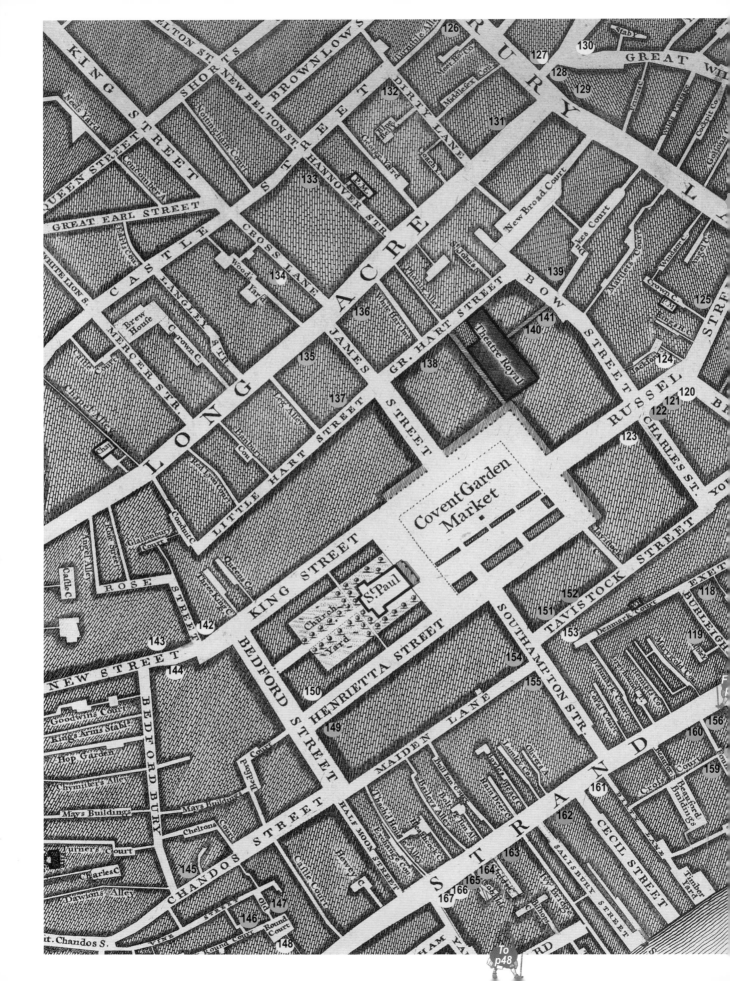

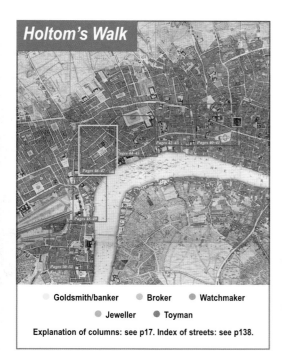

Pages 42-43 | Pages 40-41
Pages 44-45
Pages 46-47
Pages 48-49
Pages 50-51

Holtom's Walk

- ○ Goldsmith/banker
- ● Broker
- ● Watchmaker
- ● Jeweller
- ● Toyman

Explanation of columns: see p17. Index of streets: see p138.

No.	Name	Address	Trades visited
118	Longland	Exeter St	B22
119	Goddard	Burley St	B23
120	Jernegan	Russel St	G43
121	Nangle	Russel St	J14
122	Grignion	Russel St	W36
123	Carter	Russel St	G44
124	Turrel	Russel St	G45
125	Borer	Russel St	B24
126	Barret	Turnstile Passage, Drury Lane	B25
127	Dally	Drury Lane by Long Acre	J&G46
128	Rawlings	Drury Lane by Long Acre	B26
129	Mitchell	Drury Lane by Long Acre	B27
130	Cawthorn	Wild St by Queen St	G47
131	Cox	Long Acre	W37
132	Vaughan	Dirty Lane, Long Acre	B28
133	Shoppo	Hannover St, Long Acre	J15
134	Duemas	Cross Lane, Long Acre	G&J48
135	Ferguson	Long Acre	B29
136	Fennery	Long Acre	B30
137	Norwood	Hart St	B31
138	Reynolds	Hart St	B32
139	Imacer	Bow St	J16
140	Gibson	Bow St	J17
141	Barcer	Bow St	J18
142	Feline	King St	G49
143	Folkingham	New St	G50
144	Bartue	New St	G51
145	Cormal	Chandois St	B33
146	Arnaud	Round Court	J19
147	Simons	Round Court	J20
148	Roger	Round Court	G52
149	Duhamel	Henrietta St	J21
150	Beal	Henrietta St	G53
151	M****	Tavistock St (Mayoffe?)	J22
152	Loddington	Tavistock St	W38
153	Pons	Tavistock St	G54
154	Cole	Maiden Lane	J23
155	Taylor	Maiden Lane	B34
156	Lockan	corner Fountain Court, Strand	J24
157	Chardon	Fountain Court, Strand	J25
158	Husnel	Fountain Court, Strand	J26
159	Barrow	Fountain Court, Strand	J27
160	Neve	Corner of Fountain Court, Strand	W39
161	England	in the Strand	G55
162	Duhamel	in the Strand	W40
163	Threlgle	in the Strand	W41
164	Jones	at a Toyshop in the Strand	J28
165	Hubbard	at a Toyshop in the Strand	W42
166	Horne	at a Toyshop in the Strand	G56
167	Lukin	at a Toyshop in the Strand	G57

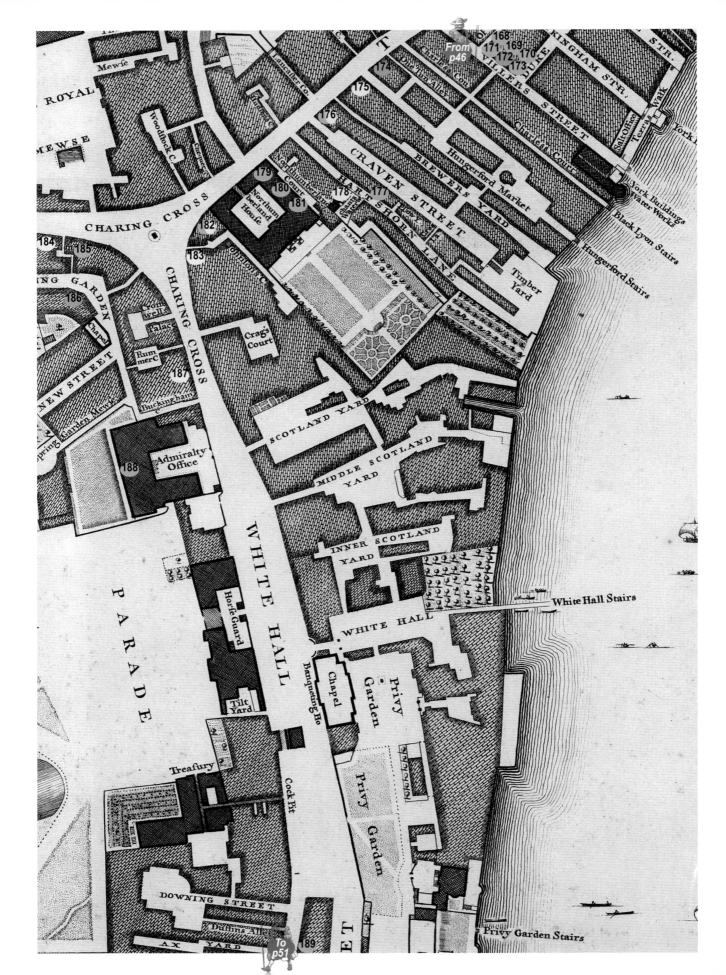

From p46

168
171 169
172 170
173
174
175
176
179
180 181
178 171
182
183
184 185
186
187
188
189

ROYAL
MEWSE
Mewse
Woodstock C.
Chequer C.

CHARING CROSS

CHARING CROSS

Lancaster Co.

Northumberland Court
Northumberland House

Craven's Watering

HART SHORN LANE

CRAVEN STREET

BREWERS YARD
Hungerford Market
Charles's Court
One Ally Alley
Charles's Court

VILLERS STREET

DUKE STR.

BUCKINGHAM STR.

KINGHAM STR.

Salt Office
Terras Walk

York

York Buildings
Water Works

Black Lyon Stairs

Hungerford Stairs

Timber Yard

SPRING GARDEN
Chapel

NEW STREET

Spring Garden Mewse

York Cromwell's Palace
Rummer C.
Buckingham

Crag's Court

Admiralty Office

SCOTLAND YARD

MIDDLE SCOTLAND YARD

INNER SCOTLAND YARD

White Hall Stairs

WHITE HALL

PARADE

WHITE HALL

Horse Guard

Banqueting Ho.

Chapel
Privy Garden

Privy Garden

Tilt Yard

Treasury

Cock Pit

DOWNING STREET

Duffins Alley

AX YARD

To p51

Privy Garden Stairs

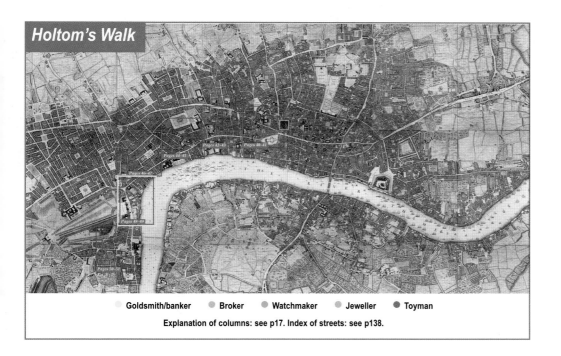

Goldsmith/banker ● Broker ● Watchmaker ● Jeweller ● Toyman

Explanation of columns: see p17. Index of streets: see p138.

No.	Name	Address	Trades visited
168	Flippo	York Buildings	J29
169	Lockrum	York Buildings	J30
170	Floreau	York Buildings	J31
171	Cherack	York Buildings	J32
172	Thornborough	York Buildings	W43
173	Hudard	York Buildings	B35
174	Tucker	angle Hungerford Market	W44
175	Midleton	angle Hungerford Market	G58
176	Manners	in the Strand	G&J59
177	Kirby	Hartshorne Lane in the Strand	B36
178	Spring	Hartshorne Lane in the Strand	G60
179	Flippo	Northumberland Court, in the Strand	J33
180	Turquand	Northumberland Court, in the Strand	J34
181	Brunnett	Northumberland Court, in the Strand	J35
182	Quillet	Charing Cross	G&J61
183	Drummond	Charing Cross	G62
184	Haistings	Charing Cross	G63
185	Charitable Corporations	Spring Gardens	B37
186	Dunlop	Spring Gardens	W45
187	Bartleme	Whitehall	G64
188	Admiralty Office	Whitehall	65
189	Bartlett	King St, Westminster	B38

Locations of most premises are approximate

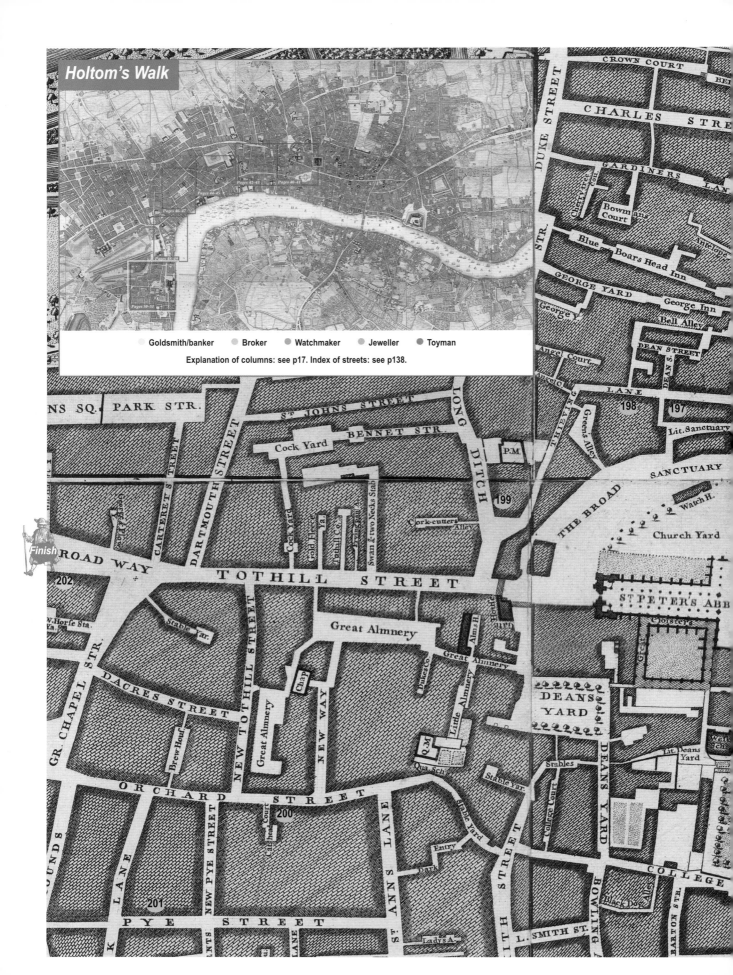

No.	Name	Address	Trades visited
190	Evans	King St, Westminster	B39
191	Bilby	King St, Westminster	G66
192	Ellis	King St, Westminster	W46
193	Williams	King St, Westminster	G67
194	York	King St, Westminster	G68
195	Tellers Office	Westminster Hall	69
196	Woodford	by the Church	B40
197	Highstreet	Thieving Lane	B41
198	Fitzhal	Thieving Lane	B42
199	Gardener	Long Ditch	B43
200	Bradley	Orchard St	B44
201	Smiths	*** St, Westminster	B45
202	********	Broadway, Westminster	B46

Locations of most premises are approximate

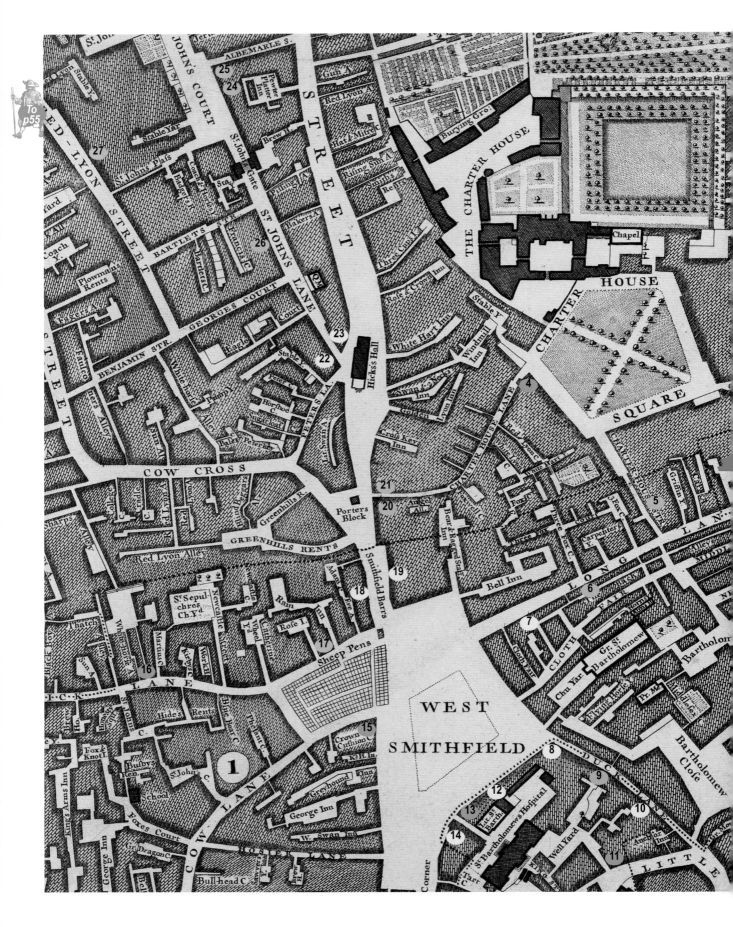

Locations of most premises are approximate

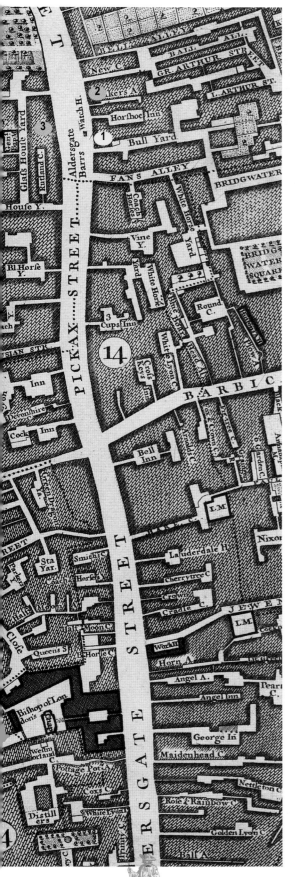

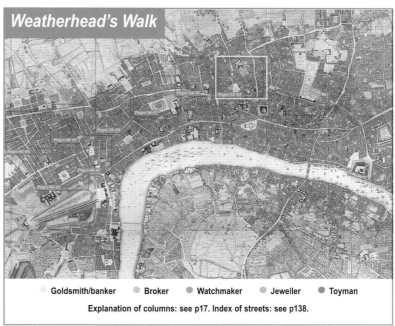

Pages 52-55 · Pages 56-57 · Pages 58-59 · Pages 60-61 · Pages 62-63 · Pages 64-65 · Pages 66-

Weatherhead's Walk

○ **Goldsmith/banker** ● **Broker** ● **Watchmaker** ○ **Jeweller** ● **Toyman**

Explanation of columns: see p17. Index of streets: see p138.

No.	Name	Address	Trades visited
1	Hutton	Goswell Street	G1
2	Makin	Goswell Street	B1
3	Harrison	Goswell Street	B2
4	Freeman	Charterhouse Square	W1
5	Bowman	Charterhouse Street	B3
6	Cole	Long Lane	B4
7	Cartwright	Long Lane	G2
8	Crag	Duck Lane	G3
9	Marquar	Duck Lane	J1
10	Lilley	Duck Lane	G4
11	Needham	Little Brittain	W2
12	Cook	by Mr. Wollfryes	G5
13	Roaker	in the Passage	W3
14	Morris	Smithfield	G 6
15	Loyd	Smithfield	W4
16	Lipscom	Smithfield	W5
17	Hartley	by the Sheep Pens	B5
18	Merry	Smithfield Bars	G7
19	Southam	Smithfield Pens	G8
20	Waters	Charterhouse Lane	B6
21	Newingham	Charterhouse Lane	B7
22	Rigly	Hick's Hall	G9
23	Bartley	Hick's Hall	G10
24	Sears	St Johns Court	B8
25	Sears	St Johns Court	B9
26	Collier	St Johns Lane	B10
27	Battle	Red Lyon Street	B11

Locations of most premises are approximate

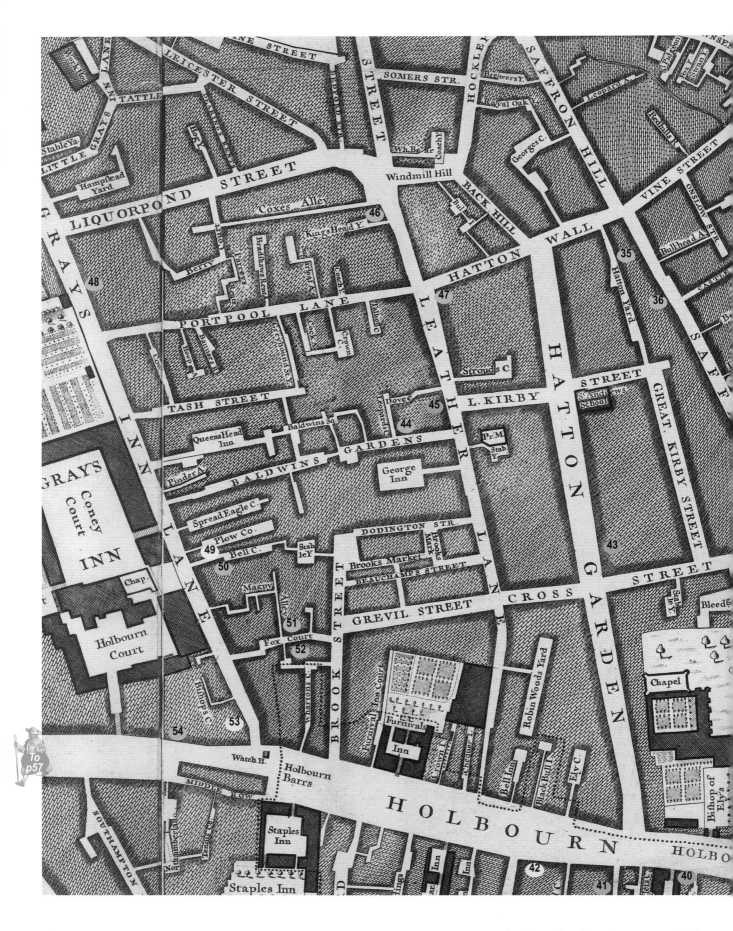

LINE STREET

LEICESTER STREET

STREET

SOMERS STR.

HOCKLEY

SAFFRON HILL

Brewers Y.

Royal Oak Y.

STABLE Ya.

LITTLE

GRAYS

LANE

TATTLE

Hampstead Yard

Wh. Bear

Coach Y.

Windmill Hill

Georges C.

VINE STREET

ONSLOW STR.

Bullhead A.

STREET

LIQUORPOND

Coxes Alley

King's Head Y.

46

BACK HILL

HATTON

WALL

35

Hatton Yard

36

CASTLE

Hog Y.

Bradbury Rent

Berry Court

Park Square

Greyhound St.y

Cook

Crown C.

47

LEATHER

Strouds C

St. Andrews School

PORTPOOL LANE

Mulin C

GRAYS

INN

TASH STREET

45

Dove C

Leopards

L. KIRBY

STREET

44

GREAT. KIRBY STREET

SAFF

QueensHead Inn

Baldwins Sq.

GARDENS

Pr. M Stab. Y.

GRAY'S

Coney Court

INN

Pinder A

BALDWINS

George Inn

SpreadEagle C.

Plow Co.

49

Bell C.

50

Magpy

Stable Y

DODINGTON STR.

Brooks Mark

Brooks Market

BEAUCHAMP'S STREET

HATTON

GARDEN

43

STREET

Chap.

Holbourn Court

LANE

Alley

Fox Court

51

52

BROOK

STREET

GREVIL STREET

CROSS

Stable Y

Bleed

Chapel

Bishops C.

53

54

Furnivals Inn Court

Furnivals Inn

Crown C.

Robin Woods Yard

Bell Inn

BlackBull Inn

Bishop of Ely's

Watch H.

Holbourn Barrs

MIDDLE ROW

SOUTHAMPTON

Nor

Staples Inn

Staples Inn

HOLBOURN

HOLBO

42

41

40

To p57

Locations of most premises are approximate

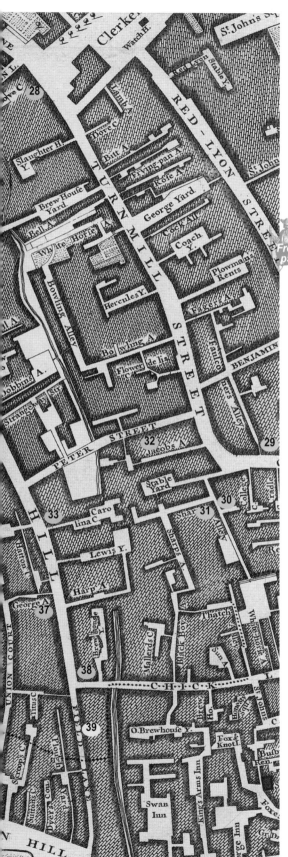

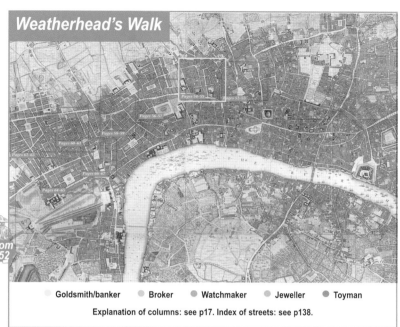

● Goldsmith/banker   ● Broker   ● Watchmaker   ● Jeweller   ● Toyman

Explanation of columns: see p17. Index of streets: see p138.

No.	Name	Address	Trades visited
28	Hall	Trumball (Turnmill) Street	B12
29	Scalf	Cow Cross	B13
30	Tower	Cow Cross	B14
31	Robinson	Cow Cross	B15
32	Tropher	Peters Street, Cow Cross	B16
33	Daniel	Saffron hill	B17
34	Wyborn	Saffron hill	B18
35	Burchmore	Saffron hill	B19
36	Woodman	Saffron hill	B20
37	Higerson	Saffron hill	B21
38	Dokins	Chick Lane	B22
39	Gray	Field Lane	G11
40	Dudds	Holborn	W6
41	Hiccox	Holborn	W7
42	Manning	Holborn	G12
43	Turner	Hatton Garden	W8
44	White	Baldwins Gardens	B23
45	White	Leather Lane	W9
46	Hoskins	Leather Lane	B24
47	Stroud	Leather Lane	B25
48	Ashbourn	Grays Inn Lane	B26
49	Nicholls	Bell Court, Brooks Market	G13
50	Fletcher	Bell Court, Brooks Market	B27
51	Hall	Fox Court, Brooks Market	B28
52	Parsons	Fox Court, Brooks Market	B29
53	Praunock	near Midle Row, Holborn (Brannock)	G14
54	Morris	near Midle Row, Holborn	B30

Locations of most premises are approximate

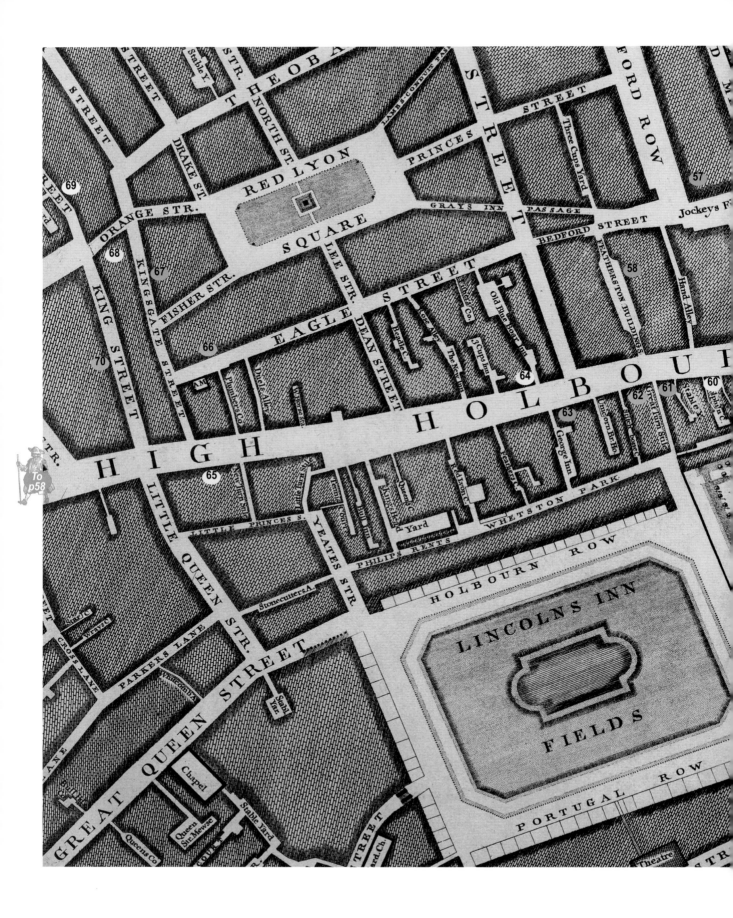

Locations of most premises are approximate

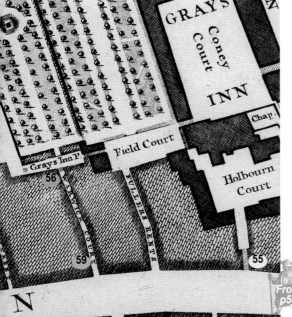

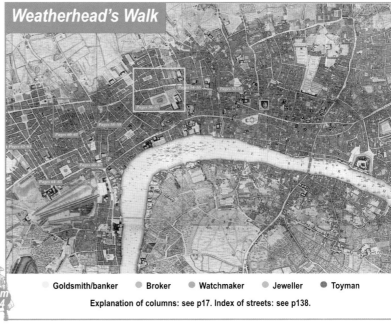

Weatherhead's Walk

| | Goldsmith/banker | | Broker | | Watchmaker | | Jeweller | | Toyman |

Explanation of columns: see p17. Index of streets: see p138.

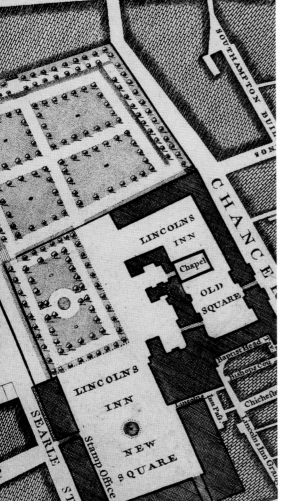

No.	Name	Address	Trades visited
55	Wike	near Midle Row, Holborn	G15
56	Harris	Grays Inn Walk	W10
57	Long	Bedford Row	W11
58	Martin	Featherstones Buildings	W12
59	Gillard	Warwick Court, Holborn	J2
60	Chabert	near Turn Stile Lane	G16
61	Jeffries	near Turn Stile Lane	W13
62	Fury	near Turn Stile Lane	J3
63	Fury	Holborn	W14
64	Gibbons	Holborn	G17
65	Spencer	New turns Stile Passage, Holborn	G18
66	Goddard	Eagle Street	B31
67	Goodread	Kings Gate Street	W15
68	Page	Orange Street	G19
69	Jennings	King Street, Bloomsbury	G20
70	Smithman	King Street, Bloomsbury	B32

From p54

Locations of most premises are approximate

58

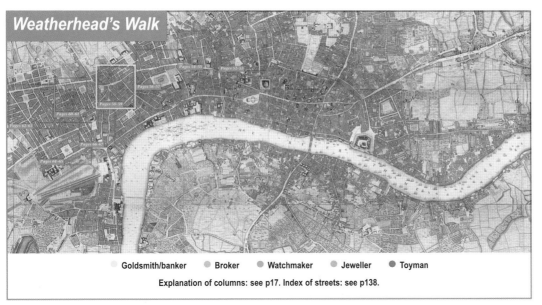

Weatherhead's Walk

Goldsmith/banker ● Broker ● Watchmaker ● Jeweller ● Toyman

Explanation of columns: see p17. Index of streets: see p138.

No.	Name	Address	Trades visited
71	Smithman	Litle Russel Street, Bloomsbury	B33
72	Mannus	Phonex Street, Bloomsbury	B34
73	Robinson	Plumbtree Street, Bloomsbury	W16
74	Clark	Plumbtree Street, Bloomsbury	B35
75	Clark	Plumbtree Street, Bloomsbury	W17
76	Clark	Plumbtree Street, Bloomsbury	B36
77	Osborn	Plumbtree Street, Bloomsbury	B37
78	Oman	at ye X Keys, & in ye Cole Yard	B38
79	Trip	in ye Cole Yard, Drury Lane	B39
80	Shelley	in ye Cole Yard, Drury Lane	B40
81	Fountain	in ye Cole Yard, Drury Lane	G21
82	Hamlin	Corner of ye Cole Yard, Drury Lane	B41
83	Gay	Shorts Gardens	B42
84	Rogers	Shorts Gardens	B43
85	Tonlain	Bromley (Brownlow) Street	W18
86	Tidmarsh	Bromley (Brownlow) Street	B44
87	Hewett	Castle Street, Long Acre	B45
88	Smithson	Castle Street, Long Acre	B46
89	Collier	Castle Street, Long Acre	B47
90	Harrison	King Street, St Giles	B8
91	Harrison	St Andrews Street, 7 Dials	W19
92	King	St Andrews Street, 7 Dials	W20
93	Hannell	St Andrews Street, 7 Dials	G22
94	Oliver	St Andrews Street, 7 Dials	J4
95	Stroud	St Andrews Street, 7 Dials	B49
96	Rous	St Andrews Street, 7 Dials	B50
97	Boshad	Lombard Street, 7 Dials	G23
98	Dupain	Lombard Street, 7 Dials	J5
99	Laroch	Lombard Street, 7 Dials	G24
100	Simmons	Earl Street, 7 Dials	G25
101	Ganderoon	Earl Street, 7 Dials	W21
102	Ganderoon	Hare Street by Monmouth St	B51
103	Ganderoon	in Browns Gardens, 7 Dials	B52
104	Cooper	Denmark St opp St Giles Church	B53

Locations of most premises are approximate

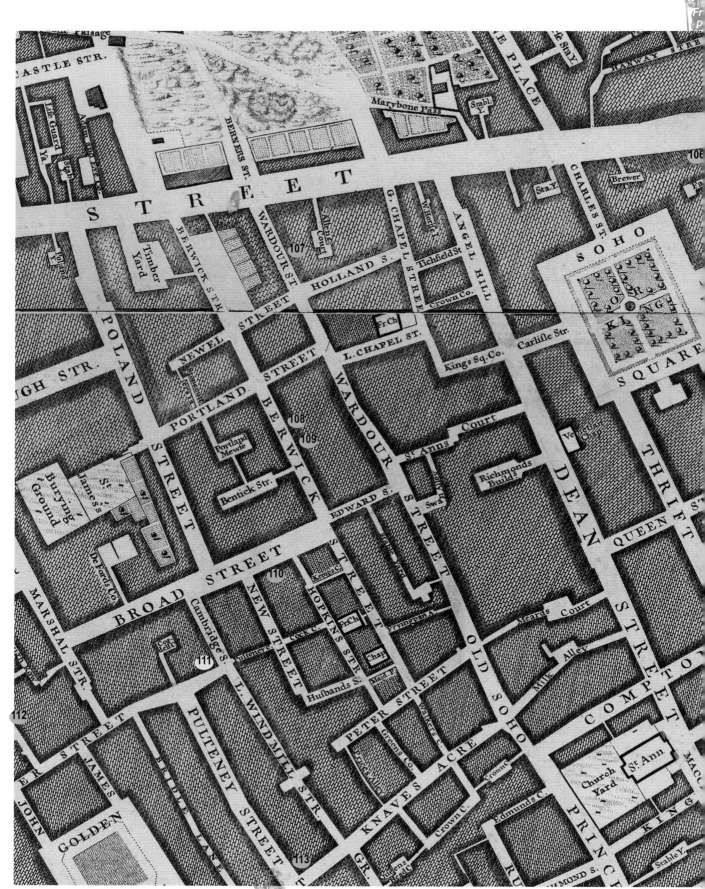

CASTLE STR.

STREET

Life Guard Sign
Ya

POLAND STR.

BERWICK STR.

WARDOUR ST.

Timber Yard

BERNERS ST.

Marybone Pass

Stabl. Y.

PLACE

HANWAY STRE

Sta. Y.

CHARLES ST.

Brewer

SOHO

107

Allen's Court

HOLLAND S.

G. CHAPEL STREET

Tichfield St

W. torley

ANGEL HILL

Crown Co.

Fr.Ch.

L. CHAPEL ST.

King's Sq. Co.

Carlisle Str.

OR.

KING

SQUARE

BUGH STR.

NEWEL STREET

PORTLAND STREET

BERWICK STREET

WARDOUR STREET

Portland Mewle

108

109

St Anns Court

Court

Venetian Chap.

DEAN

THRIFT

Burying Ground

St. James's

De Ford's Co.

Bentick Str.

Richmonds Builds

QUEEN ST

EDWARD S.

MARSHAL STR.

BROAD STREET

Cambridge S.

110

Con Meltr

Hopkins Str.

Kings C.

Cross C.

Fr.Ch.

Chap.

Fryingpan A.

Mcards Court

Milk Alley

OLD SOHO

COMPT

111

Husbands S.

Mad. C.

PETER STREET

Greens Co.

Wake's C.

St Ann

Church Yard

PRINCH

112

STREET

JAMES

PULTENEY STREET

L. WIND MILL STR.

KNAVES ACRE

Crown C.

Edmunds C.

JOHN

GOLDEN

113

GR.

Queens Head C.

RICHMOND S.

KING

Stable Y.

To p63

Locations of most premises are approximate

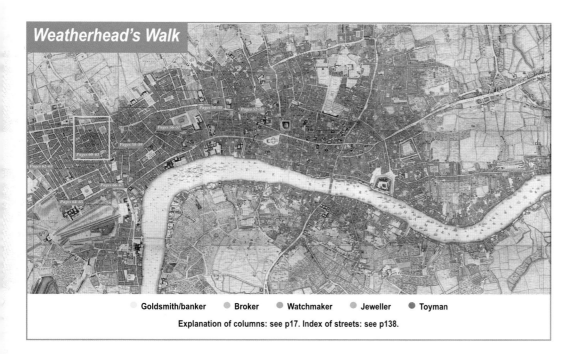

Weatherhead's Walk

Goldsmith/banker   Broker   Watchmaker   Jeweller   Toyman

Explanation of columns: see p17. Index of streets: see p138.

No.	Name	Address	Trades visited
105	Cooper	Hanaway Str. Tatnam Court Road	B54
106	Cooper	Oxford Road ner. St Giles's pound	B55
107	Dean	Warder Street, Soho	B56
108	Dawson	Berwick Street, Soho	B57
109	Dawson	Berwick Street, Soho	B58
110	Caley	Broadstreet	B59
111	Montgomery	Silver Street	G26
112	Read	Carnaby Street	B60
113	Gossford	great Poultney Street	B61

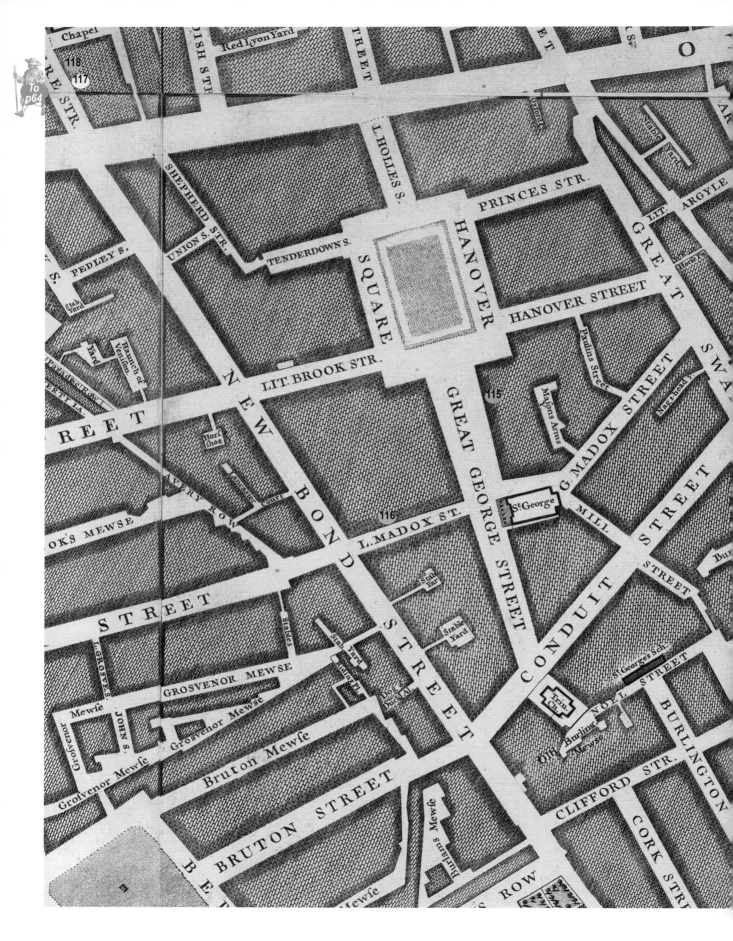

Chapel

118
117

Red Lyon Yard

ISH STR

STREET

118
117

STR.

PEDLEY S.

SHEPHERD STR.

UNION S.

TENDERDOWN S.

L. HOLLES S.

PRINCES STR.

HANOVER

SQUARE

GREAT

LIT. ARGYLE

Stable Yard

HANOVER STREET

Stab. Yard

Yard

Haunch of Venison

NEW

LIT. BROOK STR.

Horse Shoe

Avery Row

Paulins Street

115

Masons Arms

G. MADOX STREET

Nagsheads

GREAT

SWA

ERTY PLA

OK'S MEWSE

BOND

116

L. MADOX ST.

GREAT GEORGE STREET

St. George

MILL.

CONDUIT

STREET

STREET

STREET

J. GROSVE S.

GROSVENOR MEWSE

Mewse

JOHN S.

Grosvenor Mewse

Grosvenor Mewse

Stables

Stab Yard
Riding H.

Stab Yard

Dog &
Duck &c

Stable Yard

St. Georges Sch.

Trint
Ch.

Old Burling Mewse

NOEL

STREET

BURLINGTON

Bruton Mewse

BRUTON STREET

Burlhams Mewse

BE

Mewse

ROW

CLIFFORD STR.

CORK STR

Locations of most premises are approximate

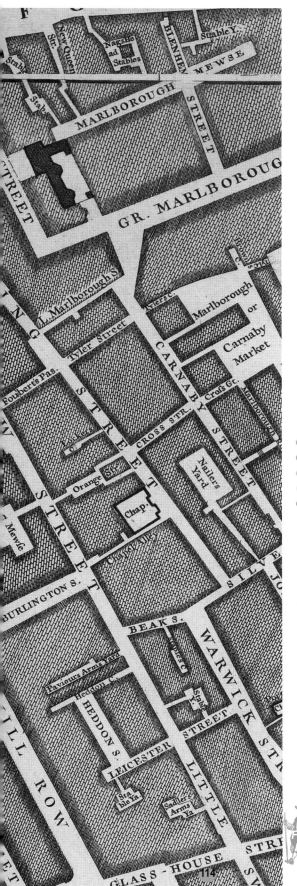

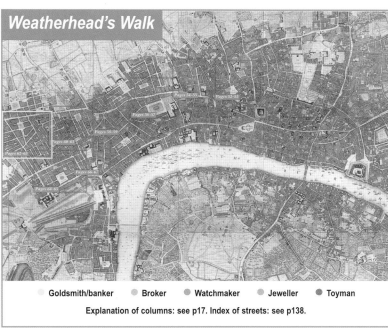

Weatherhead's Walk

Goldsmith/banker • Broker • Watchmaker • Jeweller • Toyman

Explanation of columns: see p17. Index of streets: see p138.

No.	Name	Address	Trades visited
114	Simson	Glasshouse Street	W22
115	Forterry	George St, Hanover Square	W23
116	Morris	Mattox Street	B62
117	Spragg	Vere Street by Oxford Chapel	G27
118	Moran	Vere Street by Oxford Chapel	W24

From p60

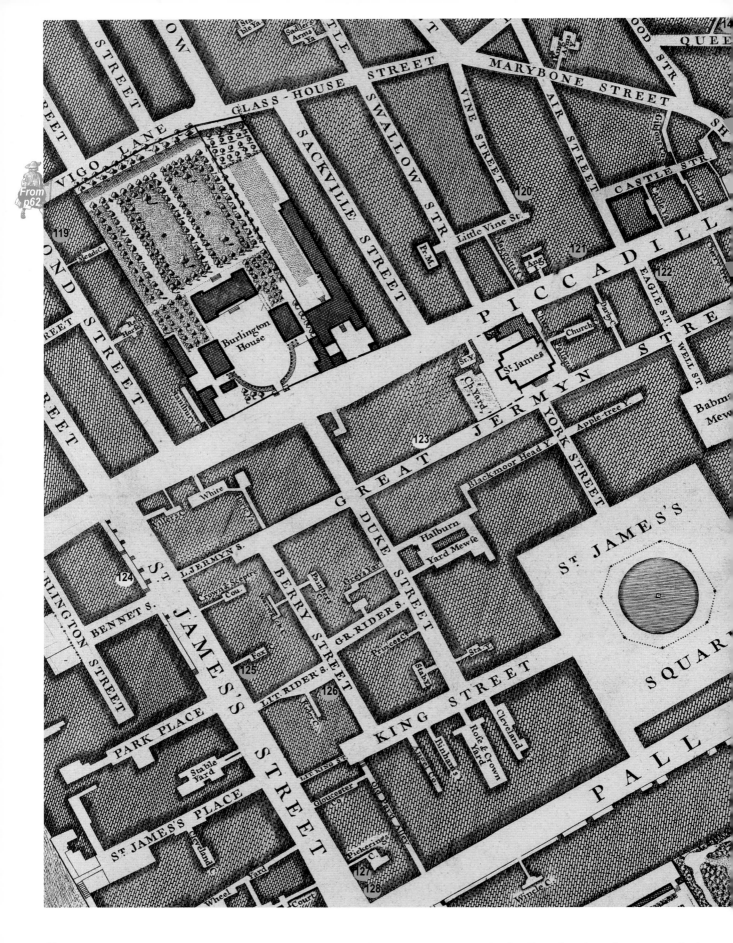

Locations of most premises are approximate

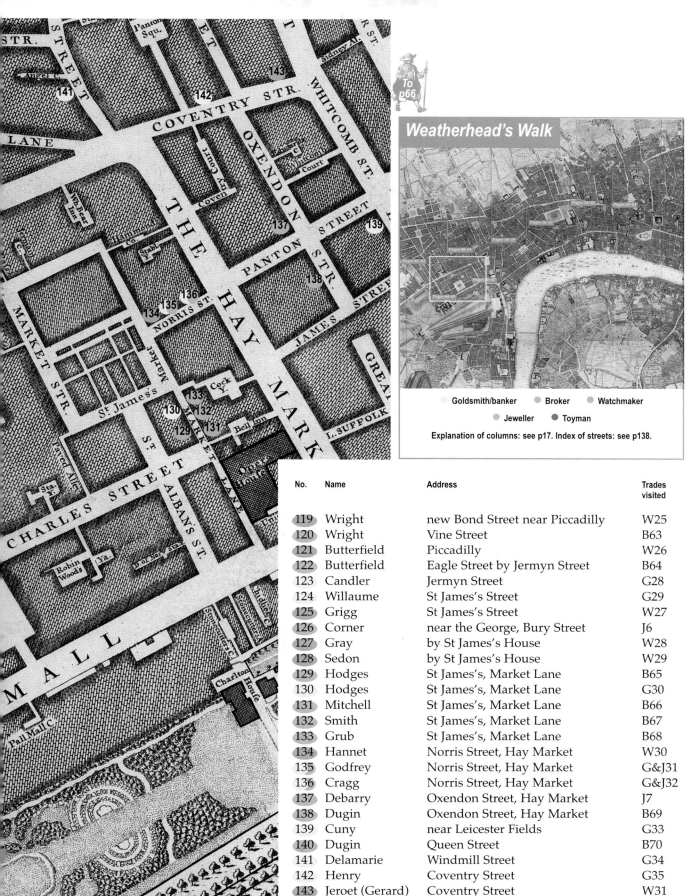

To p66

Weatherhead's Walk

Goldsmith/banker   Broker   Watchmaker

Jeweller   Toyman

Explanation of columns: see p17. Index of streets: see p138.

No.	Name	Address	Trades visited
119	Wright	new Bond Street near Piccadilly	W25
120	Wright	Vine Street	B63
121	Butterfield	Piccadilly	W26
122	Butterfield	Eagle Street by Jermyn Street	B64
123	Candler	Jermyn Street	G28
124	Willaume	St James's Street	G29
125	Grigg	St James's Street	W27
126	Corner	near the George, Bury Street	J6
127	Gray	by St James's House	W28
128	Sedon	by St James's House	W29
129	Hodges	St James's, Market Lane	B65
130	Hodges	St James's, Market Lane	G30
131	Mitchell	St James's, Market Lane	B66
132	Smith	St James's, Market Lane	B67
133	Grub	St James's, Market Lane	B68
134	Hannet	Norris Street, Hay Market	W30
135	Godfrey	Norris Street, Hay Market	G&J31
136	Cragg	Norris Street, Hay Market	G&J32
137	Debarry	Oxendon Street, Hay Market	J7
138	Dugin	Oxendon Street, Hay Market	B69
139	Cuny	near Leicester Fields	G33
140	Dugin	Queen Street	B70
141	Delamarie	Windmill Street	G34
142	Henry	Coventry Street	G35
143	Jeroet (Gerard)	Coventry Street	W31

Locations of most premises are approximate

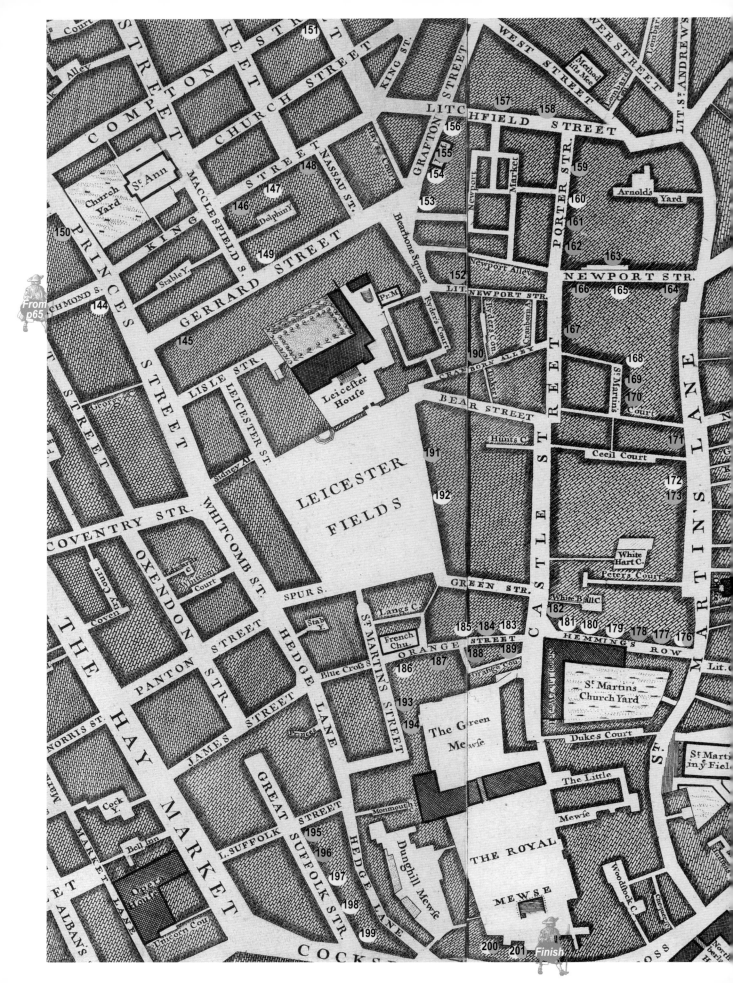

No.	Name	Address	Trades visited	No.	Name	Address	Trades visited
144	Vaughan	Princes Street by St Anns Church	G36	172	Hatfield	St Martins Lane	G46
145	Shelty	Jarrot (Gerrard) Street by St Anns Church	B71	173	Lefavor	St Martins Lane	B75
146	Dubarry	King Street by St Anns Church	J8	174	Pilleau	Chandois Street	G47
147	Chirne	King Street by St Anns Church	G37	175	Courtould	Chandois Street	G48
148	Haydon	King Street by St Anns Church	B72	176	Parry	Hemmingss Row	G&J49
149	Shaw	Jarrot (Gerrard) Street by St Anns Church	G38	177	Haydon	Hemmingss Row	B76
150	Fraydon	Princes Street by St Anns Church	B73	178	Rousseau	Hemmingss Row	W38
151	Crispin	Compton Street, Soho	G39	179	Chartier	Hemmingss Row	G50
152	Humfries	litle Newport Street	B74	180	Archambo	Hemmingss Row	G51
153	Halliday	Grafton Street	G40	181	Dugh	Hemmingss Row	G52
154	Burkitt	Grafton Street	G41	182	Delafonds	Castle Street	J16
155	Ladvocat	Grafton Street	J9	183	Vedeau	Orange Street	G53
156	Dovet	Grafton Street	G42	184	Turmeau	Orange Street	J17
157	Treble	Litchfield Street	J10	185	Lieger	Orange Street	G54
158	Lefong	Litchfield Street	J11	186	White	Orange Street	G55
159	Megault	Porter Street by Newport Market	J12	187	Cumbleford	Orange Street	J18
160	Barbott	Porter Street by Newport Market	G43	188	Martineau	Orange Street	W39
161	Archambo	Porter Street by Newport Market	W32	189	Joslin	Orange Street	J19
162	Blanchard	Porter Street by Newport Market	W33	190	Massy	Cranbourn Alley	W40
163	Hillot	Newport Street	W34	191	Dutens	Leicester Fields	J20
164	Jones	Newport Street	J13	192	Pelletier	Leicester Fields	G56
165	Howard	Newport Street	G44	193	Billings	St Martins Street, Leicester Fields	B77
166	Fountain	Castle Street	J14	194	Gole	St Martins Street, Leicester Fields	J21
167	Beavois	Castle Street	W35	195	Megrett	Suffolk Street	J22
168	Merchant	St Martins Court	G45	196	Descharmes	Suffolk Street	W41
169	Batut	St Martins Court	J15	197	Rainaud	Suffolk Street	G57
170	Purden	St Martins Court	W36	198	Makeland	Suffolk Street	G58
171	Pupin	St Martins Lane	W37	199	Lesage	Suffolk Street	G59
				200	Chenear	by the Mewse	G&TM60
				201	Admiral	by the Mewse	J61

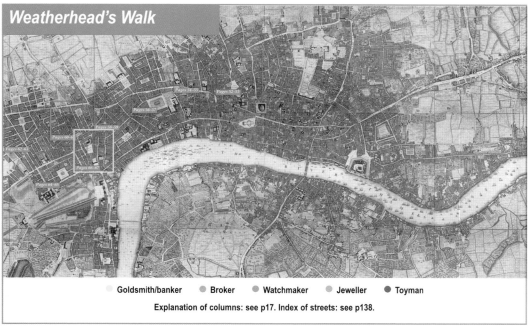

Weatherhead's Walk

○ Goldsmith/banker ● Broker ● Watchmaker ○ Jeweller ● Toyman

Explanation of columns: see p17. Index of streets: see p138.

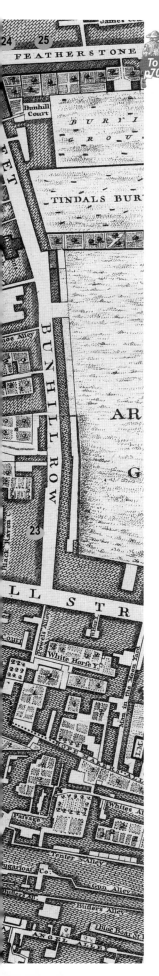

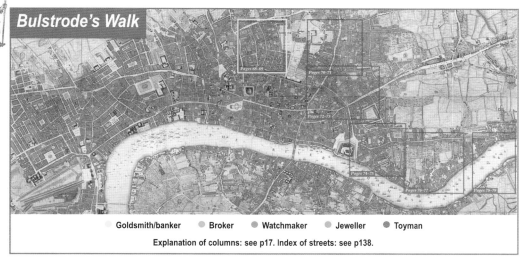

Bulstrode's Walk

Goldsmith/banker ● Broker ● Watchmaker ● Jeweller ● Toyman

Explanation of columns: see p17. Index of streets: see p138.

No.	Name	Address	Trades visited
1	Stone (Mrs)	Barbicon	B1
2	Askew	Barbicon	G1
3	Goslin	Barbicon	G2
4	Curtoys	Barbicon	B2
5	Skinner	Barbicon	W1
6	Nichols	Barbicon	G3
7	Cookson	Bridgewaters Gardens	B3
8	Edwards (Mrs)	Bridgewaters Gardens	B4
9	Smith	Bridgewaters Gardens	B5
10	Howard (Mrs)	Bridgewaters Gardens	B6
11	Armsted	Red Cross Street	B7
12	Doughty	Red Cross Street	B8
13	Gibbons	Red Cross Street	G4
14	Cooper	Red Cross Street	W2
15	Smith (Mrs)	Red Cross Street	G5
16	Alcock	Red Cross Street	G6
17	Stone	White Cross Street	B9
18	Wild	White Cross Street	B10
19	Adsit	White Cross Street	B11
20	Eysham	White Cross Street	B12
21	Bubb	White Cross Street	B13
22	Cross	White Cross Street	B14
23	Meredith (Mrs)	Bunhill Fields	B15
24	Clark	Featherstone Street	B16
25	Endersby	Featherstone Street	W3

Walk goes to page 70 and returns from page 72

Walk goes to page 70 and returns from page 72

No.	Name	Address	Trades visited
136	Farmer (Mrs)	Grub Street	B87
137	Farmer	Grub Street	B88
138	Bell (Mrs)	Grub Street	B89
139	Johnson	Grub Street	B90
140	Francis (Mrs)	Grub Street	B91
141	Erwin	Grub Street	B92
142	Road	Golden Lane	G33
143	Steventon	Golden Lane	G34
144	Howard	Turkshead Court	B93
145	Bowditch	Brick Lane	B94
146	Adrian	Brick Lane	J2

See page 37 for a note on the route of this Walk.

See page 37 for a note on the route of this Walk.

Locations of most premises are approximate

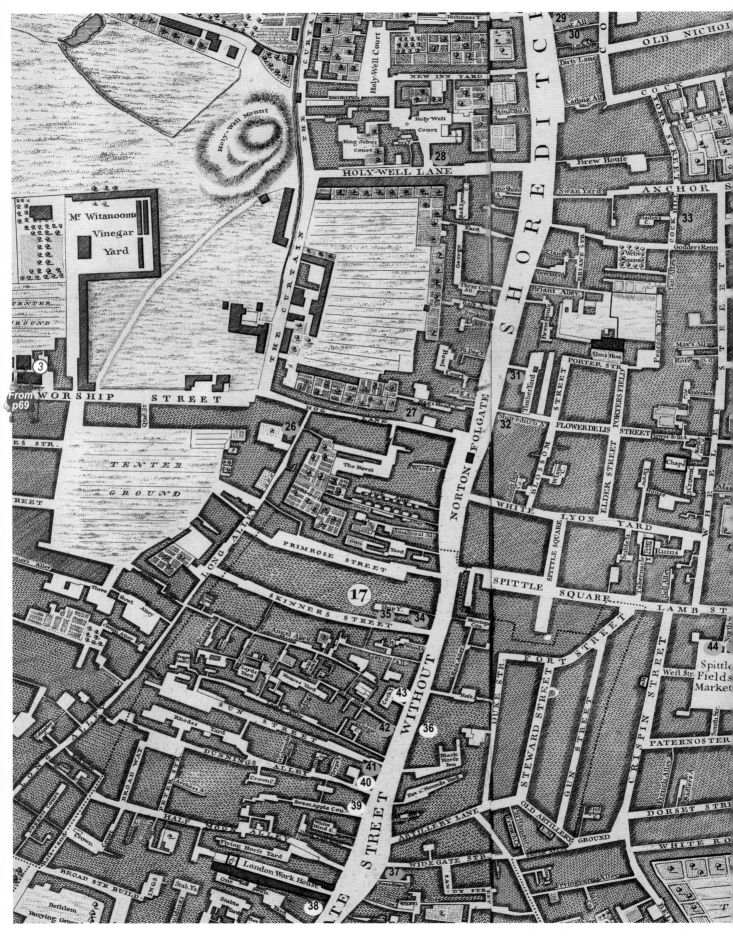

Locations of most premises are approximate

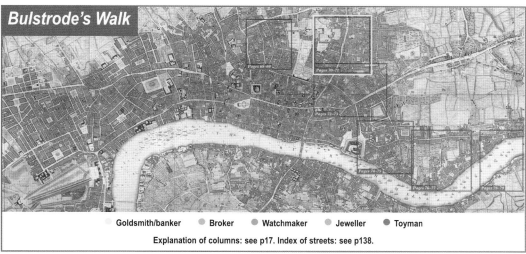

Bulstrode's Walk

● Goldsmith/banker ● Broker ● Watchmaker ● Jeweller ● Toyman

Explanation of columns: see p17. Index of streets: see p138.

No.	Name	Address	Trades visited
26	Myne	Long Alley	B17
27	Higgs (Mrs)	Hogg Lane	B18
28	Good	Paved Ally, holywell Lane, Shor	B19
29	Hill	Hare Alley, holywell Lane, Shor	B20
30	Reynolds	Hare Alley, holywell Lane, Shor	B21
31	Abbot	Norton Follgate	W4
32	Gallwith (Mrs)	Norton Follgate	B22
33	Sadler	Goddards Rents	B23
34	Boyghton	Skinners Street	B24
35	Garbert (Mrs)	Skinners Street	B25
36	Wilkinson	Bishop Gate Street	G7
37	Everitt (Mrs)	Bishop Gate Street	B26
38	Gibson (Mrs)	Bishop Gate Street	G8
39	Holland	Bishop Gate Street	G9
40	Fellows	Bishop Gate Street	G10
41	Tollson	Bishop Gate Street	W5
42	King (Mrs)	Bishop Gate Street	B27
43	Stevens	Bishop Gate Street	G11
44	Courtier	Spittle Fields	J1
45	Payne	Spittle Fields	W6
46	Mappson (Mrs)	Grey Eagle Street, Spittle Fields	B28
47	Jourdaine	Corbitts Court, Spittle Fields	G12

Walk goes to page 73

See page 37 for a note on the route of this Walk.

Locations of most premises are approximate

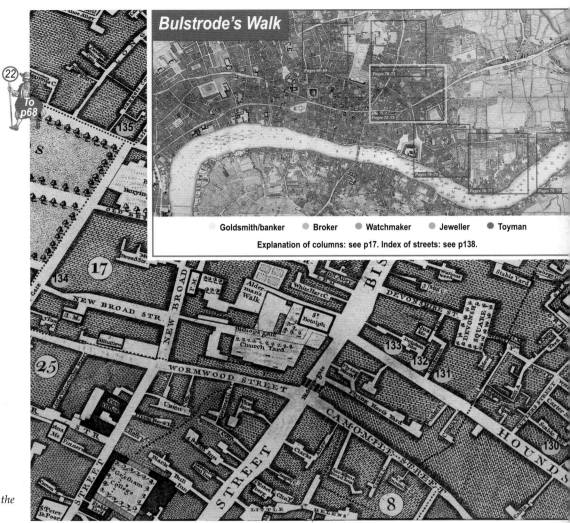

Bulstrode's Walk

Goldsmith/banker ● Broker ● Watchmaker ● Jeweller ● Toyman

Explanation of columns: see p17. Index of streets: see p138.

See page 37 for a note on the route of this Walk.

No.	Name	Address	Trades visited
48	Mitchell	Winfords (Wentworth) Street, Spittle Fields	B29
49	Rivers	old George Street, Spittle Fields	B30
50	Gough	old George Street, Spittle Fields	B31
51	Howard	old George Street, Spittle Fields	B32
52	Jennings	Thorle (Thrale) Street, SpittleFields	B33
53	Docher	Wyatt Street (White Row), Spittle Fields	B34
54	Heymore	Brick Lane	B35
55	Jourdaine	Pater Noster Rowe	W7
56	Allin	Smock Alley	B36
57	Goodman (Mrs)	Smock Alley	B37
58	Cooper	Smock Alley	B38
59	Woolley	Smock Alley	B39
60	Pickard (Mrs)	Smock Alley	B40
61	Martin	White Chaple	B41
62	Stock	White Chaple	W8
63	Quelch	Red Lyon Street	W9
64	Gray	Red Lyon Street	G13
65	Leopard	Red Lyon Street	G14

No.	Name	Address	Trades visited
66	Brassay	Aldgate	G15
67	Marlow	Aldgate	G16
68	Wilder (Mrs)	Colchester Street, Goodmans Fields	B42

Walk goes to page 74 and returns to page 73

No.	Name	Address	Trades visited
73	Reeve	Minories	G17
74	Hardy	Minories	G18
75	Wynn	Minories	G19
76	Dearing	Little Minories	G20
77	Truclock	Little Minories	B47
78	Perkins	Little Minories	B48

Walk goes to and returns from page 74

No.	Name	Address	Trades visited
126	Calcott	Hounds Ditch	B77
127	Harvey	Hounds Ditch	B78
128	Messiter	Hounds Ditch	B79
129	Smallman	Hounds Ditch	B80
130	Perry	Hounds Ditch	B81
131	Church	Hounds Ditch	B82
132	Willmot	Hounds Ditch	B83
133	Rudge	Hounds Ditch	B84
134	Yarp	Moor Fields	B85
135	Broadhurst	Rose & Crown	B86

Locations of most premises are approximate

From p73
To p73
From p73
To p73
From p76

⑪ ⑧ ⑦

GOODMANS YARD

Glass House Yard
Glass Ho.
Glass House Y.

Red Lyon Alley
Red Gate Court
BlackHorse
Perltons Y.

⑳ To p73

LITTLE

TOWER HILL

LIT PRESCOT STR.
Rosemary Court
W Hoop Co.
ors A.H.

79

80
81

Sweedland Court
QUEEN STR.

Blue Anchor
Lit Bailey Str.
Tower Hill Pass.

ROSEMARY

Great Exchange
Swallows

Pound Ya.
Pickle Ya.
Stable Ya.

VICTUALING OFFICE

Slaughter House Yard

82

Coopers Yard

83 84

EAST

CHAMBER STREET
Timber Yard

Aldgate Church Yard

85
86

SMITHFIELD

87

Green Yard

Glass House Yard
Black Horse Alley

LANE

69

SALT PETER BANK

70

WatchH

Glass Ho.

LYON ST.

Black Horse Yard

ST CATHERINES LANE

Crown Court
Johns Court
Bell All.
Church
Star C.
Shovel All.
Timber Yard
BUTCHER ROW
St Catherines Church Yard

125

124
123
122

The Cloisters
St Catherin Church Yar.
Church Yard

121
120

St Catherine's Court

ST CATHERINES

RED CROSS STREET
Moule Alley
Angel
King Henry's Yard
The King's Brew House

MAUDLINGS

BURR STREET

NIGHTINGALE L.

IRON GATE
Iron Gate Stairs
St Catherines Stairs

PILLORY LANE

Browns Wh.
Nels Wh.
Guilams' Wh.
Parsons' Brew House

⑲
119

T

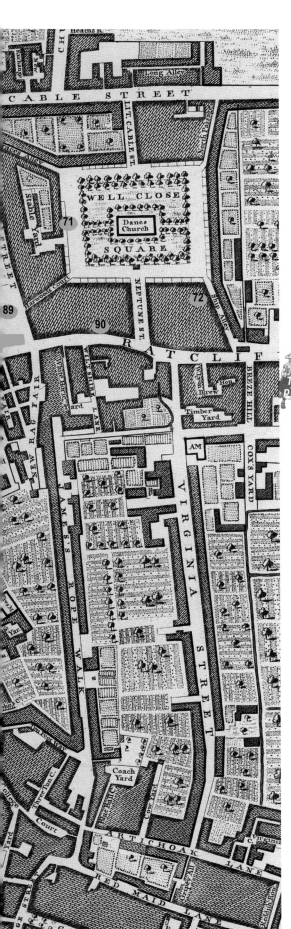

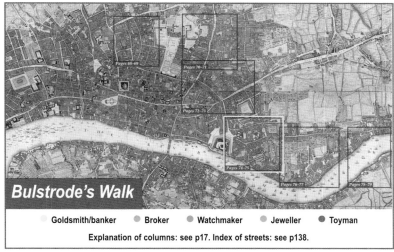

Bulstrode's Walk

○ Goldsmith/banker ● Broker ● Watchmaker ● Jeweller ● Toyman

Explanation of columns: see p17. Index of streets: see p138.

Retraces his steps to top left of this map

To p76

No.	Name	Address	Trades visited
69	Shipton	Abells Buildings	B43
70	Booth (Mrs)	Mill Yard	B44
71	Bashly (Mrs)	Wellclose Square	B45
72	Stevens (Mrs)	Ship Alley	B46
Walk goes to page 73			
79	Green	Tower hill	G21
80	Jacobsen	King Street	B49
81	Warner	King Street	B50
82	Jovett	East Smithfield	G22
83	Alsop (Mrs)	East Smithfield	W10
84	Foot	East Smithfield	G23
85	Herne	Starr Ally	B51
86	Robinson	Starr Ally	B52
87	Goddard (Mrs)	Nightingale Lane	B53
88	Allome (Mrs)	Ratcliffe highway	B54
89	Hering	Well Street, Ratcliffe highway	B55
90	Hally	Ratcliffe highway	B56
Walk goes to and returns from page 76			
119	Barrow	St Catherines	W16
120	How	St Catherines	G31
121	How	St Catherines	G32
122	Smith	St Catherines	B73
123	Priswell	St Catherines	B74
124	Batty	St Catherines	B75
125	Waters (Mrs)	St Catherines	B76

See page 37 for a note on the route of this Walk.

Locations of most premises are approximate

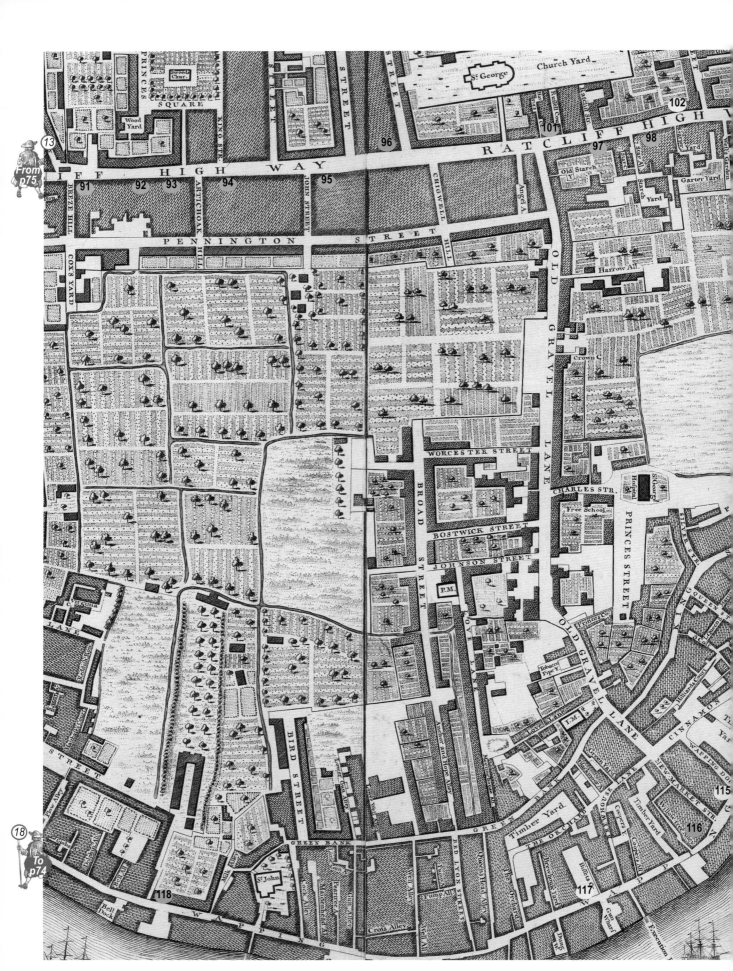

13
From p75

18
To p74

PRINCES

SQUARE

Sweeds Chur.

Wood Yard

St George

Church Yard

102

101

107

RATCLIFF HIGH WAY

97

98

Yard

96

Angel A.

Old Starch Y

Starch Yard

Garter Yard

CLIFF   HIGH   WAY

91   92   93   94   95

JOHN STREET

FREEZE HILL

ARTICHOAK HILL

CHIGWELL HILL

KING STR

COX'S YARD

PENNINGTON   STREET

OLD   GRAVEL   LANE

Harrow All.

Crown C

WORCESTER STREET

BROAD STREET

BOSTWICK STREET

JOHNSON STREET

P.M.

CHARLES STR.

Hospital

St George

Free School

PRINCES STREET

SILVESTER

KING

QUEEN

Crown C

Tobacco Pipe Y.

OLD GRAVEL LANE

T.M.

CINNAMON

Yar

WAPPING DO

115

Christian

LANE

BIRD   STREET

Anchor and Hope Ally

GREEN BANK

Lovers

PD LYON STREET

GREEN BANK

Queens Head Ally

Timber Yard

TimberYard

Coopers

Willow Ho

116

STREET

St John

117

WAPPING

118

Bell Dock

Cross Alley

Pump All

Gun Wharf

Execution

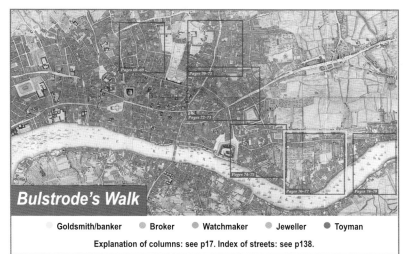

Bulstrode's Walk

| | Goldsmith/banker | Broker | Watchmaker | Jeweller | Toyman |

Explanation of columns: see p17. Index of streets: see p138.

No.	Name	Address	Trades visited
91	Budd	Ratcliffe highway	B57
92	Winch	Ratcliffe highway	B58
93	Gosling (Mrs)	Ratcliffe highway	B59
94	Ward	Ratcliffe highway	B60
95	Benson	Ratcliffe highway	B61
96	Smith	Ratcliffe highway	W11
97	Bentley	Ratcliffe highway	B62
98	Holmes (Mrs)	Ratcliffe highway	B63
99	Hewett (Mrs)	Ratcliffe highway	B64
100	Scarlett (Mrs)	Ratcliffe highway	B65
101	Lane	Ratcliffe highway	B66
102	Ludlow	Ratcliffe highway	G24
103	Brigham	Ratcliffe highway	B67
104	Horne (Mrs)	Ratcliffe highway	B68
105	Rickman	Ratcliffe highway	B69
106	Biddle	Ratcliffe highway	B70

Walk goes to and returns from page 78

112	Payne	New Gravell Lane	B71
113	Foster	New Gravell Lane	B72
114	George	Wapping	G28
115	Hill	Wapping	G29
116	Davis	Wapping	W14
117	Blisset (Mrs)	Wapping	G30
118	Gibbs	Wapping	W15

See page 37 for a note on the route of this Walk.

Locations of most premises are approximate

ROPE WALK

SHADWELL

Royal Oak Coll.

Coopers Alms Ho.

107

BROAD
110

Coal Yard

Cooper Coll.

Stone Yard

Ship Alley

Timber Wharf

Coal Wh.

Trinity Stairs

Trinity Yard

Great Stone Stairs

Timber Wharf

Timber Yard

3 Cup All.

SHADWELL

DEAN STREET

COCK HILL

GOLDS HILL

SHADWELL

15

From
p77

Pennant Alley

Market Hill

Shadwell

Market

SHADWELL

VIRGINIA PLANTER

BROAD BRIDGE

The Works

Back side

Bell Wharf Stairs

GRIFFIN STREET

MIDDLE

The Orchard

The Green

Timber

Coal Stairs

SHADWELL

Coal W.

Shadwell Dock Stairs

Timber
Yard

FOX LANE

Coopers Yard

Coal Wh.

16

To
p77

111

Shadwell Dock

Pelean Stairs

King & Queen Stairs

Ship Alley

Browns C.

A Dry Dock
Shipwrights

Timber
Wharf

W

R E D R I F F

78

Locations of most premises are approximate

Bulstrode's Walk

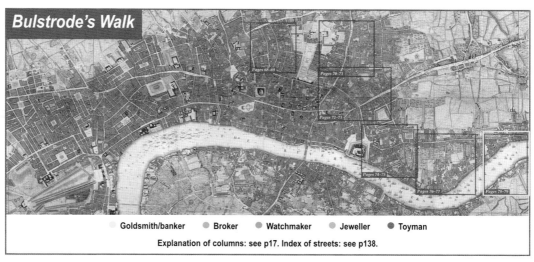

Goldsmith/banker ● Broker ● Watchmaker ● Jeweller ● Toyman

Explanation of columns: see p17. Index of streets: see p138.

No.	Name	Address	Trades visited
107	Beale	Ratcliffe highway	G25
108	Kipling	Ratcliffe highway	W12
109	Roberts	Ratcliffe highway	G26
110	Jackson	Wapping	W13
111	Fowler	Wapping	G27

Walk goes to page 77

See page 37 for a note on the route of this Walk.

Locations of most premises are approximate

29 'The Lottery', mezzotint, anon, circa 1760, published by Bowles & Carver.
A boy picks the pocket of a young lady as she goes into the state lottery office to try her luck.

3

The tradesmen

*Alphabetical list of
goldsmiths, jewellers, watchmakers, toymen, brokers and pawnbrokers
listed in the notebook, with biographical details.*

In the following pages all the names in the three Walks are combined and listed alphabetically, using the spelling of the notebook. The phonetic spelling of some names may necessitate using the concordance on pp132–36, for example the well-known silversmith Kandler is spelt Candler by the compiler of the notebook, and Mr Eyemaker is spelt Imacer.

The name is followed by the trade (as given in the notebook). Below this is a cross-reference to the relevant map on pp40–79. The address on the next line is that given in the notebook, using the original spelling. Addresses and names in other references are spelt according to the source quoted and for the most part have not been standardised. The script in the notebook has faded and some pages are worn. Added to this is the difficulty of differentiating between F, P, T and J, although in some cases verification has been possible from the research sources used. Remember, too, that it was common practice for fathers and eldest sons to bear the same first name.

The Trades
It must be assumed that the majority of those described as 'Broker' were in fact pawnbrokers, particularly those in the east end of London and those who were women. Where it is known that the trade was that of pawn-broking, it is given by the present author as (Broker/pawnbroker), otherwise the listing of the note-book is given: (Broker).

Banking was carried out by many goldsmiths, being part of, or solely, their business. Bankers were described as goldsmiths in the eighteenth century. Where a person or firm is listed in the notebook as 'goldsmith' but is known to have been a banker, it is given as (Goldsmith/banker).

The identity of some of those listed is not absolutely proven, as readers will discover. Research into this period inevitably produces vague and conflicting data. It is acknowledged that information given below may be subject to alteration by future researchers. Readers are asked to bear this in mind and also to recognise the parameters that the author set for this work.

Notes on parish records

Parish rate collectors' books vary greatly in style and detail. Some wards are divided into numbered precincts and some into areas, others have street names or are simply lists of people. Where there are several names within the same street, the order in which they are visited is apparent and occasionally there is indication of which side of the street the collector is walking, eg, north, south, east or west. Some streets have been renamed since the eighteenth century and it should be remembered that in this period there were no street numbers. Where detailed street names are given, it is possible to locate establishments more precisely, eg Charles Pinchbeck's name is listed between St Dunstan's Court and Holt Court, Fleet Street [HOLTOM NO44]; Edward Pinchbeck comes between Three Legged Alley and Bolt Court, Fleet Street [HOLTOM NO46], see p43.

The preferred year for research was 1734. Where records are not available the previous six years have been used. The rate books do not distinguish between householder and tenant, dwelling houses or work prem-ises or indicate whether a ratepayer is carrying on a business. It is noticeable that tradesmen such as jewellers and watchmakers, who perhaps required only a work-room, are not as frequently found as, say, goldsmiths able to own or rent entire premises. Where a householder is also an owner of other properties, the number of prem-ises and sometimes the location is indicated.

The three Walks cover a diverse area. In Westminster, St James's and Mayfair, a duke could be paying £16 16s 0d, whereas a goldsmith, who might be renting in a vicinity where property was too expensive to buy or who might not have sufficient comparative wealth, may not have qualified or be listed for a rating. In Soho, Smithfield and Bishopsgate a relatively successful goldsmith, jeweller, watchmaker or broker would qualify and in the east (Shadwell and Wapping) even brokers could be required to pay a top Land Tax rate for that parish of 5s. The basis on which the assessments were made, and the fact that occasionally lump sums were paid, make records covering this period rather confusing. [The Guildhall Library Manuscripts section has information on early Land Tax Assessments for the City of London, leaflet no13].

*An asterisk shows that a reference has been found indicating that the person kept a shop.

See p140 for abbreviations to sources used in the following pages.

A

Abbot (Watchmaker)
31 BULSTRODE, P71
Norton Follgate
1695–1750 possibly Philip Abbott and
1724, John Abbot, his son (*Britten*)

Admiral (Goldsmith and jeweller)
201 WEATHERHEAD, P67
by the Mewse
1734 ffrancis Admirauld, Warwick Street,
registered for Poor Rate (*WAC: MF1577
F488 item3*)
1741 Mr Francis Admiral, Sign of the
Ring and Pearl, over-against the End
of Hedge Lane, near Charing-Cross,
advertised in *The London Daily Post*
and *General Advertiser* for the return of
a pair of ear-rings, jeweller (*BL: Burney
355B, 06 Apr 1741*)

Admiralty Office (No trade)
188 HOLTOM, P49
Whitehall
1734 Admiralty registered for Poor Rate
(*WAC: MF1577 F488 item3*)

Adrian (Jeweller)
146 BULSTRODE, P69
Brick Lane
Not found

Adsit (Broker)
19 BULSTRODE, P69
White Cross Street
1734 possibly Edward Aris, White Cross
Street, White Cross Street precinct,
Cripplegate Without ward, registered
for Land Tax (*GLMS: MF11316 vol 103*)
1749 possibly Samuel Aris, Cranbourn
Street, Westminster Pollbook, watchmaker (*WAC: CD Rom*)

Alcock (Goldsmith*)
16 BULSTRODE, P69
Red Cross Street
1725 John Alcock, Wood Street, smallworker; 1731 Goldsmiths' Company
Livery; Mr Alcock Goldsmith at ye
Cup & Ring at Cripplegate with whom
Philip Shaw was living in 1730 (*Grimwade*)
1733 John Alcock, Old Bailey trial
concerning buckles and tea tongs
stolen from a shew-glass in his shop
(*OBP: t17330912-27*)

1734–43 John Alcock, Cripplegate, goldsmith (*Heal*)
1742–43 Mr John Alcock, at Cripplegate,
advertised twice in *The Daily Advertiser*
for the return of a silver spoon and
stating he had stopt a diamond ring,
goldsmith (*BL: Burney 381B, 10 Dec
1742; 379B, 25 Jan 1743*)

Allin (Broker/pawnbroker)
56 BULSTRODE, P72
Smock Alley
1734 possibly Robt Allyn, Catherine
Wheel Alley, 4th division, Bishopsgate
Without ward, registered for Land Tax
(*GLMS: MF11316 vol 105*)
1737 John Allen, Old Bailey trial where
he was acquitted of receiving stolen
goods knowing them to have been
stolen, pawnbroker (*OBP: t17370114-42*)
1744 Mr Allen, Petticoat Lane,
Spittlefields, advertised in *The Daily
Advertiser* for customers to redeem
their pledged items he leaving off
trade (*BL: Burney 397B, 28 Dec 1744*)
1745 Allen, Three Blue Balls, Petticoat
Lane, pawnbroker (*Heal*)

Mrs Allome (Broker)
88 BULSTRODE, P75
Ratcliffe highway
1734 possibly Saml Allome, Glasshouse
Yard, East Smithfield, St Mary
Whitechapel, registered for Land Tax
(*GLMS: MF6016, vol 5*)

Almson (Goldsmith)
60 HOLTOM, P43
Perfumers' Shop, Corner of
Salisbury Court
1733 Widow Amson, Fleet Street precinct,
Ludgate Hill, Farringdon Without
ward, registered for Land Tax (*GLMS:
MF11316 vol 104*)

Mrs Alsop (Watchmaker)
83 BULSTRODE, P75
East Smithfield
1689–1710 Joshua Allsop, East
Smithfield, a great clockmaker (*Britten*)
1734 Wido Alsop, East Smithfield, St
Botolph-Without-Aldgate, registered
for Land Tax (*GLMS: MF6011 vol 4*)

Archambo (Watchmaker)
161 WEATHERHEAD, P67
Porter Street by Newport Market
1720–50 John Archambo, Princes Street,
Leicester Fields; 1749 Gerard Street, St
Annes, Westminster Pollbook (*Britten*)
1727 John Archambo, the Dealer [Dial?],
Porter Street, parish of St Ann's,
Westminster, insured stock in house,
goods in trust, etc for £500, watchmaker (*GLMS: 11936 vol 25 [SI.43575]*)
1733 Mr John Archambo, the Dial, Porter
Street, advertised in *The Daily Post* for
the return of a watch by John
Archambo, watchmaker (*BL: Burney
297B, 28 May 1733*)
1733–35 Archambo, listed in
Clockmakers' Company New Walk
(*GLMS: 2715 vol 4*)
1734 John Archimbowe, Porter Street
East, registered for Poor Rate (*WAC:
MF32 A134*)
1749 John Archambo, Gerrard Street,
parish of St Anne, Soho, Westminster
Pollbook, watchmaker (*WAC: CDRom*)

Archambo (Goldsmith)
180 WEATHERHEAD, P67; FIG 33
Hemmingss Row
1720 Peter Archambo I, free of the
Butchers' Company, Golden Cup in
Green Street; moved to Hemings Row;
1739 Golden Cup, Coventry Street,
Piccadilly (*Grimwade*)
1722–39 Peter Archambo, Hemings Row,
St Martin's Lane; Peter Archambo
junior, plateworkers (*Heal*)
1726 Peter Archambo, Golden Cup,
Green Street, near Leicester Fields,
parish of St Martin-in-the-Fields,
insured household goods in house,
stock, etc for £500, silversmith (*GLMS:
11936 vol 22 [SI.39497]*)
1734 Peter Archambo, Hemings Row,
registered for Poor Rate (*WAC: MF1577
F488 item3*)

Armsted (Broker)
11 BULSTRODE, P69
Red Cross Street
1733 Wm Armsted, Red Cross Street, Red
Cross Street precinct, Cripplegate
Without ward, registered for Land Tax
(*GLMS: MF11316 vol 106*)

Arnaud (Jeweller)
146 HOLTOM, P47
Round Court
1701–31 fl, possibly Benjamin Arlaud, 'Miniature' [Miniaturist] or J.A. Arlaud, fl 1668–1748 (Quiet Conquest)
1734 possibly Claudeos Arnoux, New Castle Court, 1st and 2nd; registered for Poor Rate with Dorothy Ratcliffe, 3rd and 4th (WAC: MF183 B38 item2)

Ashbourn (Broker)
48 WEATHERHEAD, P55
Grays Inn Lane
Not found

Ashly (Goldsmith)
100 HOLTOM, P45
near ye new Church, Strand
1733 Jeconiah Ashly, nr Somerset House, Strand, London, account on headed paper for goods supplied dated 20 April 1733, goldsmith (GLPrints&Maps; Trade cards)
1734 Jeconiah Ashly, Dutchy Liberty Strand, registered for Poor Rate (WAC: MF1901 G14 item12)
1740 Jeconiah Ashley, corner of Green Street, Leicester Fields, largeworker (Grimwade)
1741–43 Jeconiah Ashley, against New Church, Strand, advertised in The London Daily Post & General Advertiser and The Daily Advertiser for the return of lost items, goldsmith (BL: Burney 355B, 23 May 1741; 379B, 04 Jun 1743)
1744 Jeconiah Ashly, the Golden Acorn, over against the New Church, Strand, auction notice in The Daily Advertiser of his stock in trade and household goods at his house, goldsmith deceased (BL: Burney 381B, 13 Feb 1744)
1744 died, Jeconiah Ashley, Golden Acorn, over against the New Church in the Strand, goldsmith (Heal)
1744 Jeconiah Ashley, late of the Strand, announcement in The Daily Advertiser of a creditors' meeting, goldsmith deceased (BL: Burney 381B, 08 May 1744)

Askew (Goldsmith*)
2 BULSTRODE, P69
Barbicon
1726 Richard Askew, 'I keep a Goldsmith's Shop in Barbican', Old Bailey trial concerning gold and silver goods stolen from his shop, including 17 snuff boxes, goldsmith (OBP: t17260302-57)
1730 Askew, Barbican, goldsmith (Heal)
1733 Richard Askew, 4th precinct, Aldersgate Without ward, registered for Land Tax (GLMS: MF11316 vol 102)

B

Bagley (Watchmaker)
10 HOLTOM, P41
Oxford Arms Inn Yard, Warwick Ct, Warwick Lane
1733 Heny Badley registered for Land Tax in St Sepulchre's, Farringdon Within ward (GLMS: MF11316 vol 103)
1735 Badley listed in Clockmakers' Company New Walk (GLMS: 2715 vol 4)

Barbott (Goldsmith)
160 WEATHERHEAD, P67
Porter Street by Newport Market
1734 possibly Charles Barbe, Litchfield Street, registered for Poor Rate (WAC: MF32 A134)

Barcer (Jeweller)
141 HOLTOM, P47
Bow St
1734 George Barker, Wards Alley, Bow Street West, registered for Poor Rate (WAC: MF1959 H43 item14)
1755 George Barker, Bow Street, Covent Garden, goldsmith (Heal)

Barnes (Goldsmith*)
16 HOLTOM, P41
without Ludgate
1702 William Barnes by Ludgate on Ludgate Hill, largeworker (Grimwade)
1702–31 William Barnes on Ludgate, Ludgate Hill, goldsmith (Heal)
1732 Mr Barnes advertised in The Daily Post for the return of an ear-ring, goldsmith (BL: Burney 286B, 4 Mar 1732)
1734 William Barnes, Without the Gate, St Martin's Ludgate registered for Poor Rate (GLMS: 1315 vol 1)
1738–46 Mr Barnes, on the other Side of Ludgate, two Old Bailey trials re stolen items, he having received a 'Warning from Goldsmiths Hall', goldsmith (OBP: t17381011-9; t17460702-1)

Barret (Broker/pawnbroker)
126 HOLTOM, P47
Turnstile Passage, Drury Lane
1736 2 Old Bailey trials concerning stolen watches pawned at 'Barret's' and with Mary Barret, pawnbrokers (OBP: t17360908-10; t17360908-59)

Barron (Jeweller)
159 HOLTOM, P47
Fountain Court, Strand
1734 possibly Barron, Fountain Court, Strand, registered for Poor Rate (WAC: MF183 B38 item2)

Barrow (Watchmaker)
119 BULSTRODE, P75
St Catherines
1733 Wm Barrow and 1735 William Barrow, listed in Clockmakers' Company East Walk (GLMS: 2715 vol 4)
1734 Wm Barrow, St Catherine's, St Botolph-Without-Aldgate, registered for Land Tax (GLMS: MF6011 vol 4)

Bartleme (Goldsmith*)
187 HOLTOM, P49
Whitehall
1734 James Bathelemi, Charing Cross and at Angel Court, registered twice for Poor Rate (WAC: MF1577 F488 item3)
1735 James Barthelmy, Angel Court, Charing Cross, French goldsmith and jeweller (Heal)
1735 James Barthelemi, convicted during Old Bailey trial of receiving a silver tankard knowing it to have been stolen; Lewis Laroch witness, Holtom gave evidence; Barthelemi sentenced to transportation for 14 years, goldsmith (OBP: t17350911-14)
1735 publication of a summary of Old Bailey Sessions listing James Barthelemi in The London Daily Post & General Advertiser (BL: Burney 310B, 23 Sept 1735)

Bartlett (Broker)
189 HOLTOM, P49
King St, Westminster
1734 Geo Bartlett, King Street, registered for Poor Rate (WAC: MF2364 E355)

Bartley (Goldsmith)
23 WEATHERHEAD, P53
Hick's Hall
Not found

Bartue (Goldsmith)
144 HOLTOM, P47
New St
1710 and 1722 Joseph Barbut, New St, St Martin-in-the-Fields, Middx and nr the Golden Fleece, New Street, parish of St Martin-in-the-Fields, insured his 'goods'; in the second instance referred to as a silversmith *(GLMS: 11936 vol 1 [SI.883]; vol 15, [SI.27527])*
1703–39 Joseph Barbut, New Street, Covent Garden, largeworker and possibly specialist spoon and fork maker *(Grimwade)*
1734 Joseph Barbot, New Street South, registered for Poor Rate *(WAC: MF1577 F488 item3)*

Mrs Bashly (Broker)
71 BULSTRODE, P75
Wellclose Square
1734 Mrs Bashley, Liberty of Well Close, Tower division, registered for Land Tax *(GLMS: MF6004 vol 6)*

Battle (Broker)
27 WEATHERHEAD, P53
Red Lyon Street
Not found

Batty (Broker / pawnbroker)
124 BULSTRODE, P75
St Catherines
1731 Benjamin Baty, St Catherines Lane, near the Tower, advertised in *The Country Journal or The Craftsman* for customers to redeem their pledged items, pawnbroker *(BL: Burney 237B, 16 Jan 1731)*
1734 Benj Batey, St Katherines by the Tower, Tower division, registered for Land Tax *(GLMS: MF6010 vol 3)*

Batut (Jeweller)
169 WEATHERHEAD, P67
St Martins Court
Not found

Beal (Goldsmith)
150 HOLTOM, P47
Henrietta St
1731–73 Richard Beal, Unicorn, Henrietta Street, Covent Garden, plateworker *(Heal)*
1733, 1739 and 1746 Richard Beale at ye Unicorn in Henaretter Street, Covent Garden, largeworker *(Grimwade)*
1734 Richard Beal, Henrietta Street North, registered for Poor Rate *(WAC: MF1959 H43 item14)*
1749 Richard Beal, Henrietta Street, St Paul Covent Garden, Westminster Pollbook, silversmith *(WPB)*

Beale (Goldsmith)
107 BULSTRODE, P79
Ratcliffe highway
1723 possibly George Beale, Cockhill, St Dunstan Stepney, insured his goods and merchandise for £500, silversmith *(GLMS: 11936, vol 15 [SI.28161])*
1734 possibly Josu Beele, Highway South and Robt Peele, Hyway South; Thos Peele, Highway North, Upper division, St George-in-the-East, each registered for Land Tax *(GLMS: MF6016 vol 5)*

Beavois (Watchmaker*)
167 WEATHERHEAD, P67; FIG 57
Castle Street
1705 Paul Beauvais, Crowned Cadran (Dial) in Castle Street, watchmaker *(no359 Quiet Conquest)*
1710 Paul Beauvais, Castle Street, parish of St Martin-in-the-Fields, Middx (French policy) *(GLMS: 11936 vol 1 [SI.925])*
1730 Paul Beavois and his brother, Simon (1690–1730) *(Britten)*
1730 Paul Beauvais, Dyal & Crown, Castle Street, Leicester Fields, parish of St Martin-in-the-Fields, insured household goods for £500, watchmaker *(GLMS: 11936 vol 31 [SI.52182])*
1730 Paul Beauvau, Old Bailey trial concerning five silver watches stolen from his shop *(OBP: t17301204-18)*
1733 Beauvais, 1735 Beavis, listed in Clockmakers' Company New Walk *(GLMS: 2715 vol 4)*
1734 Paul Beauvois, Castle Street East, registered for Poor Rate on two houses in the street *(WAC: MF1577 F488 item3)*

1743 possibly Mr Beavis, at a shoe-makers, facing the Bull Inn, Bishopsgate-Street, advertised in *The Daily Advertiser* for the return of a watch by William Creake *(BL: Burney 387B, 07 Oct 1743)*

Mrs Bell (Broker)
138 BULSTRODE, P69
Grub Street
1733 Mary Bell, Grub Street, near Welsh Harp Alley, Grub Street precinct, Cripplegate Without ward, registered for Land Tax *(GLMS: MF11316 vol 103)*

Benn (Watchmaker*)
74 HOLTOM, P43
Fleet St
1716–40 Robert Benn, Fleet Street *(Britten)*
1725 Mr Benn's Shop, under St Dunstans Church, Tithe assessment, watchmaker *(GLMS: 3011)*
1733 Robt Ben, Shop under the Church, St Dunstan-in-the-West precinct, Farringdon Without ward, registered for Land Tax *(GLMS: MF11316 vol 104)*
1735 Benn, listed in Clockmakers' Company South West walk *(GLMS: 2715 vol 4)*

Benson (Broker)
95 BULSTRODE, P77
Ratcliffe highway
1734 Edwd Benson, Highway South, Upper division, St George-in-the-East, Middx, registered for Land Tax *(GLMS: MF6016 vol 5)*

Bentley (Broker)
97 BULSTRODE, P77
Ratcliffe highway
1734 Jno Bentley, Highway South, Upper division, St George-in-the-East, Middx, registered for Land Tax *(GLMS: MF6016 vol 5)*

Berrey (Watchmaker)
108 HOLTOM, P45
Duke St, Lincolns Inn Fields
1733 Samll Berrey, Great Queen Street, St Giles and St George Bloomsbury, registered for Poor Rate *(CLS; UTAH MF98 item8)*
1743 Samuel Berry, Duke Street, Lincolns Inn Fields, advertised in *The Daily*

Advertiser for the return of a silver watch by Samuel Berry (*BL: Burney 387B, 24 Nov 1743*)

1749 Samuel Berry, Duke Street, St Margaret's, Westminster Pollbook, watchmaker (*Britten*)

Biddle (Broker)
106 BULSTRODE, P77
Ratcliffe highway
1733 William Biddell & Son, Musick House Court, Upper Shadwell with John Biddell and William Biddell Junr of Upper Shadwell North side, St Paul Shadwell, each registered for Land Tax (*GLMS: MF6009 vol 3*)

Bilby (Watchmaker)
191 HOLTOM, P51
King Street, Westminster
1734 Jno Bilby, King Street, registered for Poor Rate, (*WAC: MF2364 E355*)

Billings (Broker)
193 WEATHERHEAD, P67
St Martins Street, Leicester Fields
1734 John Billings, St Martin's Street East, registered for Poor Rate (*WAC: MF1577 F488 item3*)
1747 possibly Mary Billings, Old Bailey trial concerning a stolen clock offered to her (*OBP: t17470225-22*)
1749 possibly George Billings, Drury Lane, St Martin-in-the-Fields, Westminster Pollbook, broker (*WAC: CDRom*)

Blanchard (Watchmaker)
162 WEATHERHEAD, P67
Porter Street by Newport Market
1728 Abraham Blanchard, Porter Street, insured household goods, goods in trust for £500, watchmaker (*GLMS: 11936 vol 27 [SI.46676]*)
1730 Abraham Blanchard, London (*Britten*)
1733–35 Blainshard, listed in Clockmakers' Company New Walk (*GLMS: 2715 vol 4*)
1734 Abraham and Peter Blanchard, Porter Street, both registered for Poor Rate (*WAC: MF32 A134*)

Mrs Blisset (Goldsmith)
117 BULSTRODE, P77
Wapping
1726 Isaac Blisset, near Execution Dock,

Wapping, insured coach house, stable and lofts in Bethnal Green, parish of Stepney in occupation for £300, goldsmith (*GLMS: 11936 vol 22 [SI.40886]*)
1733 Elizabeth Blisset, Wapping Dock, St Dunstan Wapping, registered for Land Tax, together with an additional £100 lump sum (*GLMS: MF6013 vol 4*)
1735 Eliza Blisset, Wapping Dock, Wapping, registered for Sewer Rate (*LMA: THCS 149*)
Bisset Co, premises marked on 1746 Rocque map

Mrs Booth (Broker)
70 BULSTRODE, P75
Mill Yard
1734 Amy Booth, Liberty of Well Close, Tower division, registered for Land Tax (*GLMS: MF6004 vol 6*)

Boothby (Goldsmith)
89 HOLTOM, P45
without Temple Barr
1720 and 1739 George Boothby at ye Parrott, Temple Bar, largeworker (*Grimwade*)
1731–34 Mr Boothby, Sign of the Parrot, Temple Bar, advertised twice in *The Daily Post* and *The Daily Journal* for the return of various items, goldsmith (*BL: Burney 286B, 04 Jun 1731; 304B, 16 Oct 1734*)
1734 George Boothby, Strand Side, registered for Poor Rate (*WAC: MF183 B38 item2*)
1740–41 George Boothby, by Temple Bar, advertised in *The London Daily Post & General Advertiser* for the return of a lost candlestick, goldsmith (*BL: Burney 355B, 31 Jan 1740–41*)
1741 George Boothby, Parrott, without Temple Bar, Strand, goldsmith and banker (*Heal*)

Borer (Broker)
125 HOLTOM, P47
Russel St
1734 William Bower, Russell Street, registered for Poor Rate (*WAC: MF1577 F488 item3*)

Boshad (Goldsmith)
97 WEATHERHEAD, P59
Lombard Street [Court], 7 Dials
Not found

Bowditch (Broker)
145 BULSTRODE, P69
Brick Lane
Not found

Bowman (Broker)
5 WEATHERHEAD, P53
1724 Edward Bowman, London, goldsmith (*Heal*)

Boyghton (Broker)
34 BULSTRODE, P71
Skinners Street
1734 Jno Beighton, Skinner Street, 3rd division, Bishopsgate Without ward, registered for Land Tax (*GLMS: MF11316 vol 105*)

Bradley (Broker)
200 HOLTOM, P51
Orchard Street
1734 John Bradley, Orchard Street, registered for Poor Rate (*WAC: MF2364 E355*)

Bradshaw (Watchmaker)
94 HOLTOM, P45
Arundel St end
1733 Bradshaw listed in Clockmakers' Company South West Walk (*GLMS: 2715 vol 4*)
1731 possibly John Bradshaw (*Britten*)
1734 possibly Jno Bradshaw, Arrundale Street, registered for Poor Rate (*WAC: MF183 B38 item2*)

Brassay (Goldsmith/banker)
66 BULSTRODE, P72
Aldgate
1716 John and Nathaniel Brassey (*Hilton-Price*)
1723 John Bracy, The Spread Eagle without Aldgate, St Botolph Aldgate, insured goods and merchandise in his house for £1,000, goldsmith (*GLMS: 11936 vol 15 [SI.28211]*)
1731 John Brassey, Aldgate, advertised in *The Daily Advertiser* that he had stopt a spoon, goldsmith (*BL: Burney 289B, 18 Aug 1731*)
1732 Mr Nath Brassay and Comp, the Acorn, Lombard Street, advertised in *The Daily Post* for the return of a lost bank note, bankers (*BLCol: Burney 805B, 22 Feb 1732*)
1730–40 Nathaniel Brassey & Lee; 1725–31 Without Aldgate, largeworker (*Grimwade*)

1730–40 Nathaniel Brassey & Lee, Acorn, Lombard Street, goldsmiths and bankers (*Heal*)

1730–40 Nathaniel Brassey with Lee, Lombard Street; 1754 Brassey Lee & Son, bankers (*Hilton-Price*)

See Notice no11582 p30

Brigham (Broker)
103 BULSTRODE, P77
Ratcliffe highway

1733 Robert Brigham, Upper Shadwell North side, St Paul Shadwell, registered for Land Tax (*GLMS: MF6009 vol 3*)

Bristow (Goldsmith)
54 HOLTOM, P43
by Bride Lane

1707 Richard Bristow, Ludgate Street, smallworker; 1736 Goldsmiths' Company Prime Warden (*Grimwade*)

1724 Richard Bristow, Fleet Street, listed as inhabitant of St Bride's parish; served as Questman**, silversmith (*GLMS: 6561*)

1733 Richard Bristow, Fleet Street precinct, Ludgate Hill, Farringdon Without ward registered for Land Tax (*GLMS: MF11316 vol 104*)

1736 Richard Bristow at 3 Balls (Bells), cnr of Bride Lane, goldsmith (*Heal*)

**Note: Questman. Member of an Inquest, especially a parish or ward official; one appointed to make official enquiry into any matter, particularly weights and measures. It was a citizen's duty to help govern the community by taking on various roles within the parish; however it was possible to evade these tasks by paying a fine (*see* Robinson, p120).

Broadhurst (Broker)
135 BULSTRODE, P72
Rose & Crown [Grub Street]

1733 James Broadhurst, White Cross Street precinct, Cripplegate Without ward, registered for Land Tax (*GLMS: MF11316 vol 103*)

Brooks (Goldsmith)
85 HOLTOM, P45
St Clements Lane

1734 Jno Brooks, Clements Lane, registered for Poor Rate (*WAC: MF183 B38 item2*)

Brown (Watchmaker)
28 HOLTOM, P43
Crabtree Court, Holborn Bridge

1728 Henry Brown, Crabtree Court, registered for Poor Rate (*GLMS: 9975 vol 1*)

1733 Henry Browne, Plumbtree Court, Farringdon Without ward, registered for Land Tax (*GLMS: MF11316 vol 104*)

1705–32 William Browne (*Baillie*)

1733 William Browne, Plumbtree Court, Farringdon Without ward, registered for Land Tax (*GLMS: MF11316 vol 104*)

1735 Brown, listed in Clockmakers' Company New Walk (*GLMS: 2715 vol 4*)

Brown (Goldsmith and toyman*)
86 HOLTOM, P45
Clements Inn Gate

1734 John Browne, (Irenz)[*sic*] of Clements Inn, registered for Poor Rate (*WAC: MF183 B38 item2*)

1738 Mr John Browne, Clements Inn Passage nr Clare Market, advertised in *The London Daily Post & General Advertiser* stating he had stopped a silver knife handle (*BL: Burney 333B, 03 Oct 1738*)

Brunnett (Jeweller)
181 HOLTOM, P49
Northumberland Court, in the Strand

1734 Peter Brunet, Somerset Court, Strand, registered for Poor Rate (*WAC: MF1577 F488 item3*)

1735 Peter Brunet, Northumberland Street, Strand, jeweller (*Heal*)

Bubb (Broker)
21 BULSTRODE, P69
White Cross Street
Not found

Budd (Broker)
91 BULSTRODE, P77
Ratcliffe highway

1734 possibly Jno Babb, Highway North or Wido Budd, Highway South or Geo Budd, Highway South, Upper division, St George-in-the-East, each registered for Land Tax (*GLMS: MF6016 vol 5*)

Burchmore (Broker/pawnbroker*)
35 WEATHERHEAD, P55
Saffron hill

1733 Joseph Burchmore, Saffron Hill, Liberty of Saffron Hill, registered for Poor Rate on two houses (*CLS: UTAH MF415 item4*)

1735 Joseph Birchmore, witness in Old Bailey trial concerning the theft of a silver tankard with lid, pawnbroker (*OBP: t17360505-10*)

1737 Joseph Birchmore, Old Bailey trial concerning a gown and petticoat pawned at his shop in Saffron Hill, pawnbroker (*OBP: t17370907-53*)

1743 Mr Burchmore, Golden Ball, Saffron Hill, advertised in *The Daily Advertiser* that he had stopt two large silk handkerchiefs (*BL: Burney 379B, 23 Jun 1743*)

1753 Burchmore, Golden Ball, Saffron Hill, pawnbroker (*Heal*)

Burkitt (Goldsmith)
154 WEATHERHEAD, P67
Grafton Street

1734 possibly Peter Birkhead, Litchfield Street, registered for Poor Rate (*WAC: MF32, A134*)

1742 died, possibly Burkitt, Grove Street, Soho, goldsmith (*Heal*)

Butterfield (Watchmaker)
121 WEATHERHEAD, P65
Piccadilly

1719 possibly Thomas Butterfeild [*sic*], apprenticed; 1720 Edmond Butterfeild apprenticed (*Britten*)

1743 possibly Mr Thomas Butterfield, Brewer-Street, Golden Square, advertised in *The Daily Advertiser* for the return of a silver watch by T Washbourn, watchmaker (*BL: Burney 387B, 30 Dec 1743*)

Also: **Butterfield** (Broker)
122 WEATHERHEAD, P65
Eagle Street
Not found

C

Calcott (Broker/pawnbroker*)
126 BULSTRODE, P72
Hounds Ditch

1725 Calcot in Houndsditch, Old Bailey trial concerning his loan of 40s on a stolen watch, pawnbroker (*OBP:

t17250224-2)

1726 Mr Colcots shop in Houndsditch, Old Bailey trial concerning a watch pawned with him, pawnbroker *(OBP: t17260114-16)*

1734 Daniell Calcott, Houndsditch, Houndsditch precinct, Portsoken ward, registered for Land Tax *(GLMS: MF11316 vol 107)*

1735 Mr Calcot, Old Bailey trial where his apprentice, Edward Hoare, stood witness, pawnbroker *(OBP: t17340416-24)*

1740 Daniel Calcott, London, pawnbroker *(Heal)*

Caley (Broker)
110 WEATHERHEAD, P61
Broadstreet

1734 possibly Richard Collet, Berwick Street, St James's Piccadilly, registered for Poor Rate *(WAC: MF655 D39 item1, Gt Marlboro division)*

Cambden (Watchmaker)
29 HOLTOM, P43
Crabtree Court, Holborn Bridge

1701–35 William Camden, Plumbtree Court, Shoe Lane *(Britten)*

1708–51 William Campden *(Baillie)*

Candler (Goldsmith)
123 WEATHERHEAD, P65; FIG 52
Jermyn Street

1727 Charles Kandler I (Frederick), with James Murray in Sant Martens Lain; 1739? Jermyn Street; 1743 St James's, Westminster, goldsmith *(Grimwade)*

1727 Charles Kandler with Murray, St Martin's Lane, plateworker *(Heal)*

1732 Charles Kandler, parish of St James's Westminster, insured a house in Jermyn Street for £500 *(GLMS: 11936 vol 37 [SI.58391])*

1734 Chas Candler, Jermyn Street North, beyond the church, registered for Poor Rate *(WAC: MF655 D39 item1, Church & Market division)*

1735–73 Frederick Kandler, Jermyn Street, against St James's Church, plateworker *(Heal)*

1743 Mr Kandler, Jermyn Street, St James's, advertised in *The Daily Advertiser* for the return of Rose-Diamond Night-Dress Ear-Rings, silversmith *(BL: Burney 387B, 06 Oct 1743)*

1745 Mr Kandler, facing St James's Church in Jermyn Street, advertised in *The Daily Advertiser* for the return of three silver spoons, goldsmith *(BLCol: Burney 407B, 05 Feb 1745)*

1748 Charles Frederick Candler, over against the Churchyard in Jermain Street, parish of St James's in Westminster, insured household goods, furniture, wrought and manufactured plate worth £700, total £1,000, silversmith. (Later policies list the premises as No 100 Jermyn Street) *(GLMS: 11936 vol 83, [SI.111582])*

Carpenter (Goldsmith)
21 HOLTOM, P41
Snow Hill

1727 John Carpender in Snow Hill, smallworker *(Grimwade)*

1733 John Carpender registered for Land Tax in Farringdon Without ward *(GLMS: MF11316 vol 104)*

1744–48 John Carpender next the Green Dragon ale-house, Snow-hill, goldsmith *(Heal)*

1744 John Carpender in Snow-hill advertised in *The Daily Advertiser* for the return of a lost watch by Whitehead, goldsmith *(BL: Burney 397B, 05 Jul 1744)*

Carter (Goldsmith)
123 HOLTOM, P47
Russel Street

1734 Edward Carter at the Unicorn, Russell Street South, registered for Poor Rate *(WAC: MF1959 H43 item14)*

1743–44 Mr Edward Carter at the Unicorn, Russel Street, Covent Garden (and Little Russel Street), advertised five times in *The Daily Advertiser* for the return of various items, goldsmith *(BL: Burney 379B, 11 Jun 1743; 387B, 16 Aug 1743, 28 Sept 1743; 381B, 03 May 1744; 397B, 07 Jul 1744)*

1744 Edward Carter, Unicorn, Russell Street, Covent Garden, goldsmith *(Heal)*

1745 and 1749 Edward Carter, parish of St Paul Covent Garden, insured household goods, wrought and manufactured plate, etc in his house at the Unicorn, Russell Street, for £800 and £500 respectively, silversmith *(GLMS: 11936 vol 74 [SI.103286]; vol 87 [SI.116778]*

Cartwright (Goldsmith)
7 WEATHERHEAD, P53
Long Lane

1732 possibly Cartwright, 3 Horse Shoes, Cow Cross, silversmith *(Heal)*

1732 possibly Benjamin Cartwright I, 3 Horse Shoes, Pedlars Lane, Cow Cross; 1739 Crown & Pearl, Bartholomew Close, largeworker *(Grimwade)*

1733 possibly Peter Cartwright, Smithfield precinct, Farringdon Without ward, registered for Land Tax *(GLMS: MF11316 vol 107)*

1739–54 possibly Benjamin Cartwright, Crown & Pearl, Bartholomew Close, or Crown & Pearl, nr ye George Inn, West Smithfield, working goldsmith/toyman *(Heal)*

Cawthorn (Goldsmith)
130 HOLTOM, P47
Wild St by Queen Street

1733 Samll Cawthorne, Wild Street, St Giles and St George Bloomsbury, registered for Poor Rate *(CLS; UTAH MF98 item8)*

1753–70 Beadle at Goldsmiths' Hall; end pages of Warning Carriers Walks book

1766 Samuel Cawthorn, Goldsmiths' Hall, jeweller *(Heal)*

Chabert (Goldsmith)
60 WEATHERHEAD, P57
near Turn Stile Lane

1731–44 John Chabbert, Crown in Holborn, over against Brownlow Street, goldsmith and jeweller *(Heal)*

1732 John Chabbart, Holborn, St Andrew Holborn, St George the Marytr, registered for Poor Rate *(CLS: UTAH MF29 item6)*

1744 Mr Chabert, end of Chancery Lane, Holborn, advertised in *The Daily Advertiser* for the return of a box containing 60 half guineas, goldsmith *(BL: Burney 381B, 20 Mar 1744)*

Chad (Jeweller)
7 HOLTOM, P41
Rose St, Newgate St

1733 Richd Chad registered for Land Tax in St Sepulchre's precinct, Farringdon Within ward *(GLMS: MF11316 vol 103)*

Concordance of variant spellings of tradesmen's names pp132–36; index of streets p138; bibliography pp140–41

Chambers (Goldsmith/banker)
43 HOLTOM, P43
Fleet St
1733–49 Abraham Chambers and
Thomas Usborne, Three Squirrels,
Fleet Street, goldsmith and banker
(Heal)
1733–56 Abraham Chambers, junior,
Falcon, Fleet Street, goldsmith *(Heal)*
1733 Abraham Chambers and partner,
Fleet Street, St Dunstan-in-the-West
precinct, Farringdon Without ward
registered for Land Tax *(GLMS:
MF11316 vol 104)*
1734–41 William Chambers and Usborne,
Three Squirrels, Fleet Street; later no19
Fleet Street, trading as Gosling &
Sharpe, bankers *(Hilton-Price)*
1739 Mess Chambers & Usborne, the
Eagle, Fleet Street advertised in *The
Daily Post* for the return of a bill for
£45, bankers *(BL: Burney 340B, 22 Feb
1739)*

Chambers (Broker)
105 HOLTOM, P45
Drury Lane
1734 Wm Chambers, Drury Lane, registered for Poor Rate *(WAC: MF183 B38
item2)*

Chardon (Jeweller)
157 HOLTOM, P47
in the Fountain Court, Strand
1734 Peter Chardon, ffountain Court,
registered for Poor Rate *(WAC: MF183
B38 item2)*

Charitable Corporations (No trade)
185 HOLTOM, P49
Spring Gardens
1733 The Charitable Organisation House,
Spring Garden, advertised in *The Daily
Post* for Creditors of the Charitable
Corporation for the relief of the
Industrious Poor to meet *(BL: Burney
297B, 10 Mar 1733)*
1734 The Charitable Corporation regis-
tered for Poor Rate *(WAC: MF1577
F488 item3)*
1744 Charitable-Corporation-House,
Spring Garden, announced in *The Daily
Advertiser* the plan for raising a new
fund for carrying on the business of
their Charter was available to view
(BL: Burney 397B, 14 Nov 1744)

*Note: The Charitable Corporation for the
Relief of the Industrious Poor, pawnbrokers in Spring Gardens, founded 1707 to
lend money at legal interest to the poor on
small pledges (T. Murdoch,* Country Life,
2 November 1989, pp202-03)

Chartier (Goldsmith)
179 WEATHERHEAD, P67; FIG 42
Hemmings Row
1698–99 John Chartier; 1723, largeworker; 1720 Daniel, his son,
apprenticed; 1740 Hemings Row, near
St Martin's Lane, largeworker *(Grimwade)*
1723 John Chartier junior, Hemings Row,
St Martin's Lane, goldsmith *(Heal)*
1734 Chartier, listed in Clockmakers'
Company New Walk *(GLMS: 2715 vol 4)*
1734 John Chartier, Hemings Row, registered for Poor Rate *(WAC: MF1577
F488 item3)*
1740 Daniel Chartier, Hemings Row, St
Martin's Lane, plateworker *(Heal)*
1749 Daniel Chartier, Heming Row, St
Martin's, Westminster Pollbook, silversmith *(WPB)*

Chenear (Goldsmith and toyman)
200 WEATHERHEAD, P67
by the Mewse
Not found. Possibly Chenevix.

Cherack (Jeweller)
171 HOLTOM, P49
York Buildings
1712–31 Denis Chirac, Golden Head,
Villiers Street, York Buildings, jeweller
(Heal)
1734 Denis Chirac, Villiers Street, regis-
tered for Poor Rate *(WAC: MF1577
F488 item3)*
1736 Denis Chirac, York Buildings,
Strand, made and fashioned 'a Coronet
for her Royal Highness the Princess of
Wales' and lent 'the Brilliant
Diamonds therein' all for the sum of
£100 *(Nat. Archives: E.404/246, f82, 14
Sept 1736)*

Child, Sir Fra & Co (Goldsmith/
banker)
78 HOLTOM, P43
Temple Bar
1721–40 died Sir Francis Child junior,
Marygold, within Temple Bar, goldsmith and banker *(Heal)*

1725 Fra Child, Fleet Street, Tithe assessment *(GLMS: 3011)*
1733 Sr ffrancis Child & Ptners, Fleet
Street, St Dunstan-in-the-West precinct,
Farringdon Without ward, registered
for Land Tax *(GLMS: MF11316 vol 104)*
1734 Sir Francis Child, Temple Bar,
advertised in *The Daily Journal* for the
return of two lost banknotes *(BL:
Burney 303B, 22 Apr 1734)*
1735 Francis Child, Samuel Child, John
Morse, William Backwell, Temple Bar,
(Francis died 1740), bankers *(Hilton-Price)*
1736 Sir Francis Child, Temple-Bar,
advertised in *The Daily Post* for the
return of two lost banknotes *(BL:
Burney 319B, 24 Jan 1736)*
1738 Sir Fra Child & Comp, Old Bailey
trial concerning a forged 'Paper
Writing' Order for £120, bankers *(OBP:
t17380628-26)*
1741–44 Samuel Child & Co, Temple-Bar,
advertised once in *The London Daily
Post & General Advertiser*, again in *The
London Gazette*, and four times in *The
Daily Advertiser* for the return of an
ear-ring drop, a watch and several
banknotes, bankers *(BL: Burney 355B,
08 Apr 1741; 363B, 17 Apr 1742; 387B,
27 Aug 1743, 24 Jan 1744; 381B, 10 Feb
1744, 21 Feb 1744)*

Chirne (Goldsmith)
147 WEATHERHEAD, P67
King Street by St Anns Church
Not found

Church (Broker)
131 BULSTRODE, P72
Hounds Ditch
Not found

Clark (Broker/pawnbroker)
74 WEATHERHEAD, P59
Plumbtree Street, Bloomsbury
1728 John Clark, Old Bailey trial
concerning stolen clothing brought to
him to pawn, pawnbroker *(OBP:
t17280117-3)*
1734 Mr John Clark, Plumbtree Street, St
Giles and St George Bloomsbury, registered for Poor Rate on 2 houses *(CLS:
UTAH MF99 item1)*
Also: **Clark** (Watchmaker)
75 WEATHERHEAD, P59
Plumbtree Street, Bloomsbury

1710 circa, possibly Josiah Clark, London, clockmaker (*Baillie, vol 2*)

1710–74 circa, possibly, George Clark, London, watch & clockmaker (*Baillie, vol 2*)

mid–18th century, possibly Alexander Clark, watchmaker (*Baillie, vol 2*)

Also: **Clark** (Broker/pawnbroker)
76 WEATHERHEAD, P59
Plumbtree Street, Bloomsbury

1726 possibly Mr Clark, Old Bailey trial concerning a stolen silver watch pawned with him (*OBP: t17260302-80*)

1727 possibly William Clark, Old Bailey trial concerning household items pawned with him (*OBP: t17270517-10*)

Clark (Broker)
24 BULSTRODE, P69
Featherstone Street
Not found

Clay (Watchmaker)
101 HOLTOM, P45
near ye new Church, Strand

1715–50 Charles Clay, Strand; previously of Flockton, Yorks (*Britten*)

1727 Charles Clay, at the Machine Watch in the Strand over against the New Church, insured household goods and stock in trade in house for £500, watchmaker (*GLMS: 11936 vol 24 [SI.42978]*)

1733 Charles Clay, Fleet Street precinct, Ludgate Hill, Farringdon Without ward, registered for Land Tax (*GLMS: MF11316 vol 104*)

1734 Charles Clay, Dutchy Liberty Strand, registered for Poor Rate (*WAC: MF1901 G14 item12*)

1736 C. Clay, no address, advertised his Musical Machines in *The London Daily Post & General Advertiser*, watchmaker (*BL: Burney 320B, 02 Nov 1736*)

1743 John Pyke, Clockmaker in Bedford Row, advertised in *The Daily Advertiser* that he had purchased and finished the famous Clockwork Machine which the ingenious Mr Clay left unfinished (*BLCol: Burney 387B, 23 Nov 1743*)

1743 Mrs Clay, widow of Charles, advertised her change of address to over-against Cecil Street in the Strand (*BL: Burney 387B, 28 Nov 1743*)

1748 running advertisement in *The London Daily Post & General Advertiser* for Clays musical clock (*BL: Burney 333B, 19 Sept 1748*)

Clifton (Goldsmith)
113 HOLTOM, P45
Catherine St

1718 possibly Jonas Clifton, Crown, Strand; circa 1730 Crown, Henrietta Street, Covent Garden; Remov'd from a little beyond Hungerford in ye Strand, goldsmith (*Heal*)

1729 possibly Jonas Clifton, Old Bailey trial concerning stolen silver spoons offered to him (*OBP: t17291203-11*)

1734 James Clifton, Bridges Street West, registered for Poor Rate (*WAC: MF1959 H43 item14*)

1743 possibly Jonas Clifton, Old Bailey trial concerning his purchase of a stolen Coral; he received a reprimand from the Court, which felt he should have been indicted himself, a silversmith in the Strand (*OBP: t17430907-25*)

1752 possibly 'Last Sunday Died Mr Clifton, an Eminent Goldsmith in Skinner Row', *The General Advertiser* (*BLCol: 12 Oct 1752*)

Cole (Jeweller)
154 HOLTOM, P47
Maiden Lane

1734 Christopher and George Cole, Maiden Lane North, registered for Poor Rate (*WAC: MF1959 H43 item14*)

Cole (Broker)
6 WEATHERHEAD, P53
Long Lane

1733 possibly Jms Cole, Smithfield precinct, Farringdon Without ward, registered for Land Tax (*GLMS: MF11316 vol 104*)

Collier (Broker/pawnbroker)
89 WEATHERHEAD, P59
Castle Street, Long Acre

1734 Charles Collier, Castle Street, registered for Poor Rate (*WAC, MF1577 F488 item3*)

1736 possibly Mr Collier in Denmark Street, Old Bailey trial concerning household goods pawned with him, pawnbroker (*OBP: t17360505-25*)

Collier (Broker/pawnbroker)
26 WEATHERHEAD, P53
St Johns Lane

1733 Wm Collier, Sunn Alley, Cripplegate

Without ward, registered for Land Tax (*GLMS: MF11316 vol 103*)

Colly (Watchmaker)
45 HOLTOM, P43; FIG 55
Fleet St

1733 Richd Colly, Fleet Street, St Dunstan-in-the-West precinct, Farringdon Without ward registered for Land Tax (*GLMS: MF11316 vol 104*)

1734 Colley and 1735, Richd Colley in Clockmakers' Company South West Walk (*GLMS: 2715 vol 4*)

Note: *Fig* **[55]** *is for Thomas Colley*

Connier (Watchmaker)
81 HOLTOM, P45
Academy Court, Chancery Lane

1684–1730 possibly Benjamin Connier/Collier, 'a noted maker' (*Britten*)

1732 John Conyers, Esq, Chancery Lane, St Andrew Holborn, St George the Martyr, registered for Poor Rate (*CLS: UTAH MF29 item6*)

1734 possibly Conyars and 1735, Conyers listed in Clockmakers' Company New Walk (*GLMS: 2715 vol 4*)

Cook (Goldsmith)
12 WEATHERHEAD, P53
by Mr Wollfryes
[1734 Mr Wollfryes by Barts Hosp: *Heal*]

1731 Robert Cook, Crown & Spur in Chick Lane, insured his household goods, stock, including wrought and manufactured plate for £200, working silversmith (*GLMS: 11936 vol 35 [SI.56094]*)

1731 Robert Cook(e), Chick Lane, Nr West Smithfield; 1737 Goldsmiths' Company Livery, smallworker (*Grimwade*)

1734 Robert Cook, Barts the Less precinct, Farringdon Without ward, registered for Land Tax (*GLMS: MF11316 vol 107*)

1738 Mr Cook, witness in an important coining trial, goldsmith (*OBP: t17380906-20*)

Cookson (Broker)
7 BULSTRODE, P69
Bridgewaters Gardens
Not found

Cooper (Broker)
104 WEATHERHEAD, P59
Denmark St, opp St Giles Church
1734 Chas Cooper, Bainbrig Street, St Giles and St George Bloomsbury, registered for Poor Rate (CLS: UTAH MF99 item1)
Also: **Cooper** (Broker)
105 WEATHERHEAD, P61
Hanaway Str Tatnam Court Road
1734 possibly Christopher Capper, Tottenham Court Road, St Giles & St George Bloomsbury, registered for Poor Rate (CLS: UTAH MF99 item1)
Also: **Cooper** (Broker)
106 WEATHERHEAD, P61
Oxford Road ner St Giles's Pound
Not found

Cooper (Goldsmith/banker)
93 HOLTOM, P45
Arundel St end
1716–68 Gissingham Cooper, cnr of Arundel Street, Strand, goldsmith, banker (Heal)
1716, 1720 and 1723 Gissingham Cooper insured property at Arundell Street, cnr of Norfolk Street, against St Clements Church all in the Strand for £–, £300 and £1,000, goldsmith (GLMS: 11936 vol 6 [SI.8099], vol 11 [SI.17272], vol 17 [SI.31162])
1734 Giss Cooper, Strand Side, nr Milford Lane, registered for Poor Rate, (WAC: MF183 B38 item2)
1735–68 Gissingham (Gifflingham) Cooper, cnr of Arundel Street, Strand, goldsmith, banker (Hilton-Price)
1739 and 1743 Mr Gis Cooper, the Strand, advertised in The Daily Post & General Advertiser and The Daily Advertiser for the return of lost items (BL: Burney 341B, 03 Nov 1739; 387B, 16 Dec 1743)

Cooper (Broker)
58 BULSTRODE, P72
Smock Alley
1734 possibly Henry Cooper, Catherine Wheel Alley, 4th division, Bishopsgate Without ward, registered for Land Tax (GLMS: MF11316 vol 105)

Cooper (Watchmaker)
14 BULSTRODE, P69
Red Cross Street
1700 circa, possibly Jon Cooper, watch-

maker (Britten)
1733 John Cooper, Red Cross Street, Red Cross Street precinct, Cripplegate Without ward, registered for Land Tax (GLMS: MF11316 vol 106)

Cormal (Broker)
112 HOLTOM, P45
Catherine St
1734 John Carmalt & Co, Bridges Street East, registered for Poor Rate (WAC: MF1959 H43 item14)

Cormal (Broker)
145 HOLTOM, P47
Chandois St
1734 William Carmalt & Co, Shandois Street North, registered for Poor Rate for himself and another tenanted property (WAC: MF1959 H43 item14)

Corner (Jeweller)
126 WEATHERHEAD, P65
near the George, Bury Street
1731 Corner, Bury St, St James's, jeweller (Heal)
1734 Jno Connor, Bury Street beside West Side down South, registered for Poor Rate (WAC: MF655 D39 item1, Pall Mall division)
1743 Mr Corner, Berry-Street, St James's, advertised in The Daily Advertiser for the return of a cane and sword, jeweller (BL: Burney 379B, 25 Apr 1743)

Courtier (Jeweller)
44 BULSTRODE, P71
Spittle Fields
1724 possibly John Corsier, Bethnal Green, Spitalfields, registered for Sewer Rate (LMA: THSC 133)

Courtould (Goldsmith)
175 WEATHERHEAD, P67; FIG 51
Chandois Street
1729 Augustine Courtauld, Chandos Street; 1739 Chandos Street, St Martin-in-the-Fields, goldsmith (Grimwade)
1729–51 Augustine (Augustus) Courtauld, Chandos Street, goldsmith (Heal)
1734 Augustine Courtaux, Shandois Street, registered for Poor Rate on two houses (WAC: MF1577 F488 item3)

Cox (Watchmaker)
131 HOLTOM, P47
Long Acre
1734 Jason Cox, Long Acre, registered for Poor Rate (WAC: MF1577 F488 item3)
1735 Jason Cox, north side of Long Acre, St Martin-in-the-Fields, insured household goods and goods for £300, clockmaker (GLMS: 11936 vol 43 [SI 67983])
1743 Mr Cox, Tavistock Row, advertised for the return of a Tompion watch, pawnbroker (BLCol: 689B, 14 Jan 1743)
1743 Mr Jason Cox, over-against the Vine Tavern, Long-Acre, advertised in The Daily Advertiser for the return of a stolen Tompion watch made 1699, watchmaker (BL: Burney 379B, 09 Apr 1743)
1744 Mr John Cox, over-against The Vine Tavern, Long Acre, advertised in The Daily Advertiser for the return of a lost watch by Des Charmes, watchmaker (BL: Burney 381B, 29 Feb 1744)
1745–60 Jason Cox (son?) Long Acre (Britten)
1749 Jason Cox, Long Acre, parish of St Martin-in-the-Fields, Westminster Pollbook, watchmaker (WAC: CDRom)

Crag (Goldsmith)
8 WEATHERHEAD, P53
Duck Lane
1730 John Cragg, New Street, Cloth Fair, smallworker (Grimwade)
1734 John Cragg, Barts the Less precinct, Farringdon Without ward, registered for Land Tax (GLMS: MF11316 vol 104)

Cragg (Goldsmith and jeweller)
136 WEATHERHEAD, P65; FIG 45
Norris Street, Hay Market
1727 Craggs (Craigs), Norris Street Haymarket, goldsmith (Heal)
1730–35 Ann and John Craig, corner of Norris Street (with George Wickes); 1736 died John, silversmith; 1740 Ann, Corner of Norris Street, St James's, Haymarket with John Neville; 1745 Ann presumed retired or deceased, smallworker (Grimwade)
1736 Mr John Craig, Hand & Ring, corner of Norris Street, St James's, Haymarket; Ann advertised in The London Daily Post & General Advertiser that her late husband's shop is kept

with the same Choice by the Widow and her two Sons, jeweller and goldsmith *(BL: Burney 320B, 21 Dec 1736)*

1738–46 Ann Craig and John Neville, Norris Street, St James's, plateworker *(Heal)*

1743 Mess Craig(e) and Neville, corner of Norris-Street, St James's, Hay-Market, advertised three times in *The Daily Advertiser* for the return of various items, including a watch by Hubert, jeweller and goldsmith *(BL: Burney 379B, 04 Feb 1743, 30 Jun 1743; 387B, 14 Nov 1743)*

Cranmore (Goldsmith)
66 HOLTOM, P43
Fleet St

1722–52 (died) Samuel Cranmer, Crown, nr Serjeants Inn, Fleet Street, goldsmith *(Heal)*

1725 Samuel Cranmer, Fleet Street, Tithe assessment *(GLMS: 3011)*

1731 Samuel Cranmer, Crown next Serjeants-Inn, Fleet Street advertised in *The Daily Post* for the return of a lost Pocket Book and Bank Note, goldsmith *(BL: Burney 286B, 19 Jan 1731)*

1733 Saml Cranmore, Fleet Street, St Dunstan-in-the-West precinct, Farringdon Without ward, registered for Land Tax *(GLMS: MF11316 vol 104)*

1742–44 Mr Samuel Cranmer, Crown, Fleet Street, advertised four times in *The Daily Advertiser* for the return of various lost items *(BL: Burney 363B (Reel 1), 28 Oct 1742; 387B, 07 Jul 1743,19 Jul 1743; 397B, 17 Oct 1744)*

Crispin (Goldsmith)
151 WEATHERHEAD, P67; FIGS 22, 50
Compton Street, Soho

1720–57 Paul Crespin, Golden Ball, Compton Street, Soho, silversmith *(Heal)*

1721 Paul Crespin, Compton Street; 1739, Golden Ball, Compton Street, St Anns, Soho, goldsmith *(Grimwade)*

1726 Crespin, portrait *(no344, Quiet Conquest)*. See p27

1729 Crespin, parish of St Ann, Westminster, insured his house at Golden Ball, corner of Compton St and Greek St for £450; trade utensils £200, stock in trade (wrought plate in house £150, glass £50) and another house in Greek St occupied by F. Clarke, chan-

dler, £150; total £1,000, goldsmith *(GLMS: 11936 vol 29 [SI.49093])*

1733 Paul Crispin, witness in Old Bailey trial concerning a silver dish stolen from his Grate in Compton Street, Corner of Greek Street [Transcript indicates a strong French accent or lisp – see p27] *(OBP: t17330628-30)*

1734 Paul Crespin, Greek Street, registered for Poor Rate *(WAC: MF32 A134)*

1744 Mr Crespin, Greek Street, Soho, advertised in *The Daily Advertiser* for the return of a lost seal, goldsmith *(BL: Burney 397B, 26 Jun 1744)*

1740 Paul Crespin Junior, London, goldsmith *(Heal)*

1747 and 1752 Paul Crespin, parish of St Ann Soho, Middx, two notices of his bankruptcy and creditors meeting in *The General Advertiser*, silversmith *(BL: Burney 421B, 09 Feb 1747; 449B, 12 Mar 1752)*

Croket (Broker)
31 HOLTOM, P43
Shoe Lane

1728 Matthew Cockett, Dean Street, registered for Poor Rate *(GLMS: 9975 vol 1)*

1733 Matthew Cockett, Dean Street, Farringdon Without ward, registered for Land Tax *(GLMS: MF11316 vol 104)*

1739 Mr Crokat, Old Bailey trial concerning a stolen silver watch pledged with him; received a Court reprimand *(OBP: t17390221-2)*

Cross (Broker)
22 BULSTRODE, P69
White Cross Street

1715 possibly William Cross, Golden Ball, Grub Street *(Heal)*

Cumbleford (Jeweller)
187 WEATHERHEAD, P67
Orange Street

1734 Abraham Cumbleford, Orange Street, registered for Poor Rate *(WAC: MF1577 F488 item3)*

1743 Mr Cumbleford, Cushion Court, Broad Street, advertised in *The Daily Advertiser* for the return of an emerald ring, jeweller *(BL: Burney 387B, 25 Nov 1743)*

Cuny (Goldsmith)
139 WEATHERHEAD, P65; FIG 44
near Leicester Fields

1703–27 Louis Cugny, Three Crowns, cnr Panton Street and Hedge Lane, near Leicester Fields, plateworker *(Heal)*

1711 Lewis Cuny, Panton Street, parish of St Martin-in-the-Fields, Middx, insured his goods *(GLMS: 11936 vol 1 [SI.760])*

1733 died Louis Cuny (1708, Lewis Caney), Spur Street, Leicester Fields, silversmith *(Grimwade)*

1734 Widow Cuny, Leicester Fields, possibly a tenant, registered for Poor Rate *(WAC: MF1577 F488 item3)*

1738 Henry Hebert(?) and Elizabeth Cuny, Spurr Street, near Leicester Fields, parish of St Martin-in-the-Fields, insured household goods, stock, wrought and manufactured plate £300, total £500, goldsmith *(GLMS: 11936 vol 50 [SI.79087])*

Curghey (Goldsmith)
69 HOLTOM, P43
Fleet St

1733 John Curghey, Fleet Street, St Dunstan-in-the-West precinct, Farringdon Without ward, registered for Land Tax *(GLMS: MF11316 vol 104)*

1734–49 John Curghey, Ship, cnr Crane Court, nr Fetter Lane, Fleet Street, goldsmith *(Heal)*

1743 John Curghey, Fleet Street, advertised in *The Daily Advertiser* for the return of a watch by Graham, goldsmith *(BL: Burney 387B, 02 Sept 1743)*

Curtoys (Broker/pawnbroker)
4 BULSTRODE, P69
Barbicon

1731 Mr Curtis, witness in Old Bailey trial, 'The Pawnbroker' *(OBP: t17310115-68)*

1733 Wells Curtis, Barbican, Cripplegate Without ward, registered for Land Tax *(GLMS: MF11316 vol 103)*

1739 Welles Curtoys, Old Southampton Buildings, bankruptcy notice, pawnbroker *(Hart)*

D

Dally (Jeweller and goldsmith*)
127 HOLTOM, P47
Drury Lane by Long Acre
1734 Samuel Dailey, Drury Lane, registered for Poor Rate (WAC: MF1577 F488 item3)
1737 Samuel Dally, Old Bailey trial concerning a ring stolen from his shop (OBP: t17370216-5)
1743 Mr Dailey, facing Long Acre, Drury Lane, advertised in The Daily Advertiser for the return of a lost watchcase, jeweller (BL: Burney 387B, 12 Sept 1743)

Daniel (Broker/pawnbroker)
33 WEATHERHEAD, P55
Saffron hill
1733 Martha Daniel, Saffron Hill, Liberty of Saffron Hill, registered for Poor Rate (CLS: UTAH MF415 item4)
1735 Martha Daniel acquitted in an Old Bailey trial of receiving stolen clothing knowing it to have been stolen, pawnbroker (OBP: t17350226-16)

Davenport (Goldsmith)
91 HOLTOM, P45; FIG 46
angle Temple Barr, [opp] Clements Church
1731 Isaac Davenport, Queens Head over against St Clements, Strand, goldsmith (Heal)
1734 Isaac Davenport, Strand Side, Milford Lane, registered for Poor Rate (WAC: MF183 B38 item2)
1736 Mr Davenport, in the Strand, witness in Old Bailey Trial re theft of a 'Coal' [Coral] (OBP: t17360610-17)
1743 Mr Davenport, Queens Head, opp St Clement's Church, Strand, advertised in The Daily Advertiser for the return of a lost sable tippet, goldsmith (BL: Burney 379B, 22 Jan 1743)

Davis (Watchmaker)
116 BULSTRODE, P77
Wapping
1705 circa, possibly James Davis, Ratcliffe Highway (Britten)
1733 possibly Amos Davis, Wapping Dock Street, St Dunstan Wapping, registered for Land Tax (GLMS: MF6013 vol 4)
1733 possibly Joseph Davis senior, Wapping Dock Street, St Dunstan Wapping, registered for Land Tax (GLMS: MF6013 vol 4)
1740 circa, possibly Joseph Davis, clockmaker (Britten)

Dawson (Broker)
108 WEATHERHEAD, P61
Berwick Street, Soho
1734 Edward Dawson, Berwick Street East, St James's Piccadilly, registered for Poor Rate (WAC: MF655 D39 item1, Gt Marlboro division)
Also: **Dawson** (Broker)
109 Weatherhead, p61
Berwick Street, Soho
1734 possibly Daniel Dawson, Little Windmill Street, St James's Piccadilly, registered for Poor Rate (WAC: MF655 D39 item1, Gt Marlboro division)

Dean (Broker)
107 WEATHERHEAD, P61
Warder Street, Soho
1734 Percival Dean, Wardour Street, St Annes Soho, registered for Poor Rate (WAC: MF32 A133 item17)

Deard (Toyman*)
71 HOLTOM, P43; FIG 63
Fleet St
1725 Mr Deards, Fleet Street, Tithe assessment (GLMS: 3011)
1726 William Deard(s), Fleet Street, smallworker (Grimwade)
1731 Mr Deard's Toyshop in Fleet Street or the Court of Requests at Westminster, advertised in The Daily Post for the return of a lost Chrystal (BL: Burney 286B, 06 Feb 1731)
1733 Wm Deards, Fleet Street, St Dunstan-in-the-West precinct, Farringdon Without ward, registered for Land Tax (GLMS: MF11316 vol 104)
1736 William Deard, Old Bailey trial concerning various items stolen from him (OBP: t17360721-13)
1736–39 Mr William Deards at variations of his Fleet Street address advertised three times in The London Daily Post & General Advertiser for the return of various stolen items including a shewglass (BL: Burney 320B, 02 Aug 1736; 333B, 16 Aug 1738, 341B, 17 Nov 1739)
1740 William Deard(s), opp St Dunstan's Church, Fleet Street, goldsmith, toyman (Heal)
1742–44 Mr Deard, cnr of Craven Street, Charing Cross (Strand), advertised five times in The Daily Advertiser for the return of lost items (BL: Burney 381B, 25 Nov 1742, 23 Aug 1743, 20 Feb 1744, 23 Apr 1744, 03 May 1744)

Dearing (Goldsmith)
76 BULSTRODE, P72
Little Minories
Not found

Debarry (Jeweller)
137 WEATHERHEAD, P65
Oxendon Street, Haymarket
1719 Peter Debary, Newport Street, jeweller (Heal)
1726 Peter de Bary, at Mrs Provost, a fan shop in Panton Street, St Martin-in-the-Fields, insured goods and merchandise in his apartments for £500, jeweller (GLMS: 11936 vol 23 [SI.–])
[1734 Mrs Provost, Panton Street, registered for Poor Rate (WAC: MF1577 F488 item3)]

Delafonds (Jeweller)
182 WEATHERHEAD, P67
Castle Street
1738 possibly John Delafons, Ring & Crown, West Street, near Seven Dials, jeweller (Heal)
1738 possibly Mr John Dela Fons, Ring & Crown, West Street, near Seven Dials, advertised in The Daily Post for the return of stolen watch and money, jeweller (BL: Burney, 332B, 23 May 1738)

Delamarie (Goldsmith)
141 WEATHERHEAD, P65; FIG 35
Windmill Street
1718 Paul de Lamerie, Windmill Street, upper end of the Haymarket, St James, Westminster, insured his goods and merchandise in his house, silversmith (GLMS: 11936 vol 8 [SI.11708])
1726 Paul D L'Marie, Gt Windmill Street, parish of St James, Westminster, insured household goods and stock for £500 (GLMS: 11936 vol 23 [SI.40042])
1728 Paul De Lamerie, St James's, Westminster, insured household goods in his house in Great Windmill Street, stock in trade £200, wrought plate only

£800 etc for £1,100, goldsmith *(GLMS: 11936 vol 27 [SI.45888])*

1733 Paul Delamarie, Golden Ball, Windmill Street, St James's; 1738–44 no42 Gerrard Street, goldsmith *(Grimwade)*

1734 Paul Lemery, Windmill Street, registered for Poor Rate on two premises *(WAC: MF655 D39 item1, Gt Marlboro division)*

1738 Mr Lamary, Gerrard Street, advertised in *The London Daily Post & General Advertiser* for the return of an ear-ring drop, silversmith *(BL: Burney 340B, 01 Jan 1738)*

1742 Paul Delamerie, Gerrard Street, St Ann's, Soho, advertised in *The Daily Advertiser* for the return of a stolen silver tankard, goldsmith *(BL: Burney 381B, 04 Oct 1742)*

1743–51 Paul De Lamerie, no42 Gerrard Street, plateworker *(Heal)*

1748 Paul de Lamerie, Old Bailey trial concerning a forged order; trial includes details of his staff *(OBP: t17480224-40)*

1749 Paul Delammerry, Gerard Street, St Ann's, Westminster Pollbook, goldsmith *(WAC: CDRom)*

1751 report of death and funeral at St Ann's Church of Mr Paul de Lamerie, silver worker to His Majesty in *The London Morning Penny Post* and *The General Advertiser (BL: Burney 442B, 02 Aug 1751; 443B, 09 Aug 1751)*

Delander (Watchmaker)
77 HOLTOM, P43; FIG 59
Temple Barr

1721–61 Nathaniel De Lander /Delaunder Fleet Street nr Temple Bar, watchmaker *(Britten)*

1725 Mr Delander, Fleet Street, Tithe assessment *(GLMS: 3011)*

1731 Nathaniel Delander, Cornhill, nr Royal Exchange, advertised in *The Daily Post* for the return of a stolen watch, watchmaker *(BL: Burney 286B, 22 Feb 1731)*

1733 Natt Delander; 1733 with Jno; 1735 John Delander, listed in Clockmakers' Company South West Walk *(GLMS: 2715 vol 4)*

1733 Nathl Delander, Fleet Street, St Dunstan-in-the-West precinct, Farringdon Without ward, registered

for Land Tax *(GLMS: MF11316 vol 104)*

1734 Nathaniel Delander, Kings Tavern, within Temple Bar, insured his household goods, plate £80, etc for £1,000, watchmaker *(GLMS: 11936 vol 40 [SI 64462])*

1739 Nathaniel Delander stated in an Old Bailey trial he had issued a reward for the return of a watch stolen whilst in his possession *(OBP: t17391017-42)*

1743–44 Mr Delander, Temple Bar, advertised six times in *The Daily Advertiser* for the return of various lost items *(BL: Burney 379B, 02 Feb 1743, 09 Mar 1743; 689B, 22 Feb 1743; 381B, 20 Feb 1744; 397B, 21 Oct 1744, 15 Dec 1744)*

Note: Fig **[59]** *is for Daniel Delander*

Descharmes (Watchmaker)
196 WEATHERHEAD, P67
Suffolk Street

1688–1730 Simon (Simone) Descharmes *(Britten)*

1705 Simon DeCharmes, Watchmaker, at his house, the Sign of the Clock, corner of Warwick St, Charing Cross; gold watch *(no353 Quiet Conquest)*

1733 Simon Descharmes, 1735 Descharms, Clockmakers' Company South West Walk *(GLMS: 2715 vol 4)*

1734 Simon Descharmes, Suffolk Street, registered for Poor Rate *(WAC: MF1577 F488 item3)*

1744 possibly Mr Deschamps, Greek Street, advertised in *The Daily Advertiser* for the return of a ring *(BL: Burney 397B, 14 Jun 1744)*

Docher (Broker)
53 BULSTRODE, P72
Wyatt Street [White Row], Spittle Fields

1724 Jno Dockra, Hamlett of Spittlefields, registered for Sewer Rate *(LMA: THCS 132)*

Dokins (Broker)
38 WEATHERHEAD, P55
Chick Lane

1733 Wm Dakin, Cheek Lane, Liberty of Saffron Hill, registered for Poor Rate *(CLS: UTAH MF415 item4)*

Doughty (Broker)
12 BULSTRODE, P69
Red Cross Street

1733 Thomas Doughty, Cradle Court, off Red Cross Street, Red Cross Street

precinct, Cripplegate Without ward, registered for Land Tax *(GLMS: MF11316 vol 103)*

Dovet (Goldsmith)
156 WEATHERHEAD, P67
Grafton Street
Not found

Drummond (Goldsmith/banker)
183 HOLTOM, P49
Charing Cross

1712–54 Andrew Drummond, Golden Eagle, Charing Cross, goldsmith and banker *(Heal)*

1717 Andrew Drummond, Golden Faulcon, Charing Cross in the parish of St Martin-in-the-Fields, insured his goods, merchandise, etc in his dwelling house, goldsmith *(GLMS: 11936 vol 6 [SI 8712])*

1734 Mr Andrew Drummond, St Martin's Lane registered for Poor Rate at this address and at Charing Cross *(WAC: MF1577 F488 item3)*

1735–44 Mr Andrew Drummond, Charing-Cross, advertised seven times in *The London Daily Post & General Advertiser* and *The Daily Advertiser* for the return of lost banknotes and other items, goldsmith and banker *(BL: Burney 310B, 14 Dec 1735; 347B, 22 Feb 1739-40; 379B, 26 Apr 1743; 387B, 18 Aug 1743, 30 Dec 1743; 381B, 24 May 1744; 397B, 04 Dec 1744)*

1741 Andrew Drummond and son, John, Drummonds & Co, Charing Cross, goldsmiths and bankers; later Robert Drummond & Co *(Hilton-Price)*

1749 Andrew Drummond, Charing Cross, parish of St Martin-in-the-Fields, Westminster Pollbook, banker *(WAC: CDRom)*

Dubarry (Jeweller)
146 WEATHERHEAD, P67
King Street by St Ann's Church

1734 John Du Barry, King Street, registered for Poor Rate *(WAC: MF 32, A1746)*

Du Bois (Jeweller)
87 HOLTOM, P45
Boswell Court

1731 Joseph Dubois, Newcastle Court, Butchers Row, nr Temple Bar, jeweller *(Heal)*

1734 Joseph Dubois, Clements Lane, registered for Poor Rate (*WAC: MF183 B38 item2*)

1738 Joseph Dubois , St Martin-in-the - Fields, jeweller (*Heal*)

1736 Mr Joseph Dubois, auction notice in *The London Daily Post & General Advertiser* for his household furniture and effects, jeweller (*BL: Burney 320B, 01 Nov 1736*)

Dudds (Watchmaker)
40 WEATHERHEAD, P55
Holborn

1721–80 (died) Joseph Dudds; 1730 Coleman Street (*Britten*)

1728 Joseph Dudds, Fetter Lane, registered for Poor Rate (*GLMS: 9975 vol 1*)

1733 Joseph Dudds, St Andrew's Holborn precinct, Farringdon Without ward, registered for Land Tax (*GLMS: MF11316 vol 104*)

1733–35 Joseph Dudds, listed in Clockmakers' Company North Walk (*GLMS: 2715 vol 4*)

1755 Joseph Dudds, insured an empty house in Andover lately let to David Dudds, watchmaker (*GLMS: 11936 vol 110 [SI.145662]*)

Duemas (Goldsmith and jeweller)
134 HOLTOM, P47
Cross Lane, Long Acre

1734 John Demass, Cross Lane, registered for Poor Rate (*WAC: MF1577 F488 item3*)

Dugh (Goldsmith)
181 WEATHERHEAD, P67
Hemmingss Row

1734 John Duge, Hemings Row, registered for Poor Rate (*WAC: MF1577 F488 item3*)

Dugin (Broker / pawnbroker)
140 WEATHERHEAD, P65
Queen Street

1734 Edwd Dugan, Queen Street, registered for Poor Rate (*WAC: MF655 D39 item1, Golden Square division*)

1737 Edward Dogan, Old Bailey trial concerning a stolen silver pint mug pawned with him, pawnbroker (*OBP: t17370526-46*)

Dugin (Broker / pawnbroker)
138 WEATHERHEAD, P65
Oxendon Street, Hay Market

1734 John Dogan, Oxenden Street, registered for Poor Rate (*WAC: MF1577 F488 item3*)

Duhamel (Watchmaker*)
162 HOLTOM, P47
in the Strand

1734 and 1735 Duhamel listed in Clockmakers' Company South West Walk (*GLMS: 2715 vol 4*)

1734 Isaac Duhamel, Strand, registered for Poor Rate (*WAC: MF1577 F488 item3*)

1743 Isaac Duhamel, Old Bailey trial concerning a watch with diamond pendant, property of William Pitt, stolen from his shop in the Strand, a watchmaker (*OBP: t17431207-24*)

1744 Mr Isaac Du Hamel [Duhamel], the Enamell'd Dial, the Corner of Salisbury Street [and Cecil Street], Strand, advertised three times in *The Daily Advertiser* for the return of lost watches by himself and Leman, London, watchmaker (*BL: Burney 387B, 26 Jan 1744, 02 Feb 1744; 381B, 09 May 1744*)

1750 circa, Isaac Duhamel, triple-case repeating watch (*no167 Quiet Conquest*)

1757 auction notice in *The Public Advertiser* of 'All the Curiosities of Mr Isaac Du Hamel of Gerard Street, Soho, collected by him for many years', watchmaker and jeweller (*BLCol: Burney 467B, 30 Dec 1757*)

Duhamel (Jeweller)
149 HOLTOM, P47
Henrietta St

1730–37 Jacob Duhamel, Crown & Ring, Henrietta Street, Covent Garden, jeweller (*Heal*)

1734 Jacob Duhamel, Henrietta Street, registered for Poor Rate (*WAC: MF1959, H43, item 14*)

1749 Jacob Duhamel, Henrietta Street, listed in the Westminster Pollbook (*WPB*)

Dunlop (Watchmaker)
186 HOLTOM, P49
Spring Gardens

1725–79 died, Conyers Dunlop, Spring

Gardens, Charing Cross (*Britten*)

1731 Mr Dunlop, Spring Gardens, advertised in *The Daily Post* for the return of a lost watch by Pepys (*BL: Burney 286B, 26 May 1731*)

1733 Andrew and 1734 Conyers Dunlop listed in Clockmakers' Company South West Walk (*GLMS: 2715 vol 4*)

1734 Andrew Dunlop, Spring Garden, registered for Poor Rate (*WAC: MF1577 F488 item3*)

1742–43 Mr Conyers Dunlop, Spring Gardens, advertised three times in *The Daily Advertiser* for the return of lost silver watches by Dunlop, watchmaker (*BL: Burney 379B, 29 Dec 1742, 27 Jan 1743; 387B, 23 Aug 1743*)

1749 Conyers Dunlop, Spring Gardens, parish of St Martin-in-the-Fields, Westminster Pollbook, watchmaker (*WAC: CDRom*)

1758 Conyers Dunlop, insured four brick houses adjoining Spring Gardens (two owner-occupied, two let to widow McCormack and coachman Robertson, another let to Robert Taylor); two other empty brick houses adjoining Red Lyon Inn upper end of Red Lyon Court, Shoe Lane, total £1,600, watchmaker (*GLMS: 11936 vol 125 [SI 165694]*)

Dupain (Jeweller)
98 WEATHERHEAD, P59
Lombard Street [Court], 7 Dials
Not found

Dutens (Jeweller)
191 WEATHERHEAD, P67
Leicester Fields

1730–31 Peter Dutens, Golden Cup, Chandos Street, St Martin's Lane; 1744–65 Leicester Square, jeweller (*Heal*)

1734 Peter Dutens, Leicester Fields East, registered for Poor Rate (*WAC: MF1577 F488 item3*)

1734 Peter Dutems, Golden Cup in Leicester Square, Old Bailey trial concerning his goods stolen from the house of Elisha Minisire, an engraver working for him, goldsmith and jeweller (p27) (*OBP: t17340424-13*)

1736–44 P Dutens and Mr Peter Dutens, advertised eight times in *The Daily Post* and *The Daily Advertiser* for the return of various items including watches by Debaufre, James Gallois, Dutens, jeweller (*BL: Burney 320B, 11 May 1736; BLCol: Burney 434B, 28 Jun 1739; 689B, 28 Feb 1743; BL: Burney 387B, 02 Aug 1743, 03 Sep 1743, 28 Jan 1744; 381B, 01 Mar 1744; 397B, 20 Jun 1744*)

Peter Dutens, at the sign of the Gold Cup in Chandos Street, near St Martin's Lane Charing Cross, trade card (*V&A, Prints & Drawings*)

E

Edlin (Goldsmith)
18 HOLTOM, P41
in Ye Old Bailey
1734 Samuel Edlin in Old Bailey; 1712 Goldsmiths' Company Livery (*Grimwade*)
1734 Samuel Edlin, Old Bailey, goldsmith (*Heal*)
1734 Samuel Edlin, Without the Gate, St Martins Ludgate, registered for Poor Rate (*GLMS: 1315 vol 1*)
1735 possibly Edlen in Clockmakers' Company New Walk (*GLMS: 2715 vol 4*)

Mrs Edwards (Goldsmith)
79 HOLTOM, P45
Hemlock Court
1729–39 Griffith Edmonds, Hemlock Ct, Little Sheer Lane, Lincolns Inn Fields, plateworker (*Heal*)
1733 and 1739 Griffith Edwards, Hemlock Court, largeworker (*Grimwade*)
1734 Griffith Edwards, Eagle Court, registered for Poor Rate (*WAC: MF1901 G14 item12*)
1734 Jno Edwards, Hemlock Court, registered for Poor Rate (*WAC: MF183 B38 item2*)

Mrs Edwards (Broker)
8 BULSTRODE, P69
Bridgewaters Gardens
1729 Mr John Edwards, White Hart and Anchor, Barbican, advertised in *Fog's Weekly Journal* for customers to redeem their goods his House to be Lett (*BLCol: Burney 331B, 06 Dec 1729*)
1733 John Edwards, Bridgewater Gardens, Red Cross precinct, Cripplegate Without ward, registered for Land Tax (*GLMS: MF11316 vol 103*)

Ellis (Watchmaker)
192 HOLTOM, P51
King St, Westminster
1673–1749 (died), Richard Ellis (*Britten*)
1733 Rich Ellis, listed in Clockmakers' Company South West Walk (*GLMS: 2715 vol 4*)
1734 Richd Ellis, King Street, registered for Poor Rate (*WAC: MF2364 E355*)
1749 'Yesterday died at his House in King Street, Westminster, Mr Richard Ellis, an eminent and wealthy Clockmaker', *The General Advertiser* (*BLCol: Burney 431B, 17 May 1749*)

Endersby (Watchmaker)
25 BULSTRODE, P69
Featherstone Street
1745 circa, possibly — Enderby, watchmaker (*Britten*)

England (Goldsmith*)
161 HOLTOM, P47
in the Strand
1725 Thomas England, Long Acre, over against the Vine Tavern; 1739 Fleet Ditch; 1740 moved to Newgate Street, largeworker (*Grimwade*)
1725 Thomas England, Long Acre; 1739 Fleet Ditch, plateworker (*Heal*)
1730 Thomas England, Old Bailey trial concerning goods stolen from his shop (*OBP: t17301204-68*)
1734 Thomas England, Strand, registered for Poor Rate (*WAC: MF1577 F488 item3*)

Erwin (Broker)
141 BULSTRODE, P69
Grub Street
1752 possibly — Erwin, Tea Table, Chiswell Street, Moorfields, pawnbroker (*Heal*)

Evans (Broker)
190 HOLTOM, P51
King St, Westminster
1734 possibly Jno Evans, Charles Street, registered for Poor Rate (*WAC: MF2364 E355*)
1749 possibly John Evans, Charles Street, parish of St Margaret, Westminster and St John the Evangelist, Westminster Pollbook, broker (*WAC: CDRom*)

Everett (Watchmaker)
98 HOLTOM, P45
near ye new Church, Strand
1716 John Everell, at the Clock nr the Maypole in the Strand, parish of St Clement Danes, insured goods and merchandise in his house, watchmaker (*GLMS: 11936 vol 6 [SI 7795]*)
1724 circa, John Everett (*Britten*)
1727 John Evereil, at his House by the New Church in the Strand, advertised in *Mist's Weekly Journal* for the return of a watch lost between Stevenage and Barnet, Herts, watchmaker (*BLCol: Burney B885, 30 Dec 1727*)
1729 John Everell, at the Dial in the Strand, insured seven tenanted houses in Purple Lane, parish of St Andrew, Holborn for £400 (*GLMS: 11936 vol 28 [SI 47562]*)
1731 John Everall, over against the new Church in the Strand insured his moiety in a house and outhouse facing Kidney Stairs in Limehouse for £100 (*GLMS: 11936 vol 33 [SI 53643]*)
1734 Jno Everall, Strand Side, registered for Poor Rate (*WAC: MF183 B38 item2*)
1738 John Everell, in the Strand, insured a house and other buildings in Westgate, Peterborough for £500, watchmaker (*GLMS: 11936 vol 51 [SI 77194]*)
1739 Mr Everell, opp the New Exchange, Strand, advertised in *The Daily Post* for the return of a lost watch by John Everell, watchmaker (*BL: Burney 340B, 19 May 1739*)
1743 John Everall, Strand, insured a house and other buildings in Saltons, St Edmonds, Lincoln, let to a yeoman miller for £500, watchmaker (*GLMS: 11936 vol 66 [SI 95584]*)

Mrs Everitt (Broker)
37 BULSTRODE, P71
Bishop Gate Street
1734 Elizb Everett, Bishopsgate Street, 3rd division, Bishopsgate Without ward, registered for Land Tax (*GLMS: MF11316 vol 105*)

Eysham (Broker)
20 BULSTRODE, P69
White Cross Street
Not found

F

Mrs Farmer (Broker)
136 BULSTRODE, P69
Grub Street
1733 Rebecca Farmer, Grub Street
precinct, Cripplegate Without ward,
registered for Land Tax on two houses
(*GLMS: MF11316 vol 103*)

Farmer (Broker/pawnbroker)
137 BULSTRODE, P69
Grub Street
1725 Thomas Farmer, Leg & Dial, Grub
Street, pawnbroker (*Heal*)
1733 possibly Edward Farmer in street by
Moor Lane, Cripplegate Without ward,
registered for Land Tax (*GLMS:
MF11316 vol 103*)
1736 John Farmer, advertised in *The Daily
Post* his auction sale, broker (*BL:
Burney 319B, 22 Apr 1736*)
1744 possibly Mess Farmer & Co, Hogg
Lane, Shoreditch, advertised in *The
Daily Advertiser* for the return of two
large watches by Lee and Sharpe (*OBP:
Burney 381B, 11 Apr 1744*)

Farnel (Goldsmith)
24 HOLTOM, P43; FIG 37
Holborn Bridge
1714 John Farnell in St Anne's Lane,
largeworker (*Grimwade*)
1714–20 John Farnell at Golden Ball, cnr
Plum-tree Ct, plateworker (*Heal*)
1733 John Fernhill of Ditch Side, nr Shoe
Lane, Farringdon Without ward registered for Land Tax (*GLMS: MF11316
vol 104*)

Feline (Goldsmith)
142 HOLTOM, P47; FIG 48
King St
1720–39 Edward and Magdalen Féline,
cnr Rose Street, Covent Garden;
1739–55, King Street, Covent Garden;
Edward fl 1720–55, goldsmith; Magdalen fl 1753–62, plateworker (*Heal*)
1720 Edward Feline, Rose Street, Covent
Garden; 1739, King Street, fl 1720–55;
1731 Goldsmiths' Company Livery,
largeworker (*Grimwade*)
1734 Edward Feline, King Street North,
registered for Poor Rate (*WAC: MF1959
H43 item14*)
1753–62 fl, Magdalen Feline, King St,

Covent Garden, plateworker
(*Grimwade*)
1755 Magdallene Feline, cnr of Rose St,
Covent Garden, insured her household
goods, etc for £100, goldsmith (*GLMS:
11936 vol 110 [SI 145987]*)

Fellows (Goldsmith)
40 BULSTRODE, P71
Bishop Gate Street
1734 Jno Fellows, Bishopsgate Street, 3rd
division, Bishopsgate Without ward,
registered for Land Tax (*GLMS:
MF11316 vol 105*)

Fennery (Broker)
136 HOLTOM, P47
Long Acre
Not found

Ferguson (Broker)
135 HOLTOM, P47
Long Acre
1734 John Ferguson, Long Acre, registered for Poor Rate (*WAC: MF1577
F488 item3*)

Fitzhall (Broker)
198 HOLTOM, P51
Thieving Lane
1734 Thos Fitzhall, Thieving Lane, registered for Poor Rate (*WAC: MF2364
E355*)

Fletcher (Broker)
50 WEATHERHEAD, P55
Bell Court, Brooks Market
1732 possibly Thomas Thatcher, Fox
Court, Grays Inn Lane, St Andrew
Holborn, St George the Martyr, registered for Poor Rate (*CLS: UTAH MF29
item6*)

Flippo (Jeweller)
168 HOLTOM, P49
York Buildings
1730 possibly Humphrey Phillips, St
Martins Charls Cort in the Strand,
smallworker (*Grimwade*)
1744 possibly Humphrey Phillips,
Charles Street, Strand, working silversmith (*Heal*)

Flippo (Jeweller)
179 HOLTOM, P49
Northumberland Court, in the
Strand
Not found

Floreau (Jeweller)
170 HOLTOM, P49
York Buildings
1742–44 Mr Fleureau, Kings Arms, lower
end of St James's Street, facing St
James's Gate, advertised twice in *The
Daily Advertiser* for the return of two
lost swords, sword-cutler (*BL: Burney
381B, 15 Nov 1742; 397B, 13 Sept 1744*)
1749 Francis Floreau, Pallmall (St James),
Westminster Pollbook, jeweller (*WPB*)

Folkingham (Goldsmith)
143 HOLTOM, P47; FIG 39
New St
1724 possibly Thomas Folkingham,
Golden Ball over against Sun Tavern
behind Royal Exchange, plateworker
(*Heal*)
1729 died, possibly Thomas Folkingham,
Golden Ball over against Sun Tavern,
Royal Exchange, banker, goldsmith,
largeworker (*Grimwade*)

Foot (Goldsmith)
84 BULSTRODE, P75
East Smithfield
1734 Peter ffoot, East Smithfield, St
Botolph-Without-Aldgate, registered
for Land Tax (*GLMS: MF6011 vol 4*)
1735 John Foote, over near the Tower,
previously Queen Street near Tower
Hill at a shoemaker; later Red Cross
Square, smallworker and possibly
bucklemaker (*Grimwade*)
1752 Anne Foot, near the Maypole, East
Smithfield, goldsmith (*Heal*)

Foot (Watchmaker)
117 HOLTOM, P45
in the Strand
1719–42 William Foote (*Britten*)
1733 Wm Foot, listed in the Clockmakers'
Company South West Walk (*GLMS:
2715 vol 4*)
1743 possibly William Foot, St George
Street, Hanover Square (previously a
journeyman watchmaker at upper end
of Pall-Mall) notice in *The Daily
Advertiser* seeking his whereabouts,

watchmaker (*BLCol: Burney B689, 18 Feb 1743*)

Forterry (Watchmaker)
115 WEATHERHEAD, P63
George St, Hanover Square
Not found

Foster (Broker)
113 BULSTRODE, P77
New Gravell Lane
Not found

Fountain (Jeweller)
166 WEATHERHEAD, P67
Castle Street
Not found

Fountain (Goldsmith)
81 WEATHERHEAD, P59
in ye Cole Yard, Drury Lane
1734 possibly John Fountain, Brownlow Street, St Giles and St George Bloomsbury, registered for Poor Rate (*CLS: UTAH MF99 item1*)

Fowler (Goldsmith)
111 BULSTRODE, P79
Wapping
1697, 1720 Epaphroditus Fowler at the Hermitage Bridge Wapping; Free Merchant Taylor, smallworker (*Grimwade*)
1733 Epaphroditus ffowler, Wapping Wall Waterside, St Paul Shadwell, registered for Land Tax (*GLMS: MF6009 vol 3*)
1748 possibly Ann Fowler, Old Bailey trial concerning a mother-of-pearl snuff-box stolen out of a shew-glass in her house, silversmith (*OBP: t17480526-32*)

Fowls (Broker)
27 HOLTOM, P43
Crabtree Court, Holborn Bridge
1728 Thos Foulkes, Plumbtree Court, registered for Poor Rate (*GLMS: 9975 vol 1*)
1733 Thos Foulkes, Plumbtree Court, Farringdon Without ward, registered for Land Tax (*GLMS: MF11316 vol 104*)

Mrs Francis (Broker/pawnbroker)
140 BULSTRODE, P69
Grub Street
1733 Jere Francis, Bell Court, Grub Street precinct, or John Francis, near Moor Lane, Cripplegate Without ward, registered for Land Tax (*GLMS: MF11316 vol 103*)
1733 possibly Jane Francis, Bridgewater Gardens, Red Cross Street precinct, Cripplegate Without ward, registered for Land Tax (*GLMS: MF11316 vol 103*)
1744 Mr Francis, Two Balls, Grub-Street, advertised in *The Daily Advertiser* for customers to redeem their pledged items, he leaving off trade (*BL: Burney 397B, 31 Jul 1744*)
1744 — Francis, Two Golden Balls, Grub Street, ceased trading, pawnbroker (*Heal*)

Fraydon (Broker)
150 WEATHERHEAD, P67
Princes Street by St Anns Church
1734 Abraham Fradin, Princes Street, registered for Poor Rate (*WAC: MF655 D39, Gt Marlboro division*)

Freeman (Watchmaker)
4 WEATHERHEAD, P53
Charterhouse Square
1733 John ffreeman, St Sepulchre precinct, Farringdon Without ward, registered for Land Tax (*GLMS: MF11316 vol 104*)
1734 John Furman, Charterhouse Lane, listed as tenant of John Curwin (*GLMS: 9110 vol 1*)

Fury (Jeweller)
62 WEATHERHEAD, P57
near Turn Stile Lane
Not found
Also: **Fury** (Watchmaker)
63 WEATHERHEAD, P57
Holborn
Not found

G

Mrs Gallwith (Broker/pawnbroker)
32 BULSTRODE, P71
Norton Follgate
1730 Mrs Gallwith, Rising Sun, near Hog Lane, Norton Folgate, pawnbroker (*Heal*)

Ganderoon (Watchmaker)
101 WEATHERHEAD, P59
Earl Street, 7 Dials
1731 Stephen Ganneron, Earl Street, near Seven Dials, parish of St Giles-in-the-Fields, insured household goods, stock, etc for £300, watchmaker, watch tool seller (*GLMS: 11936 vol 34 [SI.55343]*)
1734 Stephen Ganeroon, Earl Street, West End North side, St Giles and St George Bloomsbury, registered for Poor Rate (*CLS: UTAH MF99 item1*)
1734 Ganderon, listed in Clockmakers' Company New Walk (*GLMS: 2715 vol 4*)
Also: **Ganderoon** (Broker)
102 WEATHERHEAD, P59
Hare Street by Monmouth St
Not found
Also: **Ganderoon** (Broker)
103 WEATHERHEAD, P59
in Browns Gardens, 7 Dials
Not found

Mrs Garbert (Broker)
35 BULSTRODE, P71
Skinners Street
1734 Ann Garbutt, Skinner Street, north side, 3rd division, Bishopsgate Without ward, registered for Land Tax but Mr Edwd Fellows to pay (*GLMS: MF11316 vol 105*)
1738 Anne Garbutt, late of Skinner Street, but now of Southwark, bankruptcy notice in *The London Daily Post & General Advertiser*, spinster and pawnbroker (*BL: 333B, 09 Aug 1738*)

Gardener (Broker*)
199 HOLTOM, P51
Long Ditch
1734 Antho Gardner, Broken Cross, Thieving Lane, registered for Poor Rate (*WAC: MF2364 E355*)
1746 possibly Mr Gardener, Old Bailey trial concerning stolen plate brought to his shop (*OBP: t17460226-35*)

Gay (Broker/pawnbroker)
83 WEATHERHEAD, P59
Shorts Gardens
1734 John Gay, Little Wild Street, St Giles and St George Bloomsbury, registered for Poor Rate (*CLS: UTAH MF99 item1*)
1743 Mr John Gay, New Belton Street, St Giles, advertisement in *The Daily Advertiser* for customers to redeem

their pledged items due to his death, pawnbroker *(BL: Burney 387B, 29 Dec 1743)*

George (Goldsmith)
114 BULSTRODE, P77
Wapping
1733 John George, Wapping Dock, St Dunstan Wapping, registered for Land Tax *(GLMS: MF6013 vol 4)*
1733 possibly James George, Wapping Wall Landside, St Paul Shadwell, registered for Land Tax *(GLMS: MF6009 vol 3)*

Gibbons (Goldsmith)
13 BULSTRODE, P69
Red Cross Street
1733 Edward Gibbon, Red Cross Street, Red Cross Street precinct, Cripplegate Without ward, registered for Land Tax *(GLMS: MF11316 vol 103)*

Gibbons (Goldsmith)
64 WEATHERHEAD, P57
Holborn
1723–26 John Gibbons, Red Lion Street, plateworker *(Heal)*
1724 John Gibbons, Eagle Street, near Red Lion Square; Goldsmiths' Company Court until 1744, largeworker *(Grimwade)*
1732 Michael Gibbons, Gray's Inn Lane, St Andrew Holborn, St George the Martyr, registered for Poor Rate *(CLS: UTAH MF29 item6)*
1736 John Gibbons, over against the Gull and Gate Inn in High Holborn, insured household goods, plate, etc for £300, goldsmith *(GLMS: 11936 vol 46 [SI.71524])*
1743 Michael Gibbons, Red Lyon, Grays Inn Lane, advertised in *The Daily Advertiser* for return of items stolen by Job Lilley's apprentice *(BL: Burney 379B, 14 Mar 1743)*

Gibbs (Watchmaker)
118 BULSTRODE, P77
Wapping
1733 possibly Robert Gibbs, Wapping Dock, St Dunstan Wapping, registered for Land Tax *(GLMS: MF6013 vol 4)*
1735 possibly Robert Gibbs, Wapping Dock, registered for Sewer Rate *(LMA: THCS 149)*

Gibson (Watchmaker)
3 HOLTOM, P41
Round Court, St Martins Le Grand
1727 James Gibson at the Sign of the Dial, parish of St Martins le Grand, insured his household goods for £500 watchmaker *(GLMS: 11936 vol 23 [SI 41291])*
1727–60 James Gibson in London; then to Newcastle, watchmaker *(Britten)*
1733 Gibbson listed in Clockmakers' Company North Walk and 1735 in New Walk *(GLMS: 2715 vol 4)*
1734 Js Gibson registered for Land Tax in St Martins le Grand precinct, Aldersgate Within ward *(GLMS: MF11316 vol 102)*

Gibson (Jeweller)
140 HOLTOM, P47
Bow Street
1714–28 John Gibson, Bow Street, Covent Garden, jeweller *(Heal)*
1734 John Gibson, Ward Alley, Bow Street West, registered for Poor Rate *(WAC: MF1959 H43 item14)*

Mrs Gibson (Goldsmith)
38 BULSTRODE, P71
Bishop Gate Street
1733 John Gibson, Bishopsgate Street, 2nd division, Bishopsgate Without ward, registered for Land Tax *(GLMS: MF11316 vol 102)*
1738 John Gibson, adjoining the workhouse in Bishopsgate, insured stock of wrought and manufactured plate, etc for £500, goldsmith *(GLMS: 11936 vol 53 [SI.80062])*
1733 Susan Gibson, tenant of Mr East, Swan Yard, Bishopsgate Street, 2nd division, Bishopsgate Without ward, registered for Land Tax *(GLMS: MF11316 vol 102)*
1755 Mrs Gibson, Bishopsgate Street, silversmith *(Heal)*

Gillard (Jeweller)
59 WEATHERHEAD, P57
Warwick Court, Holborn
Not found

Gilpin (Goldsmith)
83 HOLTOM, P45; FIG 49
Lincolns Inn Back Gate
1725 Mr Gilpin, Fleet Street, Tithe assessment *(GLMS: 3011)*

1728 Thomas Gilpin one of three executors of Handanby Langley's estate, eventually acquiring his business in Serle Street, Lincolns Inn (J. Culme, 'The embarrassed goldsmith, 1729–1831', *The Silver Society Journal*, no10 1998, pp68–9)
1730 Thomas Gilpin, 'Goldsmith at ye Acorn in ye Strand'; 1739 Lincolns Inn Back Gate, smallworker, largeworker *(Grimwade)*
1731–73 Thomas Gilpin, Lincolns Inn Back Gate, Searle Street, next door to Will's Coffee-house, goldsmith *(Heal)*
1734 Thos Gilpin, Duke Street, registered for Poor Rate *(WAC: MF183 B38 item2)*
1735 John Wilmot states he lives with Mr Gilpin by Lincolns Inn Back Gate in Old Bailey trial concerning theft of a silver salver belonging to Rt Hon Sir Robert Walpole, goldsmith *(OBP: t17350911-49)*
1743–44 Mr Gilpin, Lincolns Inn (Carey, Portugal and Serle Streets), advertised six times in *The Daily Advertiser* for the return of lost items, including a stolen gold and silver collection, goldsmith *(BL: Burney 379B, 20 May 1743, 22 Jun 1743; 387B, 13 Oct 1743, 04 Jan 1744; 381B, 27 Feb 1744, 22 Mar 1744)*
1749 Thomas Gilpin, Searle Street, Westminster Pollbook *(WPB)*
1750 Thomas Gilpin, Searle Street, Lincolns Inn Fields, insured his own and tenanted property, outbuildings and hay in Bedfordshire and Buckinghamshire, twelve policies 1744–77, goldsmith *(GLMS: 11936 vol 92 [SI 127258])*

Mrs Goddard (Broker)
87 BULSTRODE, P75
Nightingale Lane
1733 Daniel Goddard, Nightingale Lane, St John Wapping, Tower division, registered for Land Tax *(GLMS: MF6013 vol 4)*

Goddard (Broker/pawnbroker)
66 WEATHERHEAD, P57
Eagle Street
1726 John Goddard, back door of the Vine Tavern, Eagle Street, Holborn, pawnbroker *(Heal)*
1732 John Goddard, Eagle Street, St Andrew Holborn, St George the Martyr, registered for Poor Rate *(CLS: UTAH MF29 item6)*

Goddard (Broker / pawnbroker)
119 HOLTOM, P47
Burley St
1734 Jonathan Goddard, Burleigh Street, registered for Poor Rate (*WAC: MF1577 F488 item3*)
1744 Jonathan Goddard, Golden Ball, Burleigh St, nr Exeter St, Strand, pawnbroker (*Heal*)

Godfrey (Goldsmith and jeweller*)
135 WEATHERHEAD, P65
Norris Street, Hay Market
1732 Benjamin Godfrey, Hand Ring & Crown, Norris Street Haymarket; 1741 died, largeworker (*Grimwade*)
1732–39 Benjamin Godfrey, Hand Ring & Crown, Norris Street, Haymarket, gold and silversmith (*Heal*)
1732 Mrs Godfry, Norwich Street, St James's-market, advertised in *The Daily Post* for the return to her, or Mrs Chevenix, a Toy-Shop, the Bottom of the Hay-market, of a watch by Debaufre, goldsmith (*BLCol: Burney 805B, 15 Feb 1732*)
[Mrs Godfrey, née Elizabeth Pantin, widow of Abraham, married Benjamin Godfrey 1732]
1734 Ben Godfrey, Norwich Street, registered for Poor Rate on two houses (*WAC: MF655 D39 item1, Church & Market division*)
1734 Elizabeth Godfrey, St Martin's Lane, registered for Poor Rate (*WAC: MF1577 F488 item3*)
1735 Benjamin Godfrey, Old Bailey trial concerning seven gold rings stolen from his shop (*OBP: t17350416-9*)
1741 Eliza(beth) Godfrey, Norris Street, Haymarket, gold and silversmith, jeweller (*Grimwade*)
1741–58 Elizabeth Godfrey, Hand Ring & Crown, Norris Street, St James's, Haymarket (*Heal*)
1743–44 Mrs Godfrey, Norris Street, near St James's Market, advertised six times in *The Daily Advertiser* for the return of various items, goldsmith (*BL: Burney 379B, 21 Apr 1743, 17 Jun 1743; 387B, 30 Aug 1743, 24 Dec 1743; 381B, 06 Mar 1744, 08 Mar 1744*)
1743–44 Mr [*sic*] Godfrey, Norris Street, near St James's Market, advertised twice in *The Daily Advertiser* for the return of lost items, silversmith and

jeweller (*BL: Burney 387B, 20 Oct 1743; 397B, 13 Sep 1744*)

Gole (Jeweller)
194 WEATHERHEAD, P67
St Martins Street, Leicester Fields
1734 Abraham Gole, St Martin's Street East, registered for Poor Rate (*WAC: MF1577 F488 item3*)

Good (Broker)
28 BULSTRODE, P71
Paved Ally, holywell Lane, Shor
1729 Richard Good, Holywell Lane, St Leonard Shoreditch; 1733 Richard Good, Paved Ally in the Court, St Leonard's Shoreditch, registered for Poor Rate (*P91/LEN/47; P91/LEN/1374*)

Mrs Goodman (Broker / pawnbroker*)
57 BULSTRODE, P72
Smock Alley
1734 possibly Ann Goodman, Whitechapel, 2nd division, St Mary Whitechapel, registered for Land Tax (*GLMS: MF6015 vol 2*)
1738 Mrs Elizabeth Goodman, St Botolphs Bishopsgate, Old Bailey trial concerning silver, jewellery and money stolen from her shop, pawnbroker (*OBP: t17380113-2*)
1745 Mrs Goodman, Widegate Street, without Bishopsgate, pawnbroker (*Heal*)

Goodread (Watchmaker)
67 WEATHERHEAD, P57
Kings Gate Street
Not found

Goslin (Goldsmith)
3 BULSTRODE, P69
Barbicon
1674 possibly Wm Gostling, goldsmith of Fleet Street; Sir Francis Gosling, bookseller, succeeding to R Gosling at the Mitre and Crown, opposite St Dunstan's Church, fl 1714–40; Sir Francis bookseller to Browne Willis, the author of *The Survey of the English Cathedrals*, who left off selling in 1757, a goldsmith and bookseller, eventually bookseller only (*Hilton-Price*)
1730–43 Richard Gosling; 1732 Gosling, Fox and Crown, Philip Lane Addle Street, plateworker; 1743-54 Cornhill,

plateworker (*Heal*)
1733 Richard Gosling, at ye Fox and Crown Barbican, smallworker; 1739 Barbican, largeworker; 1743 moved to Cornhill (*Grimwade*)
1733 Richard Gosling, Barbican, Cripplegate Without ward, registered for Land Tax (*GLMS: MF11316 vol 103*)
1740 Richard Goslin, Old Bailey trial concerning a stolen tankard he bought (*OBP: t17401015-2*)
1748 Mr Gosling, 'I am a goldsmith', character witness in Old Bailey trial, which records that 'A person who stood by said it was not in the warning from Goldsmiths' Hall' (*OBP: t17480907-53*)

Mrs Gosling (Broker)
93 BULSTRODE, P77
Ratcliffe highway
1734 Mme Gosling, Highway South, Upper division, St George-in-the-East, Middx, registered for Land Tax (*GLMS: MF6016 vol 5*)

Gossford (Broker)
113 WEATHERHEAD, P61
Great Poultney Street
1734 John Gasford, Gt Pultney Street East, St James's Piccadilly, registered for Poor Rate (*WAC: MF655 D39 item1, Great Marlboro division*)

Gough (Broker)
50 BULSTRODE, P72
Old George Street, Spittle Fields
1733 possibly Goffe, listed in Clockmakers' Company North Walk (*GLMS: 2715 vol 4*)

Grainger (Broker / pawnbroker)
58 HOLTOM, P43
Salisbury Court
1711–20 Thomas Grainger, Rose, Salisbury Court, Fleet Street, pawnbroker (*Heal*)
1727–29 Thomas Granger appeared in three Old Bailey trials stating he had stopped various items (*OBP: t17270517-7; t17280605-6; t17291203-28*)
1733 Thomas Grainger, Salisbury Court, Fleet Street precinct, Ludgate Hill, Farringdon Without ward registered for Land Tax (*GLMS: MF11316 vol 104*)
1734 Thomas Grainger, Salisbury Court,

listed as inhabitant of St Bride's parish, pawnbroker *(GLMS: 6561)*

1738 possibly Mr Grainger, Puddle Hill, appeared in an Old Bailey trial concerning items pawned with him, pawnbroker *(OBP: t17380222-1)*

1739–40 Thos Grainger, Salisbury Court, Fleet Street, cessation of business, pawnbroker *(Hart)*

Gray (Watchmaker)
127 WEATHERHEAD, P65
by St James's House

1720–60 Benjamin Gray (married Vulliamy's daughter and became his partner) *(Britten)*

1732 Mr Benjamin Gray, near St James's, advertised in *The Daily Post* for the return of a lost mother of pearl snuff-box, watchmaker *(BL: Burney 805B, 08 Feb 1732)*

1733 Benj Gray and 1735 Gray, listed in Clockmakers' Company South West Walk *(GLMS: 2715 vol 4)*

1734 Daniel Gray, Little Crown Court, off St James's Street, registered for Poor Rate *(WAC: MF655 D39 item1, Pall Mall division)*

1742–44 Mr Gray, St James's Street, advertised seven times for the return of watches by Quare and Horseman, Charles Gretton, Gray and other items, watchmaker *(BL: Burney 381B, 04 Dec 1742, 22 Feb 1744; 379B, 13 May 1743, 22 Jun 1743; 387B, 17 Jul 1743, 26 Oct 1743; 397B, 10 Jul 1744)*

1744 Mr Benjamin Gray, St James's Street, London, advertised in *The Daily Advertiser* for the return of a watch by Francis Ridon[?], watchmaker to His Majesty *(BL: Burney 397B, 18 Jul 1744)*

1745 Benjamin Gray & Justin Vulliamy, parish of St James, Westminster, insured stock and goods in trust at the Dial & Sun, near St James's House, St James's Street for £200, watchmaker *(GLMS: 11936 vol 75 [SI.103530])*

1749 Benjamin Gray, St James Street, parish of St James, Piccadilly, Westminster Pollbook *(WAC: CDRom)*

Gray (Goldsmith)
39 WEATHERHEAD, P55
Field Lane

1716 John Gray, Field Lane; Free Poulterer, smallworker *(Grimwade)*

1730 Mr John Grey, Field Lane, London,

advertised in *Fog's Weekly Journal* for the whereabouts of his absconded apprentice, goldsmith *(BLCol: Burney 331B, 07 Nov 1730)*

1733 John Gray, Field Lane, Liberty of Saffron Hill, registered for Poor Rate *(CLS: UTAH MF415 item4)*

1735 John Gray, Field Lane, parish of St Andrew Holborn, insured his household goods, stock in house and shed adjoining, including manufactured and wrought plate, etc for £200, gold and silversmith *(GLMS: 11936 vol 43 [SI.68607])*

1739 John Gray, London, goldsmith *(Heal)*

1743 Mr Gray, Old Bailey trial concerning theft of diamonds left with him but not traceable because of his death in June 1743, goldsmith *(OBP: t17431207-41)*

Gray (Goldsmith)
64 BULSTRODE, P72
Red Lyon Street

1731 — Gray, without the Bars, Whitechapel, silversmith *(Heal)*

1734 possibly William Gray, Reddish Row, St George-in-the-East, Middx, registered for Land Tax *(GLMS: MF6015 vol 5)*

1743 Mr Gray [Whitechapel], his demise mentioned in an Old Bailey trial *(OBP: t17431207-41)*

1743 'Yesterday Morning died, at his House in Whitechapel, aged Eighty Years, Mr Gray, an eminent and wealthy Silversmith. He was Master of the Academy in Brooks Street, Ratcliff upwards of Forty Years; which Business he gave over about Twelve Years since', *The London Evening Post (BL: Burney 378B, 29 Oct 1743)*

Grayham (Watchmaker)
48 HOLTOM, P43; FIGS 56, 62
Fleet St

1688–1751 George Grayham; 1720–51 Dial & One Crown, nr Fleet Bridge, honest Geo Graham, Tompion Graham, a Quaker, buried in Westminster Abbey, clockmaker *(Britten)*

1733 Mr George Grayham, Fleet Street, advertised twice in *The Daily Post* for the return of a lost watch made by him and watch and case by Tho Tompion, E. Banger, watchmaker *(BLCol: Burney*

805B, 15 Feb 1732; BL: 297B, 02 Mar 1733)

1732 George Grayham, Fleet Street, listed as inhabitant of St Bride's parish *(GLMS: 6561)*

1733 Geo Grayham, Fleet Street, New Street precinct, Farringdon Without ward registered for Land Tax *(GLMS: MF11316 vol104)*

1740–41 and 1744 George Grayham, Fleet Street advertised twice in *The London Daily Post & General Advertiser* for lost watch and seals, *The Daily Advertiser* for a lost watch made by him, watchmaker *(BL: Burney 355B, 31 Jan 1740-41; 379B, 27 Jan 1744)*

1744 Mr Grayham, Dial and Three Crowns, Fleet Street advertised in *The Daily Advertiser* for two watches made by him and Stevenson stolen by two footpads on Hackney Marsh, watchmaker *(BL: Burney 397B, 18 Aug 1744)*

1751 Saturday died in Fleet Street, aged 78, Mr George Graham, one of the most eminent & experienced Watchmakers of this City, *Read's Weekly Journal (BLCol: Burney 441B, 08 Nov 1751; 442B, 23 Nov 1751)*

1751 *The London Advertiser* advertised that 'Samuel Barkley, Foreman & Executor to Mr George Graham, Clock and Watchmaker dec'd, succeeds Mr Graham in his Business & Shop at the Dial and 3 Crowns, next door to the Globe Tavern in Fleet Street, opp Salisbury Court, in Partnership with Mr Colley, the other Executor' *(BLCol: Burney 441B, 03 Dec 1751)*

1751 *The London Evening Post* advertised that Thomas Mudge, Watchmaker, late Apprentice to Mr Graham deceas'd, carries on Business in the same Manner Mr Graham did, at the Dial & One Crown, opposite the Bolt & Tun, Fleet Street *(BLCol: Burney 439B, 19 Nov 1751)*

Green (Goldsmith)
79 BULSTRODE, P75
Tower hill

1711 Joseph Green at the Golden Ball & Ring, corner of Little Tower Hill, next the Minories, St Botolph Aldgate, insured his house, goldsmith and Citizen of London) *(GLMS: 11936 vol 1 [SI.1160])*

1723–34 Joseph Green, Ring & Ball, Little Tower Hill, goldsmith and pawnbroker *(Heal)*

1725 Mr Green, Minories, Old Bailey counterfeit trial where he confirmed a Bill was not a fake, goldsmith *(OBP: t17250224-51)*

1737 died, — Green, Minories, goldsmith *(Heal)*

1738 Mrs Mary Green, Little-Tower Hill, advertised in *The London Daily Post & General Advertiser* the auction of her entire Stock of Plate being the Widow of Mr Joseph Green of the same address, goldsmith *(BL: Burney 340B, 24 Jan 1738-9)*

Green (Jeweller)
1 HOLTOM, P41
Angel Street, St Martins Le Grand

1734 Richard Greene, Foster Lane, plateworker *(Grimwade)*

1734 Richard Green St John Zachary precinct, Aldersgate Within ward, registered for Land Tax *(GLMS: MF11316 vol 102)*

1750 circa, Richard Green, Strand, opp New Exchange, possibly a son, goldsmith and jeweller *(Heal)*

Griffiths (Watchmaker)
26 HOLTOM, P43
Crabtree Court, Holborn Bridge

1712–20 possibly Thomas (George) Griffith *(Britten)*

1728 George Griffith, Plumbtree Court, registered for Poor Rate *(GLMS: 9975, vol 1)*

Grigg (Watchmaker*)
125 WEATHERHEAD, P65
St James's Street

1732 Richard Gregg, parish of St James, Westminster, insured household goods, stock in shop and apartments adjoining Thatched House Tavern, St James Street for £300, watchmaker *(GLMS: 11936 vol 37, [SI59135])*

1733 Ricd Grigg, 1734 Grig and 1735 Grig, listed in Clockmakers' Company South West Walk *(GLMS: 2715 vol 4)*

1734 Richard Gregg, parish of St James, Westminster, insured household goods, goods in shop, apartment in a Gent's house at the Tompions Head, St James Street and goods in trust there for £500, watchmaker and haberdasher

(GLMS: 11936 vol 40 [SI.63679])

1742–44 Mr Gregg (Grig, Tompion's Head, near White's Chocolate House), St James's Street, advertised three times for the return of gold watches by Richard Gregg, Willson and Francis Gregg, watchmaker *(BL: Burney 381B, 10 Dec 1742, 04 May 1744; 387B, 22 Dec 1743)*

Grigman (Watchmaker)
122 HOLTOM, P47
Russell Street

1720–1825 Daniel and Thomas Grignion, Kings Arms & Dial *(Britten)*

1727 circa, Daniel Grignion, watchmaker; circa 1730–63 trade card for Daniel and Thomas Grignion at the King's Arms and Dial, Russel(l) Street, Covent Garden; 1737 portrait of Thomas Grignion (1721–84) *(no365 Quiet Conquest)*

1734 Daniel Grignion, Russell Street South, registered for Poor Rate *(WAC: MF1959 H43 item14)*

1735 Grignion, listed in Clockmakers' Company New Walk *(GLMS: 2715 vol 4)*

1741–44 Mr Daniel Grignion, Russell Street (Russel-Court), opp Tom's Coffee-House, advertised four times for the return of watches and a purse, watchmaker *(BL: Burney 352B, 05 Dec 1741; 379B, 21 May 1743; 397B, 03 July 1744, 03 Aug 1744)*

1748 Daniel Grignion, insured his household goods, stock, etc at Kings Arms and Dial, Russell Street, in the parish of St Paul, Covent Garden for £500; 1756 insured his household goods, plate, etc at Church Lane, Chelsea for £200 *(GLMS: 11936 vol 84 [SI.115290], vol 114 {SI.151496])*

Grimstead (Toyman*)
13 HOLTOM, P41
The Black Swan St Paul's Chyard

1731 Mr Grimstead at a Toyshop in St Paul's Churchyard advertised in *The Daily Post* for a lost watch *(BL: Burney 286B, 24 Apr 1731)*

1733 Valentine Grimstead, West precinct, Castle Baynard ward, registered for Land Tax *(GLMS: MF11316 vol 103)*

1740–44 Mr Grimstead, St Paul's Churchyard placed four advertisements in *The Daily Advertiser* for the

return of lost property including Night-Cloaths Ear-rings, toyman *(BL: Burney 347B, 06 Jun 1740; 379B, 23 Jan 1744; 19 Aug 1744; 15 Sept 1744)*

Grub (Broker/pawnbroker)
133 WEATHERHEAD, P65
St James's, Market Lane

1730 Henry Grub, Old Bailey trial concerning 56ozs plate, value £85 19s, offered to him, 'The Pawnbroker' *(OBP: t17301014-68)*

1734 Henry Grubb, Market Lane, registered for Poor Rate on two houses *(WAC: MF655 D39 item 1, Church & Market division)*

1739–44 Mr Henry Grub, St James's Market, two Old Bailey trials concerning an apron and cap and silver items pawned with him, pawnbroker *(OBP: t17390906-9, t17440404-23)*

Gun (Broker/pawnbroker)
57 HOLTOM, P43
Bride's Alley

1726 Joseph Gun, Salisbury Court, listed as inhabitant of St Brides parish; served as a Scavenger, pawnbroker *(GLMS: 6561)*

1727 Mrs Gun, St Bride's Church-yard, Old Bailey trial concerning three silver watches, the Pawnbroker *(OBP: t17271206-2)*

1733 Widow Gunn, Fleet Street precinct, Ludgate Hill, Farringdon Without ward registered for Land Tax *(GLMS: MF11316 vol 104)*

H

Hadsel (Goldsmith)
115 HOLTOM, P45
in the Strand

1744 Mr William Hodsell, opp end of Catherine Street, Strand, advertised in *The Daily Advertiser* for the return of a lost Mourning ring, goldsmith *(BL: Burney 387B, 14 Jan 1744)*

Haistings (Goldsmith)
184 HOLTOM, P49
Charing Cross

1734 John Hastings, Warwick Street, registered for Poor Rate *(WAC: MF1577 F488 item3)*

1743 —Hastings, Charing Cross, goldsmith *(Heal)*

1743 John Hastings, Old Bailey trial concerning the exchange of stolen silver items (Old Plate) for new plus cash, goldsmith *(OBP: t17430413-18)*

1743 Mr Hastings, Unicorn, Charing Cross, advertised twice in *The Daily Advertiser* for the return of part of a table spoon and a lost watch by Keelam, goldsmith and silversmith *(BLCol: Burney 689B, 19 Feb 1743; 387B, 13 Sept 1743)*

1744 John Hastings, St Martin-in-the-Fields, insured his house, goods, furniture, manufactured plate, etc at the Unicorn, Charing Cross for £400, goldsmith *(GLMS: 11936 vol 79 [SI 99589])*

1749 John Hastings, Charing Cross, St Martin-in-the-Fields, Westminster Pollbook, silversmith *(WPB)*

Hall (Broker / pawnbroker)
28 WEATHERHEAD, P55
Trumball Street

1737 Mrs Hall, Turnmill Street, next to the Ironmongers Arms, facing Clerkenwell Green, advertised in *The Daily Post* requesting customers to redeem their pledged items as she had left off her business *(BL: Burney 325B (reel 1), 11 Jul 1737)*

Hall (Broker)
51 WEATHERHEAD, P55
Fox Court, Brooks Market

1732 Edmund and Henry Hall, Fox Court, St Andrew Holborn, St George the Martyr, each registered for Poor Rate *(CLS: UTAH MF29 item6)*

Halliday (Goldsmith)
153 WEATHERHEAD, P67; FIG 38
Grafton Street

1717, 1725 Sarah Holaday, Hrafton [*sic*] Street *(Grimwade)*

1719–40 Sarah Holaday, Grafton Street, plateworker *(Heal)*

1722 Sarah Holladay, Golden Cup, Grafton Street, parish of St Anne's, Westminster, insured goods and merchandise in house for £1,000, goldsmith *(GLMS: 11936 vol 15 [SI.27663])*

1733 Widow Holiday, Grafton Street, registered for Highway Rate *(WAC: MF32 A134 item1747)*

Hallifax (Watchmaker)
61 HOLTOM, P43
at a Fan Shop

1733 John Hallifax, Hanging Sword Alley, Fleet Street precinct, Farringdon Without ward, registered for Land Tax *(GLMS: MF11316 vol 104)*

1737 John Hallifax, Fleet Street, listed as inhabitant of St Bride's parish, watchmaker *(GLMS: 6561)*

1740 John Hallifax, Fleet Street, bankrupt; circa 1740 free of the Fanmakers' Company; died 1758 Old Bailey, clock and automata maker *(Britten)*

Hally (Broker)
90 BULSTRODE, P75
Ratcliffe highway
Not found

Hamlin (Broker)
82 WEATHERHEAD, P59
Corner of ye Cole Yard, Drury Lane

1733 Edward Hamlin, Great Queen Street, St Giles and St George Bloomsbury, registered for Poor Rate *(CLS: UTAH MF98 item8)*

1734 Edward Hamlin, Drury Lane, St Giles and St George Bloomsbury, registered for Poor Rate *(CLS: UTAH MF99 item1)*

Hannell (Goldsmith)
93 WEATHERHEAD, P59
St Andrews Street, 7 Dials

1715–28 Paul Hanet, Great St Andrews Street, plateworker *(Heal)*

1716 Paul Hannell, Great St Andrews Street, St Giles; free of the Longbow String Makers, goldsmith *(Grimwade)*

1734 Paul Hanet, St Andrews Street North side, St Giles and St George Bloomsbury, registered for Poor Rate *(CLS: UTAH MF99 item1)*

Hannet (Watchmaker)
134 WEATHERHEAD, P65
Norris Street, Hay Market

1725 Joseph Hanet, the Dial, Oxenden Street, parish of St Martin-in-the-Fields, insured household goods, stock, etc for £500, watchmaker *(GLMS: 11936 vol 18 [SI.35555])*

Hardy (Goldsmith*)
74 BULSTRODE, P72
Minories

1727 —Hardey, Parrot, Great Minories, near Aldgate, goldsmith *(Heal)*

1728–31 William Hardy, four Old Bailey trials concerning silver buckles and plate stolen from his shop and stolen rings and a silver spoon offered to him for sale, goldsmith *(OBP: t17281204-6; t17291203-2; t17291203-4; t17310714-14)*

1733 possibly Andrew Harding, 6th precinct, Aldgate ward, registered for Land Tax *(GLMS: MF11316 vol 102)*

1743–47, Mrs Hardey, Parrot, Minories, goldsmith *(Heal)*

1743 Mrs Hardy, the Parrot in the Minories, advertised in *The Daily Advertiser* for the return of a lost stay-hook, goldsmith *(BL: Burney 379B, 04 Feb 1743)*

1752 possibly Thomas Harding of the Minories, Old Bailey trial where he states he has a shop, goldsmith *(OBP: t17520514-1)*

Harris (Watchmaker)
56 WEATHERHEAD, P57
Grays Inn Walk

1721–45 Christopher Harris, Grays Inn; afterwards Leadenhall Street *(Britten)*

1732 —Harris, Grays Inn, St Andrews Holborn, St George the Martyr, registered for Poor Rate *(CLS: UTAH MF29 item6)*

1732 possibly William Harris, Grays Inn Passage, St Andrew Holborn, St George the Martyr, registered for Poor Rate *(CLS: UTAH MF29 item6)*

1734 Christph Harris, listed in Clockmakers' Company North Walk *(GLMS: 2715 vol 4)*

1742 Mr Christ Harris, East-India-House, Leadenhall Street, advertised in *The Daily Advertiser* for the return of a lost watch by Christ Harris, Grays Inn London No 132, watchmaker *(BL: Burney 381B, 19 Nov 1742)*

1743 Chris Harris, The Dial, near East-India-House, Leadenhall-Street, advertised in *The Daily Advertiser* for the return of a small silver watch case by Edward Underwood *(OBP: Burney 379B, 01 Feb 1743)*

Harris (Watchmaker)
116 HOLTOM, P45
in the Strand
Not found

Harrison (Watchmaker)
3 WEATHERHEAD, P53
Goswell Street
Not found

Harrison (Broker/pawnbroker)
90 WEATHERHEAD, P59
King Street, St Giles's
1734 Thos Harrison, King Street South, registered for Poor Rate (*WAC: MF32 A134*)
1745 Mr Harrison, by St Giles Church, Old Bailey trial concerning a silver spoon pawned with him, pawnbroker (*OBP: 17450116-7*)
1749 possibly Thomas Harrison, Turnstile Alley, parish of St Martin-in-the-Fields, Westminster Pollbook, broker (*WAC: CDRom*)
1753 possibly —Harrison, Three Balls, Denmark Street, St Giles's Church, pawnbroker (*Heal*)
Also: **Harrison** (Watchmaker)
91 WEATHERHEAD, P59
St Andrews Street, 7 Dials
1693 born–1776 died, possibly John Harrison, born Yorks: 1700–35 Barrow; 1735–76 Orange Street, Red Lyon Square; buried Hampstead Cemetery; longitude timekeeper inventor, etc (*Baillie*)
1720–50 possibly James Harrison (*Britten*)
1720–51 possibly James Harison; 1737–51 Clockmakers' Company (*Baillie*)

Hart (Goldsmith/banker)
64 HOLTOM, P43
at a Fan Shop
1733 Wm Hart, Fleet Street, St Dunstan-in-the-West precinct, Farringdon Without ward registered for Land Tax (*GLMS: MF11316 vol 104*)
1736–37 Mr William Hart, at the Grasshopper, Fleet Street, advertised three times in *The Daily Post* for the return of various lost items, goldsmith (*BL: Burney, 90B, 30 Jan 1736, 325B [reel 1], 29 Apr 1737, 7 Nov 1737*)
1738–44 Mr William Hart, Grasshopper, Fleet Street, advertised six times in *The Daily Advertiser* for the return of

various lost items, including grain gold, goldsmith, banker (*BL: Burney 332B, 06 Jan 1738, 397B, 05 Aug 1743, 04 Jun 1744, 21 Jul 1744, 27 Aug 1744, 03 Nov 1744*)
1738–47 William Hart, Grasshopper, Fleet Street, goldsmith and banker (*Heal*)
1747 William Hart at the Grasshopper, Fleet Street insured his household goods, furniture, stock, etc for £1,000, goldsmith (*GLMS: 11936 vol 80 [SI 109390]*)

Hartley (Broker)
17 WEATHERHEAD, P53
by the Sheep Pens
1718 possibly Samuel Hartley, Cock Lane, West Smithfield, parish of St Sepulchre's, insured his goods and merchandise in his house; 1719 removed to New St, Cloth Fair, parish of St Bartholomew's the Great, silver-smith (*GLMS: 11936 vol 8 [SI.12071]*)
1734 Thomas Hartley, St Sepulchre's, Smithfield precinct, Farringdon Without ward, registered for Land Tax (*GLMS: MF11316 vol 106*)

Harvey (Broker/pawnbroker)
127 BULSTRODE, P72
Hounds Ditch
1734 Thomas Harvy, Houndsditch, Houndsditch precinct, Portsoken ward, registered for Land Tax (*GLMS: MF11316 vol 107*)
1744–48 Mrs Harvey in Houndsditch, two Old Bailey trials concerning stolen linen and a silver tankard pawned with her, pawnbroker (*OBP: t17440728-21; t17480706-8*)
1747 Mrs Harvey, Houndsditch, pawn-broker (*Heal*)

Hatfield (Goldsmith)
172 WEATHERHEAD, P67; FIG 43
St Martins Lane
1727 Charles Hatfield, Golden Ball St Martin's Lane; 1739 St Martin's Lane, goldsmith; died 1740?; 1740 Susannah Hatfield, Golden Ball, St Martin's Lane, goldsmith (*Grimwade*)
1739 died, Charles Hatfield, Golden Ball, St Martin's Lane, plateworker; 1740 Susannah Hatfield, Golden Ball, St Martin's Lane, plateworker (*Heal*)

Hatton (Watchmaker)
107 HOLTOM, P45
Duke St, Lincolns Inn Fields
1733 John Hatton, Duke Street, St Giles and St George, Bloomsbury parish, registered for Poor Rate (*CLS; UTAH MF98 item8*)
1733, 1734 and 1735 Hatton, Clockmakers' Company New Walk (*GLMS: 2715 vol 4*)
1739 John Hatton, Duke Street, Lincolns Inn Fields, insured a house at the Looking Glass, Drury Lane, parish of St Martin-in-the-Fields and house in Turnstile Alley, Drury Lane and another for £700, watchmaker (*GLMS: 11936 vol 53 [SI 81385]*)

Haydon (Broker/pawnbroker)
177 WEATHERHEAD, P67
Hemmingss Row
1715 Amos Hayton, Three Bowls, Heming's Row, nr St Martin's Lane, pawnbroker (*Heal*)
1728 Mr Hayden, Old Bailey trial concerning a silver spoon brought to him to pawn, pawnbroker (*OBP: t17280717-6*)
1734 Amos Hayton, Three Bowls, Hemings Row; Warning Notice delivered to him from Goldsmiths' Hall, pawnbroker (*Hart*)

Haydon (Broker)
148 WEATHERHEAD, P67
King Street by St Anns Church
1734 Joseph Hayton, King Street South, registered for Poor Rate (*WAC: MF32 A134*)

Haydon (Watchmaker)
99 HOLTOM, P45
near ye new Church, Strand
1729 Thomas Hayden, against the New Church in the Strand, advertised in *Fog's Weekly Journal* stating he had succeeded the Eminent Watchmaker, Mr George Etherington dec'd in his business, workman and finisher (*BLCol: Burney 331B, 05 Apr 1729*)
1731 Mr Tho Haydon, Dial over against the New Church, Strand, advertised in *The Daily Post* for the return of a lost watch by Etherington, watchmaker (*BL: Burney 286B, 15 Jun 1731*)
1733, 1734 and 1735 Mr Tho Haydon

listed in Clockmakers' Company South West Walk *(GLMS: 2715 vol 4)*

1736 Haydons in the Strand, Old Bailey trial concerning a stolen watch pawned with him, pawnbroker *(OBP: t17360908-10)*

Henry (Goldsmith)
142 WEATHERHEAD, P65
Coventry Street

1734 Peter Henry, Coventry Street, registered for Poor Rate *(GLMS: MF655 D39 item1, Gt Marlboro division)*

1745–51 possibly —Henry, Unicorn, Tothill Street, goldsmith *(Heal)*

1749 Peter Henry, King Street, parish of St Ann's, Westminster Pollbook, silversmith *(WPB)*

Hering (Broker)
89 BULSTRODE, P75
Well Street, Ratcliffe highway

1728 Jos Herring, Well Street West Side, Whitechapel, registered for Sewer Rate *(LMA: THCS 140)*

1734 possibly Missr Herring and Wm Clarke, Highway South or Frans Coxson Herrings, Highway South; Godfry Herrings' land, Upper division, St George-in-the-East, Middx, each registered for Land Tax *(GLMS: MF6016 vol 5)*

Herne (Broker)
85 BULSTRODE, P75
Starr Ally

1734 Wm Hern, Starr Alley, St Botolph-Without-Aldgate, East Smithfield, registered for Land Tax *(GLMS: MF6011 vol 4)*

Mrs Hewett (Broker)
99 BULSTRODE, P77
Ratcliffe highway
Not found

Hewett (Broker)
87 WEATHERHEAD, P59
Castle Street, Long Acre

1734 Richd Hewitt, Castle Street, St Giles and St George Bloomsbury, registered for Poor Rate *(CLS: UTAH MF99 item1)*

Heymore (Broker)
54 BULSTRODE, P72
Brick Lane

1734 Robt Highmore, possibly Sugar

Bakers Court, off Brick Lane, 2nd division, St Mary Whitechapel, registered for Land Tax *(GLMS: MF6015 vol 2)*

Hiccox (Watchmaker)
41 WEATHERHEAD, P55
Holborn

1650–1710 John Hiccock or Hickock *(Britten)*

1731 —Hiccox, Holborn, goldsmith *(Heal)*

1730 John Hiccox at the Dial & Crown against Hatton Garden, Holborn, smallworker *(Grimwade)*

1733–34 John Hickox listed in the Clockmakers' Company North Walk *(GLMS: 2715 vol 4)*

1733 Jno Hiccox, Bartlett's Buildings, Farringdon Without ward, registered for Land Tax *(GLMS: MF11316 vol 104)*

1743 Mr John Hiccox, Little Kirby Street, Hatton Garden, advertised in *The Daily Advertiser* for the return of several rings stolen from a shop in Hull *(BL: Burney 387B, 08 Nov 1743)*

Higerson (Broker)
37 WEATHERHEAD, P55
Saffron Hill

1733 John Higgenson, Saffron Hill, Liberty of Saffron Hill, registered for Poor Rate *(CLS: UTAH MF415 item4)*

1736 Joseph Higginson, witness in an Old Bailey trial concerning theft of silver spoons, silversmith *(OBP: t17360505-28)*

Mrs Higgs (Broker)
27 BULSTRODE, P71
Hogg Lane

1733 Martha Higs and John Bagnel, Hogg Lane, St Leonard's Shoreditch, registered for Poor Rate *(LMA: P91/LEN/1374)*

Highstreet (Broker)
197 HOLTOM, P51
Thieving Lane

1734 Andw Highstreet, Thieving Lane, registered for Poor Rate *(WAC: MF2364 E355)*

Hill (Broker)
29 BULSTRODE, P71
Hare Alley, holywell Lane, Shor

1729 John Hill, Hare Alley and John Hill, Holywell Lane, St Leonard's

Shoreditch, each registered for Poor Rate *(LMA: P91/LEN/47)*

1733 John Hill, Holywell Lane, St Leonard's Shoreditch *(LMA: P91/LEN/1374)*

1733 William Hill, Holywell Street, St Leonard Shoreditch, registered for Poor Rate on two properties *(LMA: P91/LEN/1374)*

Hill (Goldsmith)
115 BULSTRODE, P77
Wapping

1733 possibly Thomas Hill, Wapping Dock, St Dunstan Wapping, registered for Land Tax *(GLMS: MF6013 vol 4)*

1735 possibly Thomas Hill, Wapping Dock, Wapping; possibly Wm Hill, Queens Head Alley, Wapping Dock, each registered for Sewer Rate *(LMA: THCS 149)*

Hillot (Watchmaker)
163 WEATHERHEAD, P67
Newport Street

1733 Hilot, 1734 Hillot and 1735 Helet, listed in Clockmakers' Company New Walk *(GLMS: 2175, vol 4)*

1734 Willm Hallett, Newport Street, registered for Poor Rate *(WAC: MF32 A134)*

Hoare (Goldsmith/banker*)
68 HOLTOM, P43; FIG 30
Fleet Street

1725 Wm Hoar, Fleet Street, Tithe assessment *(GLMS: 3011)*

1728 Benjamin Hoare, the Golden Bottle, Fleet Street, advertised in *The Daily Courant* for the return of lost plate *(BL: Burney 637B, 03 Aug 1728)*

1729–46 Henry and Richard Hoare and Christopher Arnold, partners at the Golden Bottle, (later no37) Fleet Street, bankers *(Hilton-Price)*

1733 Benj Hoar Esq and partners, Fleet Street, St Dunstan-in-the-West precinct, Farringdon Without ward, registered for Land Tax *(GLMS: MF11316 vol 104)*

1733 Richard Hoar, Snow Hill, Holborn Cross precinct, Farringdon Without ward, registered for Land Tax *(GLMS: MF11316 vol 104)*

1734–54 died Sir Richard Hoare, Fleet Street; 1745–46 Lord Mayor, goldsmith *(Heal)*

1736 Mess Hoare and Comp, Fleet Street, advertised in *The Daily Post & General Advertiser* for the return of a lost banknote, bankers (*BL: Burney 320B, 30 Dec 1736*)

1738 Henry and Richard Hoare with Christopher Arnold, Messrs Hoare & Co, Fleet Street, Old Bailey trial concerning intent to cheat and defraud them of £75, in the Banking Business and keeping Cash, and also then keeping a public Shop (*OBP: t17380518-16*)

1742–43 Mess Hoare & Co, Fleet Street, advertised twice in *The Daily Advertiser* for the return of lost banknotes, bankers (*BL: Burney 381B, 10 Nov 1742, 387B, 18 Jul 1743*)

**Note:* Hoare's appear to have had their own system for distributing notices.

Whereas there was on the 22th of *November* 1692. a Note given by Mr. *Richard Hoar* Goldsmith, at the *Golden Bottle* in *Fleet-ſtreet*, or one of his Servants for him, for Payment of One hundred ſeventy five Pounds twelve Shillings and ſix Pence, to Mr. *Thomas Dring*, or Bearer, and the ſaid Note is at preſent miſlaid or loſt. This is to give Notice thereof, and to deſire all Perſons to whom the ſaid Note may happen to be brought, not to accept the ſame, but to ſtop it, and to give Notice thereof to the ſaid Mr. *Hoar*.

30

Hobkins (Goldsmith)
53 HOLTOM, P43
by Bride Lane

1724 John Hopkins, Rose & Crown, Brides Lane, largeworker (*Grimwade*)

1726 Mr Hopkins, Old Bailey trial stating he had stopped a stolen silver mug, goldsmith (*OBP: t17261012-34*)

1728 John Hopkins, Bride Lane, parish of St Bride's, insured his house for £300, goldsmith (*GLMS: 11936 vol28 [SI 46871]*)

1730 John Hopkins, Goldsmiths Arms & Ring, Bride Lane; 1732–36, cnr of Bride Lane, Fleet Street; 1736–63 Golden Cup & Cover, near Fleet Bridge, Fleet Street, goldsmith (*Heal*)

1731 John Hopkins, Bride Lane, listed as inhabitant of St Brides parish; served as Constable, silversmith (*GLMS: 6561*)

1733 John Hopkins, Fleet Street precinct, Ludgate Hill, Farringdon Without ward registered for Land Tax, also Fleet Street by Ditch Side (*GLMS: 11316 vol 104*)

1741–44 Mr Hopkins, cnr of Bride Lane, Fleet Street and at the Golden Cup,

Fleet Street, near Fleet Bridge, advertised five times in *The London Daily Post & General Advertiser* and *The Daily Advertiser* for the return of stolen items and a Silver Surtout to be sold cheap, goldsmith (*BL: Burney 355B, 26 Aug 1741: 379B, 16 Feb 1743, 24 Jun 1743; 381B, 05 Apr 1744; 397B, 03 Jul 1744*)

1744 John Hopkins, Fleet Street, near Fleet Bridge advertised his stock in detail in *The General Advertiser*, goldsmith (*BLCol: Burney 396B, 14 Jul 1744*)

1747 John Hopkins at the Golden Cup Fleet Street, near Fleet Bridge, his trade card stating he continues business for more than fifteen years past, goldsmith (*GLPrints&Maps*)

1755 Mr John Hopkins, Fleet Street advertised his retirement and disposal of his stock cheap in *The Public Advertiser* and gives 'his most humble and sincere thanks to the Nobility, Gentry & Others for all Favours', goldsmith (*BLCol: Burney 472B, 02 Jan 1755*)

Hodges (Broker/pawnbroker)
129 WEATHERHEAD, P65
St James's, Market Lane

1704 Mrs Hodges, Golden Ball, Charles Street, nr St James's Sq, pawnbroker (*Heal*)

1734 possibly Edward Hodges, Cannon Row, Westminster, registered for Poor Rate (*WAC: 2364 E355*)

1742–43 Mr Edward and Mrs Ann Hodges, Golden Ball, Charles Street, St James's, two advertisements in *The Daily Advertiser* concerning a creditors' meeting at their house (deceased), requesting those with demands on their Estates to notify the Administrator and asking customers to collect pawned items from Mrs Hodges (*BL: Burney 381B, 06 Dec 1742; BLCol: Burney 689B, 17 Feb 17453*)

Hodges (Goldsmith)
130 WEATHERHEAD, P65
St James's, Market Lane

1728 George Hodges, Charles Street, St James's, broker and largeworker (*Grimwade*)

1728 George Hodges, Charles Street, plateworker (*Heal*)

1735 George Hodges, Charles Street, St James's Square, Old Bailey trial

concerning two silver spoons Goods of Sovereign Lord the King, pawnbroker (*OBP: t17350116-25*)

Holland (Goldsmith*)
39 BULSTRODE, P71
Bishop Gate Street

1711–39 John Holland, Bishopsgate Street, plateworker (*Heal*)

1720 John Holland I, Bishopsgate; 1741 Goldsmiths' Company Court, largeworker (*Grimwade*)

1734 possibly Samuel Holland (three houses and stables in Catherine Wheel and George Yard); also Wm Holland (tenant), both of Bishopsgate Street, 3rd division, Bishopsgate Without ward, registered for Land Tax (*GLMS: MF11316 vol 105*)

1736 John Holland, Bishopsgate, advertised in *The Daily Post* he had stopt a brilliant ear-ring; 1741 Mr John Holland, without Bishopsgate, advertised in *The London Daily Post & General Advertiser* for the return of pair of Tops of Ear-Rings, goldsmith (*BLCol: Burney 90B, 09 Jan 1736, repeated 29 Jan 1736; 355B, 06 Apr 1741*)

1738–47 John Holland, Bishopsgate, three Old Bailey trials concerning items stolen or brought to his shop, goldsmith (*OBP: t17380222-24; t17390502-52; t17470116-7*)

1739 John Holland II, Bishopsgate; 1758 Goldsmiths' Company Livery, largeworker (*Grimwade*)

1751 Mr Holland, near Bishop-Gate, Old Bailey trial where a witness says he sent a notice to Goldsmiths' Hall and likewise advertised it, goldsmith (*OBP: t17510703-3*)

1765–79 John Holland, no5 Bishopsgate Without, jeweller, goldsmith and clockmaker (*Heal*)

Mrs Holmes (Broker/pawnbroker)
98 BULSTRODE, P77
Ratcliffe highway

1734 Thos Holmes, Highway South, Upper division, St George-in-the-East, Middx, registered for Land Tax (*GLMS: MF6016 vol5*)

1740 Thomas Holmes in Radcliffe Highway, Old Bailey trial concerning a stolen silver spoon pawned with him, pawnbroker (*OBP: t17400227-10*)

Mrs Horne (Broker)
104 BULSTRODE, P77
Ratcliffe highway
Not found

Horne (Goldsmith/banker)
166 HOLTOM, P47
at a Toyshop in the Strand
1716–28 possibly George Horne, Angel & Crown, opp New Exchange, goldsmith *(Heal)*
1734 John Horne, Strand South, registered for Poor Rate *(WAC: MF1577 F488 item3)*
1735 —Horne, opposite to the New Exchange, Crown Court, nr Durham Yard, Strand; 1736–38 Temple and Hawn, bankers *(Hilton-Price)*
1740 Horn(e) & Temple, Angel & Crown, nr Durham Yard, Strand, goldsmith *(Heal)*

Hoskins (Broker)
46 WEATHERHEAD, P55
Leather Lane
1732 possibly Mary Hoskins, Air Street, St Andrew Holborn, St George the Martyr, registered for Poor Rate *(CLS: UTAH MF29 item6)*
1732 possibly Job Hoskins, Little Gray's Inn Lane, St Andrew Holborn, St George the Martyr, registered for Poor Rate *(CLS: UTAH MF29 item6)*

Houstown (Goldsmith*)
70 HOLTOM, P43
Fleet St
1734 George Houston, Golden Cup, nr St Dunstan's Church, Fleet Street, insured his household goods, furniture, wrought and manufactured plate for £200, goldsmith *(GLMS: 11936 vol 41 [SI.64269])*
1737 George Houstown, Golden Cup, Fleet Street, smallworker *(Grimwade)*
1742–73 Golden Cup, cnr Mitre Tavern Passage, Fleet Street or nr St Dunstan's Church, Fleet Street, goldsmith *(Heal)*
1742 Mr Houstoun, next Door to Mitre Tavern, Fleet-Street, an advertisement in *The Daily Advertiser* concerning a lost 'white Spaniel Dog of the Setting Breed', goldsmith *(BL: Burney 381B, 03 Apr 1742)*
1743 Mr Houston, opp St Dunstan's Church, Fleet Street, advertised in *The*

Daily Advertiser for the return of a watch by Walter Partridge *(BL: Burney 387B, 30 Aug 1743)*
1744 Mr Howston, Old Bailey trial concerning silver spoons offered to him, 'a Silversmith in Fleet Street' *(OBP: t17440728-6)*
1744 Mr Howstown, Fleet Street, advertised in *The Daily Advertiser* for return of a pair of 'work'd Lappets and Cawl', goldsmith *(BL: Burney 397B, 03 Aug 1744)*

How (Goldsmith*)
120 BULSTRODE, P75
St Catherines
1733 possibly Samuel How, Old Bailey trial concerning silver buckles stolen from his shop *(OBP: t17330510-2)*
1734 possibly 'Goldsmith', St Katherine by the Tower, Tower division, registered for Land Tax *(GLMS: MF6010 vol 3)*
1753–63 possibly How & Masterman, no1 White Hart Court, Gracechurch Street, goldsmiths; 1765 How, Masterman & Archer, same address, goldsmiths *(Heal)*

How (Goldsmith)
121 BULSTRODE, P75
St Catherines
1734 possibly Wido How, Ollivers Court, St Katherine by the Tower, Tower division, registered for Land Tax *(GLMS: MF6010 vol 3)*

Mrs Howard (Broker/pawnbroker)
10 BULSTRODE, P69
Bridgewaters Gardens
1736 possibly Mrs Howard, Old Bailey trial concerning clothes brought to her for pawning, pawnbroker *(OBP: t17360610-3)*

Howard (Goldsmith)
165 WEATHERHEAD, P67
Newport Street
1733 —Howard, Great Newport Street, goldsmith *(Heal)*
1734 Gerrard and William Howard, Newport Street, each registered for Poor Rate *(WAC: MF32 A134)*

Howard (Broker)
51 BULSTRODE, P72
old George Street, Spittle Fields

1724 possibly Thomas Howard, Hamlett of Spitalfields, registered for Sewer Rate *(LMA: THCS 132)*

Howard (Broker)
144 BULSTRODE, P69
Turkshead Court
1733 Wm Howard, Golden Lane, Grub Street precinct, Cripplegate Without ward, registered for Land Tax *(GLMS: MF11316 vol 103)*

Hubbard (Watchmaker)
165 HOLTOM, P47
at a Toyshop in the Strand
1731 possibly Mr Hubert, against Durham Yard, Strand, advertised in *The Daily Post* for the return of a lost silver watch, watchmaker *(BL: Burney 286B, 06 Apr 1732)*
1733 David Hubart, 1734 David Hubert and 1735 Hubart, listed in Clockmakers' Company South West Walk; also 1733 Herbeart, 1734 Edward Herbert and 1735 Harbet & Hubard in New Walk *(GLMS: 2715 vol 4)*
1734 David Hubert, Strand, registered for Poor Rate *(WAC: MF1577 F488 item3)*
1740 David Hubert, portrait; 1747 father and son to collect in subscriptions for the formation of French Protestant Charity School *(nos 111, 112 Quiet Conquest)*
1743–44 Mr David Hubert, Dial and Sun, over-against Durham-Yard, Strand, advertised four times in *The Daily Advertiser* for the return of lost watches, the latter with 'hanger' and money stolen from a coach stopped by eight footpads, watchmaker *(BL: Burney 387B, 10 Aug 1743; 381B, 17 Mar 1744, 23 May 1744; 397B, 21 Jul 1744)*

Hudard (Broker/pawnbroker)
173 HOLTOM, P49
York Buildings
1749 Joseph Hudart, Strand, parish of St Martin-in-the-Fields, Westminster Pollbook, pawnbroker *(WAC: CDRom)*

Hull (Jeweller)
97 HOLTOM, P45
near ye new Church, Strand
1734 Jno Hull, Strand Side, registered for Poor Rate *(WAC: MF183 B38 item2)*

Humfries (Broker)
152 WEATHERHEAD, P67
litle Newport Street
1734 Edwd Humfries, Little Newport
Street, registered for Poor Rate (*WAC:
MF32 A134*)

Hurt (Toyman)
14 HOLTOM, P41
The Fish at St Paul's Chyard
1733 and 1735 Heny Hurt listed in
Clockmakers' Company South West
Walk (*GLMS: 2715 vol 4*)
1733 Henry Hurt registered for Land Tax
in West precinct, Castle Baynard ward
(*GLMS: MF11316 vol 103*)
1742–44 Mr Henry Hurt, Golden Salmon,
St Paul's Church Yard advertised
seven times in *The Daily Advertiser* for
the return of lost items (*BL: Burney
381B, 06 Nov 1742; 11 Nov 1742; 379B,
08 Mar 1743; 28 Sept 1743; 29 Oct 1743;
04 Apr 1744; 30 May 1744*)
1745–55 Henry Hurt moved to Golden
Salmon (no32) north side of Ludgate
Hill from St Paul's Churchyard, goldsmith and toyman (*Heal*)

Husnel (Jeweller)
158 HOLTOM, P47
Fountain Court, Strand
1731 Mr Hoosnell, Fountain Court, registered for Poor Rate (*WAC: MF183 B38
item2*)
1731 Gertrude Hoosnell, ffountains
Court, registered for Poor Rate (*WAC:
MF183 B38 item2*)

Hutton (Goldsmith)
1 WEATHERHEAD, P53
Goswell Street
1733 possibly Francis Hutton, 1st
precinct, Aldersgate Without ward,
registered for Land Tax (*GLMS:
MF11316 vol102*)
1734 Samuel Hutton, at the Hat &
Feather, Goswell Street; 1740 Goswell
Street, plateworker (*Grimwade*)
1734–40 Samuel Hutton, Hat & Feather,
Goswell Street, plateworker (*Heal*)
1740 Sarah Hutton, Hat & Feather,
Goswell Street, plateworker (*Heal*)
1740 Sarah Hutton, spouse of Samuel
died 1740?, Hat & Feather, Goswell
Street, largeworker (*Grimwade*)

I

Imacer (Jeweller)
139 HOLTOM, P47
Bow St
1734 John Eyemaker, Wards Alley, Bow
Street East, registered for Poor Rate
(*WAC: MF1959 H43 item14*)

J

Jackson (Watchmaker)
110 BULSTRODE, P79
Wapping
1715 possibly Mathew Jackson, free of
the Clockmakers' Company; 1723–36,
possibly Matthew Jackson, clockmaker
(*Britten*)
1733 Mattw Jackson, 1734 Matt Jackson
and 1735 Matthew Jackson, listed in
Clockmakers' Company New Walk
(*GLMS: 2715 vol 4*)
1734 possibly Thos Jackson, Trinity Yard,
Broad Street, St Dunstan Stepney,
registered for Land Tax (*GLMS:
MF6014 vol 4*)

Jacobsen (Broker/pawnbroker)
80 BULSTRODE, P75
King Street
1734 Jno Jacobson, King Street, St
Botolph-Without-Aldgate, registered
for Land Tax on two houses (*GLMS:
MF6011 vol 4*)
1744 Mr Jacobsen, Blue Ball, King Street,
Tower-Hill, advertisement in *The Daily
Advertiser* for customers to redeem
their pledged items he leaving off
Trade (*BL: 397B, 20 Dec 1744*)

Jarvis (Broker/pawnbroker)
35 HOLTOM, P43
New Street
1728 John Jarvis, Robinwoods Court registered for Poor Rate (*GLMS: 9975, vol 1*)
1733 Abel Jarvis, New Street, New Street
precinct, Farringdon Without ward
registered for Land Tax (*GLMS:
MF11316 vol 104*)
1733 Henry Jarvis, Gun Powder Alley,
New Street precinct, Farringdon
Without ward registered with another
Jarvis for Land Tax (*GLMS: MF11316
vol 104*)

1733 Jono Jarvis, Spectacle Alley,
Farringdon Without ward registered
for Land Tax (*GLMS: MF 11316 vol 104*)
1733 Thomas Jarvis, Box Wood Court,
New Street precinct, Farringdon
Without ward registered for Land Tax
(*GLMS: MF11316 vol 104*)
1734 Abel and Henry Jarvis, New Street,
each listed as inhabitant of St Bride's
parish, pawnbrokers (*GLMS: 6561*)
1744 Thomas Jarvis, New Street, Fetter
Lane advertised in *The Daily Advertiser*
seeking the whereabouts of his
absconded apprentice, chaser (*BL:
Burney 397B, 27 Sept 1744*)

Jarvis (Broker)
65 HOLTOM, P43
Water Lane
Not found – see above

Jeffries (Watchmaker)
61 WEATHERHEAD, P57
near Turn Stile Lane
1717–35 John and Joseph Jeffreys,
Holborn (*Britten*)
1733 —Jefferys and 1735 Jno Jeffreys,
listed in Clockmakers' Company
North Walk (*GLMS: 2715 vol 4*)
1743 John Jefferies, the Dial and Golden
Key, near Warwick-Court, Holborn,
advertised twice in *The Daily Advertiser*
for the return of a gold watch No 128
by John Jefferies (Jefferys) (*BL: Burney
379B, 09 Feb 1743: BLCol: 19 Feb 1743*)

Jennings (Goldsmith)
69 WEATHERHEAD, P57
King Street, Bloomsbury
1720 possibly Edward Jennings, Tower
Street, Seven Dials; 1727 Little Britain,
plateworker (*Heal*)
1720 possibly Edward Jennings, Little
Britain; 1725 Goldsmiths' Company
Livery, largeworker (*Grimwade*)

Jennings (Broker)
52 BULSTRODE, P72
Thorle [Thrale] Street Spittle Fields
1724 possibly Jona, Jos and Robert Jenings,
Hamlett of Spittlefields, each registered for Sewer Rate (*LMA: THCS 132*)

Jernegan (Goldsmith/banker)
120 HOLTOM, P47
Russell Street

1734 Henry Journingham, Russell Street South, registered for Poor Rate *(WAC: MF1959 H43 item14)*

1736 Henry Jernegan, Gt Russell Street, Covent Garden, goldsmith *(Heal)*

1737 Mr Jernegan, advertised in *The Daily Post* his Bridge Lottery linked to the same Number of Receipts in his Sale of Plate, banker *(BL: Burney 325B (reel 1), 31 Aug 1737)*

1737–38 Mr Jernegan at his house in Jermyn Street, advertised in *The London Daily Post & General Advertiser* stating he was obliged to defer the Delivery [of Medals] for want of an immediate Supply from the Tower … the Public is desired to have Patience *(BL: Burney 332B, 22 Feb 1737-8)*

1738 Old Bailey trial concerning 12 Silver Medals referred to as 'Jernegans' *(OBP: t17381206-41)*

1746 'On Saturday last died of the Gout in his stomach, Mr Henry Jernegan, a noted Banker in Russell Street, Covent Garden', *The London Evening Post (BLCol: Burney 418B, 15 Feb 1746)*

Jeroet [Gerrard] (Watchmaker)
143 WEATHERHEAD, P65
Coventry Street

1714–35 circa, John Gerrard, London *(Baillie)*

1725-40 circa, John Gerrard, London; circa 1725 bracket clock; 1740 verge watch *(Britten)*

1734 possible John Guiraud, Litchfield Street, registered for Poor Rate *(WAC: MF32 A134)*

1735 —Jarrat, listed in Clockmakers' Company New Walk *(GLMS: 2715 vol 4)*

1743 Mr John Gerrard, Litchfield-Street, near Newport-Market, advertised in *The Daily Advertiser* for the return of two lost seals, watchmaker *(BL: Burney 379B, 13 Apr 1743)*

1749 John Garrard, Litchfield Street, parish of St Anne, Soho, Westminster Pollbook, watchmaker *(WAC: CDRom)*

Johnson (Broker/pawnbroker)
102 HOLTOM, P45
Drury Lane

1734 possibly Matthew Johnson, Dutchy Liberty Strand, registered for Poor Rate *(WAC: MF1901 G14 item12)*

1737 Joseph Johnson, Wych Street, Old

Bailey trial concerning various items of clothing pawned with him, pawn-broker *(OBP: t17371207-4)*

1742 Joseph Johnson, his late Dwelling House, Three Bowls, cnr of Maypole-Alley, Wych-Street, advertised in *The Daily Advertiser* for customers to redeem their pledged items his Widow not following Business *(BL: Burney 381B, 06 Nov 1742)*

Johnson (Broker/pawnbroker)
139 BULSTRODE, P69
Grub Street

1733 Nicholas Johnson in street between Hannover Court and Butlers Alley or Henry Johnson, Butlers Alley, Cripplegate Without ward, each registered for Land Tax *(GLMS: MF11316 vol 103)*

1736 Mr Johnson, The Golden Ball, Grub-Street, advertised in *The Daily Post* for customers to redeem their pledged items 'He is leaving off that Business' *(BL: Burney 320B, 26 Oct 1736)*

Jones (Jeweller)
164 WEATHERHEAD, P67
Newport Street

1734 Phil Jones, Newport Street, regis-tered for Poor Rate *(WAC: MF32 A134)*

Jones (Jeweller)
164 HOLTOM, P47
at a Toyshop in the Strand

1734 possibly Thomas Jones, Salisbury Street, registered for Poor Rate *(WAC: MF1577 F488 item3)*

Joslin (Jeweller)
189 WEATHERHEAD, P67
Orange Street

1734 possibly Mary Jewslin, Orange Street South, registered for Poor Rate *(WAC: MF1577 F488 item3)*

1772 William Jousselin, of London, insured house (not his dwelling house), south side of Orange Street for £450, jeweller *(GLMS: Hand-in-Fire & Life Assurance Co, 8674 vol 28)*

Jourdaine (Watchmaker)
55 BULSTRODE, P72
Pater Noster Rowe
Not found

Jourdaine (Goldsmith)
47 BULSTRODE, P71
Corbitts Court, Spittle Fields

1724 possibly Wm Jourdain, Hamlett of Spitalfields, registered for Sewer Rate *(LMA: THCS 132)*

Jovett (Goldsmith)
82 BULSTRODE, P75
East Smithfield

1725 possibly Simon Jouet, over against ye Victualling Office Little Tower Hill; 1748 Aldersgate, largeworker *(Grimwade)*

1734 Henry Jowitt and Peter Jovitt, East Smithfield, St Botolph-Without-Aldgate, each registered for Land Tax *(GLMS: MF6011 vol 4)*

K

Keddin (Watchmaker)
17 HOLTOM, P41
in Bell Savage Yard

1714–40 —Kedden or Keddon, Little Britain *(Britten)*

1727 Daniel Keddon, Fitches Court, Noble Street, parish of St Olave's, insured his goods and stock in trade in house for £500, watchmaker *(GLMS: 11936 vol 24, [SI.41708])*

1734 Daniel Keddin and 1735 Dan: Keddin listed in Clockmakers' Company South West Walk *(GLMS: 2715 vol 4)*

1734 Daniel Kedden, Bell Savage Yard, Fleet Street precinct, Ludgate Hill, Farringdon Without ward, registered for Land Tax *(GLMS: MF11316 vol 107)*

1737 Daniel Keddin of Wey (Ivy) Lane, parish of St Faiths under St Pauls insured his household goods in dwelling house, etc for £300; 1748, at the Dial in Little Britain, he insured his household goods and manufactured plate £100, etc for £300, watchmaker *(GLMS: 11936 vol 49 [SI 76074]; vol 83 [SI 112678])*

King (Watchmaker)
80 HOLTOM, P45
Lincolns Inn Gateway

1733 Heny King and 1734 Henry King listed in Clockmakers' Company South West Walk *(GLMS: 2715 vol 4)*

1734 possibly Henry King, Feathers Court, registered for Poor Rate *(WAC:*

MF1901 G14 item12)

1743 Henry King, Serles Gateway (Passage), Lincolns Inn, advertised three times in *The Daily Advertiser* for the return of lost items, watchmaker *(BL: Burney 379B, 16 May 1743; 01 Jun 1743; 387B, 06 Oct 1743)*

King (Watchmaker)
92 WEATHERHEAD, P59
St Andrews Street, 7 Dials
1704 possibly William King, apprenticed *(Baillie)*
1713 possibly William King, apprenticed *(Baillie)*
1721 possibly William King, apprenticed *(Baillie)*
1733 and 1735 possibly William King, listed in Clockmakers' Company North Walk *(GLMS: 2715 vol 4)*
1733 possibly Wm King, 3rd division, Bishopsgate Without ward, registered for Land Tax *(GLMS: MF11316 vol 102)*

Mrs King (Broker)
42 BULSTRODE, P71
Bishop Gate Street
1744 possibly John King, a shop in Bishopsgate and 1749 Mr King [his wife stopped a stolen silver spoon] in Bishopsgate Street, two Old Bailey trials concerning stolen items, pawnbroker *(OBP: t17440510-34; t17490411-3)*
1757 possibly John King with Gilbert Lloyd, Bishopsgate Street without, insured household goods, stock of linen and muslin, etc in late dwelling house of John Christian van Reinhardt, Aylaffe St, Goodmansfields for £600, goldsmith *(GLMS: 11936 vol 121 [Sl.160154])*

Kipling (Watchmaker)
108 BULSTRODE, P79
Ratcliffe highway
1705–50 William Kipling, Ratcliffe Cross, watchmaker *(Britten)*
1734 Wm Kipling, Broad Street, St Dunstan Stepney, registered for Land Tax *(GLMS: MF6014, vol 4)*

Kirby (Broker)
177 HOLTOM, P49
Hartshorne Lane in the Strand
1734 John Kirby, Hartshorn Lane, regis-

tered for Poor Rate *(WAC: MF1577 F488 item3)*

Kitchin (Broker / pawnbroker)
106 HOLTOM, P45
Stanhope St
1734 Henry Kitchen, Stanhope Street and possibly Jno Kitchen, Surrey Street, registered for Poor Rate *(WAC: MF183 B38 item2)*
1736 possibly Mr Kitchin, Old Bailey trial concerning red damask clothes pawned with him, pawnbroker *(OBP: t17361013-2)*
1743 Henry Kitchin, Three Bowls, Stanhope Street, nr Clare Market, announced in *The Daily Advertiser* his cessation of business, pawnbroker *(BL: Burney 387B, 29 Sept 1743)*

L

Ladvocat (Jeweller)
155 WEATHERHEAD, P67
Grafton Street
1733–44 Isaac Ladvocat, Two Blue Posts, Grafton Street, Soho, jeweller *(Heal)*
1734 possibly Peter L'Advocat, Grafton Street, registered for Poor Rate *(WAC: MF32 A134)*
1744 Mr Isaac Ladvocat, Two Blue Posts, Grafton Street, Soho, advertised in *The Daily Advertiser* for the return of a lost seal, jeweller *(BL: Burney 381B, 24 Apr 1744)*

Lane (Broker)
101 BULSTRODE, P77
Ratcliffe highway
1734 Saml Lane, Highway North, Upper division, St George-in-the-East, Middx, registered for Land Tax *(GLMS: MF6016, vol 5)*

Laroch (Goldsmith)
99 WEATHERHEAD, P59
Lombard Street [Court], 7 Dials
1725–39 Louis Laroch, Lumber Court, the Corner of Seven Dials, near Porter Street, largeworker *(Grimwade)*
1725–39 Louis Laroche, Lumber Court, the Corner of Seven Dials, plateworker *(Heal)*
1735 Lewis Laroch, witness in Old Bailey trial concerning James Barthelemi's receipt of a stolen silver tankard, silversmith *(OBP: t17350911-14)*

Lefavor (Broker)
173 WEATHERHEAD, P67
St Martins Lane
1734 possibly Joseph Lefevre, Newport Street South, registered for Poor Rate *(WAC: MF1577 F488 item3)*

Lefavor (Jeweller)
51 HOLTOM, P43
Racket Court
1733 Nicholas Leafuber, Racquet Court, Fleet Street precinct, Ludgate Hill, Farringdon Without ward registered for Land Tax *(GLMS: MF11316 vol 104)*
1735 Nicholas Lefeverie, Racquett Court, listed as inhabitant of St Bride's parish; served as Constable, jeweller *(GLMS: 6561)*
1749 possibly Lefeavor appeared in an Old Bailey trial concerning a lost banknote payable to him *(OBP: t17490113-2)*

Lefong (Jeweller)
158 WEATHERHEAD, P67
Litchfield Street
Not found

Leopard (Goldsmith)
65 BULSTRODE, P72
Red Lyon Street
1725 possibly John Leaper, Old Bailey trial concerning a stolen silver tankard *(OBP: t17250407-34)*
1734 possibly Jos Leopard, 6th division, St Mary Whitechapel, registered for Land Tax *(GLMS: MF6015 vol 2)*
1736 John Lepar, without Aldgate, Old Bailey trial where a witness stated Lepar had died, silversmith *(OBP: t17361208-4)*
1737–38 Mr Lepper, Whitechapel, announcement in *The London Daily Post & General Advertiser* of auction of part of his stock in trade, goldsmith deceased *(BL: Burney 332B, 03 Mar 1737–8)*

Lesage (Goldsmith)
199 WEATHERHEAD, P67
Suffolk Street
1718 John Hugh Lesage, Golden Cup, St Martin's Lane, St Martin-in-the-Fields, insured goods and merchandise in his apartment and mews; moved to Golden Cup, corner of Gt Suffolk

Street, goldsmith (GLMS: 11936 vol 8 [SI.12065])

1718 John Hugh Lesage, Little St Martin's Lane, near Long Acre, largeworker; 1722 corner of Great Suffolk Street, free goldsmith; 1739, Great Suffolk Street, near Haymarket; 1740 Goldsmiths' Company Livery (Grimwade)

1718 John Hugh Lesage, St Martin's Lane, Long Acre; 1722 Old Street; 1739–43 St James's, Haymarket, plateworker (Heal)

1734 John Lesage, Suffolk Street, registered for Poor Rate (WAC: MF1577 F488 item3)

1743 Mr Lesage, Corner of Great Suffolk Street, near the Hay-Market, advertised in The Daily Advertiser for the return of a seal, goldsmith (BLCol: Burney 689B, 21 Jan 1743)

1739–61 possibly Simon Lesage, Golden Cup, Corner of Great Suffolk Street, near the Haymarket, plateworker (Heal)

Lieger (Goldsmith*)
185 WEATHERHEAD, P67
Orange Street

1730 John Liger at ye sign of ye Pearl in Hemmings Row, St Martin's Lane, largeworker (Grimwade)

1730–32 John Liger, Pearl, Hemming's Row (St Martin's Lane), plateworker, (Heal)

1731 John Liger, Sign of the Pearl, Hemmings-Row, St Martins Lane, advertised in The Daily Post stating he had found a silver Scrole [plate], goldsmith (BL: Burney 286B, 20 Feb 1731)

1734 John Liger, Old Bailey trial concerning silver buckles stolen from a shew-glass in his shop (OBP: t17341204-7)

1734 John Liger, Castle Street West, registered for Poor Rate (WAC: MF1577 F488 item3)

Lilley (Goldsmith)
10 WEATHERHEAD, P53
Duck Lane

1733 Job Lilley, Barts the Less precinct, Farringdon Without ward, registered for Land Tax (GLMS: MF11316 vol 104)

1737 Job Lilley, Hand & Spur, Duck Lane, parish of St Bartholomew the Less, insured his household goods and

working tools for £300, goldsmith (GLMS: 11936 vol 48 [SI 75325])

1743–44 Mr Job Lilley, Smithfield-Bars, advertised twice in The Daily Advertiser for the return of items stolen by an absconded apprentice and stating he had stopt a large spoon with Crest almost erased, goldsmith (BL: Burney 379B, 14 Mar 1743; 387B, 07 Jan 1744)

1743–55 Job Lilley, St John Street, near Smithfield Bars, goldsmith (Heal)

1744 Job Lilley, St John's Street, Middlesex, advertised in The Daily Advertiser seeking, with Giles Southam (p123) and others, the Creditors of the goldsmith, Joseph Pargiter, goldsmith (BL: Burney, 397B, 20 Nov 1744)

Lipscom (Watchmaker)
16 WEATHERHEAD, P53
Smithfield

1733 Benj Lipscom, Crown Court and Lyiscombe, Whitehorse Alley, Smithfield precinct, Farringdon Without ward, both registered for Land Tax on two houses (GLMS: MF11316 vol 104)

1744 Mr Edmund Lipscomb, the Dial, Corner of Ram Inn, West Smithfield, advertised in The Daily Advertiser for the return of two lost watches by Wichcut and Anthony Marsh (BL: Burney 381B, 15 May 1744)

1757 Lipscom, The Dial, corner of The Ram Inn, West Smithfield, insured his household goods, stock and plate for £200, watchmaker (GLMS: 11936 vol 118 [SI.157441])

1760 circa, Benjamin Lipscombe, London (Britten)

Lockan (Jeweller)
156 HOLTOM, P47
corner Fountain Court, Strand

1734 John Lacam, cnr of Fountain Court, registered for Poor Rate (WAC: MF183 B38 item2)

1743 John Lacam, Ring & Crown, cnr of Fountain Court, parish of St Clement Dane, insured his household goods, etc for £300, jeweller, diamond cutter and goldsmith (GLMS: 11936 vol 67 [SI 96018])

1743–44 Mr John Lacam, Ring and Pearl or Ring and Crown, cnr of Fountain Court, Strand, advertised four times in

The Daily Advertiser for the return of lost items, jeweller (BL: Burney 379B, 14 Mar 1743, 11 Apr 1743; 381B, 21 Feb 1744, 13 Mar 1744)

Lockrum (Jeweller)
169 HOLTOM, P49
York Buildings
Not found

Loddington (Watchmaker)
152 HOLTOM, P47
Tavistock St

1719–34 Isaac Loddington (and his wife Ann), Dial, Tavistock Street, Covent Garden; he took two women apprentices, one his wife (Britten)

1733 and 1735 Isaac Lodington, listed in Clockmakers' Company South West Walk (GLMS: 2715 vol 4)

1734 Isaac Loddington, Tavistock Street North, registered for Poor Rate (WAC: MF1959 H43 item14)

Long (Watchmaker)
57 WEATHERHEAD, P57
Bedford Row

1690–1725 possibly John Long (Britten)

1732 John Long, Bedford Street, St Andrew Holborn, St George the Martyr, registered for Poor Rate (CLS: UTAH MF29 item6)

Longland (Broker)
118 HOLTOM, P47
Exeter St

1734 Sarah Longland, Exeter Street, registered for Poor Rate (WAC: MF1959 H43 item14)

Loyd (Watchmaker)
15 WEATHERHEAD, P53
Smithfield

1713–30 James Lloyd, Sheep Pens, Smithfield (Britten)

1733 Thomas Lloyd, Crown Court, Smithfield precinct, Farringdon Without ward, registered for Land Tax (GLMS: MF11316 vol 104)

1734 Jams Loyd, listed in the Clockmakers' Company North Walk (GLMS: 2715 vol 4)

1744 possibly Mr William Lloyd, Red Lyon Square, near St Sepulchre's Church, advertised in The Daily Advertiser seeking his absconded

apprentice, watchmaker (BL: Burney
381B, 30 Mar 1744)

1747 possibly William Lloyd of
Smithfield, appeared in an Old Bailey
trial stating he had stopped stolen
plate which had been advertised (OBP:
t17470116-15)

Loyd & Clark (Goldsmith and
toyman)
96 HOLTOM, P45
corner of Arundel St

1734 Richd Loyd & Partner, Strand Side,
registered for Poor Rate (WAC: MF183
B38 item2)

1750 circa, Thomas Clark, Golden Head,
near Arundel Street, jeweller and
toyman (Heal)

Loyd (Jeweller)
95 HOLTOM, P45
Arundel Street End
Not found

Ludlow (Goldsmith)
102 BULSTRODE, P77
Ratcliffe highway

1713 possibly John Ludlow at the sign of
the Spread Eagle without Aldgate,
goldsmith; 1720 John Ludlow, Ball
Alley, Lombard Street, Free
Imbroiderer and largeworker
(Grimwade)

1713 possibly John Ludlow, without
Aldgate; 1720 John Ludlow, Ball Alley
Lombard Street, goldsmith (Heal)

1734 John Ludlow, Upper Shadwell
North side, St Paul Shadwell, registered
for Land Tax (GLMS: MG6009, vol 3)

Luff (Goldsmith)
37 HOLTOM, P43
New St

1724 John Luff, Gunpowder Alley, New
Street, Shoe Lane; 1739 Pemberton
Street; 1750 to Mrs Bushnell's, New
Street, smallworker (Grimwade)

1733 —Luff, Three Legg'd Alley, New
Street precinct, Farringdon Without
ward registered for Land Tax (GLMS:
MF11316 vol 104)

1738 John Luffe, Three Legg'd Alley,
listed as inhabitant of St Bride's parish;
served as Constable, silversmith
(GLMS: 6561)

1743 Mr John Luff, nr Gough Square,

Fleet Street advertised twice in The
Daily Advertiser for a lost piece of steel
chain, seals, and pint mug, goldsmith
(BL: Burney 379B, 17 Mar 1743: 25 Aug
1743)

1743 John Luff, Fleet Street: ex Pemberton
Street, Gough Square, plateworker (Heal)

Lukin (Goldsmith)
167 HOLTOM, P47; FIG 41
at a Toyshop in the Strand

1712–34 William Lukin, Blackamoors
Head, cnr of York Buildings, Strand;
1749 bankrupt, silversmith (Heal)

1715 William Lukin at the Golden Cup in
the Strand, parish of St Mary le Savoy,
insured goods and merchandise £–;
1721, moved to Buckingham Street,
Strand, goldsmith (GLMS: 11936 vol 5
[SI 6371])

1718 William Lukin with Samuel Gray,
near Savoy Gate, Strand insured his
brewhouse nr 3 Cranes, Thames Street
£–, goldsmith (GLMS: 11936 vol 9
[SI.13200])

1734 William Luking, Strand South,
registered for Poor Rate (WAC: MF1577
F488 item3)

M

M**** (Jeweller)
151 HOLTOM, P47
Tavistock St

1722–45 possibly Andrew Mayastre,
Mayafree or Mayoffe, Golden Head,
Tavistock Street, jeweller (Heal)

1734 possibly Andrew Mayofara,
Tavistock Street North, registered for
Poor Rate (WAC: MF1959 H43 item14)

Makeland (Goldsmith*)
198 WEATHERHEAD, P67
Suffolk Street

1728 James Maitland, at the Grasshopper
the Corner of Suffolk Street, largeworker (Grimwade)

1728–30 James Maitland, at the
Grasshopper corner of Suffolk Street,
silversmith (Heal)

1734 James Maitland, Suffolk Street,
registered for Poor Rate (WAC: MF1577
F488 item3)

1734 James Martland, Old Bailey trial
concerning a silver mug stolen from
his shop (OBP: t17340424-9)

Makin (Broker)
2 WEATHERHEAD, P53
Goswell Street
Not found

Manners (Goldsmith and jeweller)
176 HOLTOM, P49
in the Strand

1726 James Manners, Great St Andrews
Street, nr Seven Dials; 1734, at ye Rose
in the Strand, with James, junior; 1745
moved to Villar's Street, York
Buildings (Grimwade)

1733 James Manners, Old Bailey trial
concerning four gold necklaces stolen
from his shew-glass (OBP: t17330912-25)

1734 James Manners, Strand, registered
twice for Poor Rate (WAC: MF1577
F488 item3)

1734–39 James Manners, Strand, silversmith; 1745 James Manners, possible
son, Villiers Street, Strand, plateworker
(Heal)

1738 and 1742 James Manners, Old
Bailey trials concerning unwrought
silver and items stolen from him; he
went to Goldsmiths' Hall to advertise
the theft, goldsmith (OBP: t17380906-6,
t17420115-11)

Manning (Goldsmith)
42 WEATHERHEAD, P55
Holborn

1728 Thos Manning, Dean Street, registered for Poor Rate (GLMS: 9755 vol 1)

1738 Thomas Manning, goldsmith in
Holborn; Goldsmiths' Company
Livery 1740 (Grimwade)

1744 Mr Thomas Manning, Crown,
Holborn, near Fetter Lane, advertised
in The Daily Advertiser for the return of
two lost diamond hair clasps and rings
(BL: Burney 397B, 29 Nov 1744)

1771 died, —Manning, Dean Street,
Fetter Lane, goldsmith and jeweller
(Heal)

Mannus (Broker)
72 WEATHERHEAD, P59
Phonex Street, Bloomsbury

1734 Samll Manus, Phoenix Street, St
Giles and St George Bloomsbury, registered for Poor Rate (CLS: UTAH MF99
item1)

Mrs Mappson (Broker)
46 BULSTRODE, P71
Grey Eagle Street, Spittle Fields
1724 possibly Jos Mappes, Hamlett of
Spittlefields, registered for Sewer Rate
(*LMA: THCS 132*)

Mrs Marcum (Toyman*)
72 HOLTOM, P43
Fleet St
1727 Geo Markham, Toy Shop under St
Dunstan's Church, Tithe assessment
(*GLMS: 3011*)
1728 Mr Markham's Toy-shop, Seven
Stars adjoining St Dunstan's Church,
Fleet Street, news-sheet description of
theft (*GLPrints&Maps: C42.03*)
(See note 64 p27)
1731 Anne Markham, Old Bailey trial re
items belonging to George Markham
stolen from a Shew-Glass at the Shop
window (*OBP: t17311208-2*)
1732 Mrs Markham, Toyshop under St
Dunstan's Church, advertised in *The
Daily Post* for the return of a lost seal
(*BL: Burney 805B, 15 Feb 1732*)
1733 Anne Markham, Shop under the
Church, St Dunstan-in-the-West
precinct, Farringdon Without ward,
registered for Land Tax (*GLMS:
MF11316 vol 104*)
1738 and 1743 Anne Markham widow,
two Old Bailey trials concerning items
stolen with a crooked wire from a
shew-glass in her shop, including
seven gold rings, one the thieves gave
to Bridewell's gaol-keeper, the others
they sold to him (*OBP: t17380113-38,
t17430629-50*)
1744 Mrs Marcum, Seven Stars, Fleet
Street, advertised in *The Daily
Advertiser* for the return of a lost lady's
watch (*BL: Burney 381B, 14 Apr 1744*)

Marlow (Goldsmith)
67 BULSTRODE, P72
Aldgate
1718–34 (died), Jeremiah Marlow junior,
Blackmores Head, within Aldgate;
1724, London; 1728 Abchurch Lane,
Lombard Street (*Heal*)
1733 Jere Marlow, 1st precinct, Aldgate
ward, registered for Land Tax (*GLMS:
MF11316 vol 102*)
1734 Jeremiah Marlowe, Blackmores
Head, within Aldgate, advertised in

The Daily Journal for the return of a
watch by David Lestourgeon, goldsmith (*BL: Burney 304B, 13 Jul 1734*)
1744 Mr Marlow, within Aldgate, advertised in *The Daily Advertiser* for the
return of a watch by Moore of Ispwich,
goldsmith (*BL: Burney 381B, 19 Mar 1744*)

Marquar (Jeweller)
9 WEATHERHEAD, P53
Duck Lane
Not found

Martin (Goldsmith)
55 HOLTOM, P43
Fleet St
1729–40 Charles Martin, London, plateworker (*Heal*)
1730 Charles Martin, Rose and Crown,
Brids [*sic*] Lane, Fleet Street; 1741 with
wife, Sarah, who held a power of
attorney for him; died 1744 (*Grimwade*)
1731 Charles Martin, Fleet Street, listed
as inhabitant of St Bride's parish,
silversmith (*GLMS: 6561*)
1733 Charles Martin, Ditch Side and at
Greens Rents, Fleet Street precinct,
Ludgate Hill, Farringdon Without
ward, registered for Land Tax (*GLMS:
MF11316 vol 104*)

Martin (Broker)
61 BULSTRODE, P72
White Chaple
1728 possibly Mr Martin, having seen an
advertisement, and 1743 Richard
Martin, two Old Bailey trials concerning plate and a ring pawned with him
(*OBP: t17281204-33; t17430114-26*)

Martin (Watchmaker)
58 WEATHERHEAD, P57
Featherstones Buildings
1732 Richard Martin, Featherston
Buildings & Fords Court, St Andrew
Holborn, St George the Martyr, regis-
tered for Poor Rate (*CLS: UTAH MF29
item6*)
1733–34 Richd Martin, listed in
Clockmakers' Company North Walk
(*GLMS: 2715 vol 4*)
1743 Mr Martin, Featherstone-Buildings,
Holborn, advertised in *The Daily
Advertiser* for the return of a lost sword
to Mr Hill at Mr Martin's, watchmaker
(*BL: Burney 379B, 28 Apr 1743*)

Martin (Watchmaker)
50 HOLTOM, P43
Fleet St
1733 Thos Martin, Fleet Street, Fleet
Street precinct, Ludgate Hill,
Farringdon Without ward registered
for Land Tax (*GLMS: MF11316 vol 104*)
1733 and 1734 Thos Martin and 1735
Thos Marton, in Clockmakers'
Company South West Walk (*GLMS:
2715 vol 4*)

Martineau (Watchmaker)
188 WEATHERHEAD, P67; FIG 60
Orange Street
1734 Martin, 1735 Martinue,
Clockmakers' Company New Walk
(*GLMS: 2715 vol 4*)
1737 Mr Martineau senior, Orange Street,
near Leicester-fields, advertised in *The
Daily Post* for the return of a watch by
Gudin à Paris (*BL: Burney 325 (reel 1),
27 Jun 1737*)
1744–94 Joseph Martineau, Orange Street
and St Martin's; 1750–70 Leicester
Fields (*Britten*)
1755 possibly Martineau, Porters Street,
near Newport Market, jeweller (*Heal*)
1777 possibly Martineau, tenant of Alice
Penny, widow, Red Lion Street,
Clerkenwell, insured his property for
£200, watchmaker (*GLMS: 11936 vol
259 [SI.387213]*)
1786 Joseph Martineau, St Martin's
Court, St Martin's Lane, insured
household goods, etc. for £600, watchmaker (*GLMS: 11936 vol 336
[SI.516790]*)

Massy (Watchmaker)
190 WEATHERHEAD, P67; FIG 58
Cranbourn Alley
1689–1725 Jacob Massy; 1715 free of the
Clockmakers' Company (*Britten*)
1715 Jacob Massy, free of the
Clockmakers' Company; watch move-
ment (*no358 Quiet Conquest*)
1733 and 1735 —Massey; 1734 Jacob
Massey, listed in Clockmakers'
Company New Walk (*GLMS: 2715 vol 4*)
1734 Jacob Massey, Cranbourne Street,
registered for Poor Rate (*WAC: MF32,
A134*)

Note: Fig **[58]** *is for Henry Massy*

Megault (Jeweller)
159 WEATHERHEAD, P67
Porter Street by Newport Market
1721 —Megault, Castle Street, Leicester
   Fields, jeweller *(Heal)*
1734 Oliver Megault, Porter Street East,
   registered for Poor Rate *(WAC: MF32
   A134)*
1743 Mr Oliver Megault, parish of St
   Ann, Westminster, advertisement in
   The Daily Advertiser seeking the whereabouts of his effects and calling a
   creditors' meeting, jeweller deceased
   (BL: Burney 387B, 17 Sep 1743)

Megrett (Jeweller)
195 WEATHERHEAD, P67
Suffolk Street
1695–96 David Mesgret, Red Balcony,
   Suffolk Street, jeweller *(Heal)*
1734 —Mesgret, Suffolk Street, listed for
   Poor Rate (possible tenant) *(WAC:
   MF1577 F488 item3)*

Merchant (Goldsmith)
168 WEATHERHEAD, P67
St Martins Court
1734 Peter Merchant, St Martin's Court,
   registered for Poor Rate *(WAC: MF1577
   F488 item3)*

Mrs Meredith (Broker)
23 BULSTRODE, P69
Bunhill Fields
Not found

Merry (Goldsmith)
18 WEATHERHEAD, P53
Smithfield Bars
1727–45 Thomas Merry, Smithfield Bars,
   largeworker; 1731 possibly Thomas
   Merry II, St Johns Street, largeworker
   (Grimwade)
1727–45 Thomas Merry, Smithfield Bars,
   plateworker; 1747 John Merry, jeweller
   (Heal)
1733 Thomas Merry, Little Britain,
   Smithfield precinct, Farringdon
   Without ward, registered for Land Tax
   (GLMS: MF11316 vol 104)
1743 Mr Thomas Merry, Smithfield Bars,
   advertised in *The Daily Advertiser* for
   the letting of his shop he going to leave
   off Trade, goldsmith *(BL: Burney 379B,
   05 Jun 1743)*
1750 Mr Merry stated in an Old Bailey

trial 'I am a goldsmith, and live by
   Smithfield-bars' *(OBP: t17501017-11)*

Messiter (Broker)
128 BULSTRODE, P72
Hounds Ditch
1734 Daniell Messiter, Houndsditch,
   Houndsditch precinct, Portsoken
   ward, registered for Land Tax *(GLMS:
   MF11316, vol 107)*

Midleton (Goldsmith/banker*)
175 HOLTOM, P49
angle Hungerford Market
1692–1745 (died) George Middleton,
   Three Crowns, Strand, nr St Martin's
   Lane; later G Campbell and D Bruce;
   later Campbell & Coutts, goldsmith
   and banker *(Heal)*
1692–1748 George Middleton &
   Campbell, at a shop near St Martin's
   Church, St Martin's Lane, goldsmith
   and banker; 1755 Campbell & Coutts,
   St Mary Axe; 1761 with death of
   Campbell, Coutts & Co moved to nr
   Durham Court, Strand *(Hilton-Price)*
1734 George Middleton, Strand, registered for Poor Rate *(WAC: MF1577
   F488 item3)*
1740–44 Mess Middleton & Co, Strand,
   advertised three times in *The London
   Daily Post & General Advertiser* and *The
   Daily Advertiser* for the return of
   several banknotes, the latter one paid
   away in error *(BL: Burney, 347B, 26 Apr
   1740; 387B, 10 Jan 1744; 397B, 01 Dec
   1744)*

Mitchell (Broker)
131 WEATHERHEAD, P65
St James's, Market Lane
1734 Mr Mitchell, St James's Market,
   registered for Poor Rate *(WAC: MF655
   D39 item1, Church & Market division)*

Mitchell (Broker)
129 HOLTOM, P47
Drury Lane by Long Acre
1734 Bartlett Mitchell, Drury Lane, registered for Poor Rate *(WAC: MF1577
   F488 item3)*

Mitchell (Broker)
48 BULSTRODE, P72
Winfords Street, Spittle Fields
1724 Edwd and Wm Mitchell, Hamlett of

Spitalfields, registered for Sewer Rate
   (LMA: THCS 132)

Molins (Watchmaker)
56 HOLTOM, P43
Bride's Alley
1687–1737 Charles Molyns, Fleet Street
   (Britten)
1733 Mr Mullins, Fleet Street precinct,
   Ludgate Hill, Farringdon Without
   Ward registered for Land Tax *(GLMS:
   MF11316 vol 104)*

Montgomery (Goldsmith)
111 WEATHERHEAD, P61
Silver Street
1718 John Montgomery, Silver Street,
   near Golden Square, St James's; 1729,
   at the corner of Cambridge Street;
   1736, corner of Silver Street near
   Golden Square; 1742 at the Angel the
   corner of Silver Street and Cambridge
   Street, largeworker *(Grimwade)*
1727 John Montgomery, at the Angel,
   corner of Silver St in Cambridge Street,
   parish of St James, Westminster,
   insured household goods, etc for £500,
   goldsmith *(GLMS: 11936 vol 23
   [SI.41233])*
1728 Mr Montgomery, Old Bailey trial
   concerning stolen silver spoons and
   forks *(OBP: t17280501-6)*
1729–49 John Montgomery, Angel, corner
   of Cambridge Street, Golden Square;
   1742–49 Angel, Silver Street, Golden
   Square; 1750 London, plateworker
   (Heal)
1734 John Montgomery, Cambridge
   Street, St James's Piccadilly, registered
   for Poor Rate *(WAC: MF655 D39 item1,
   Gt Marlboro division)*
1744 Mr Montgomery, Corner of
   Cambridge Street, near Golden Square,
   St James's, advertised in *The Daily
   Advertiser* for the return of a lost
   Diamond ring and bag, goldsmith *(BL:
   Burney 397B, 08 Dec 1744)*
1749 John Montgomery, Cambridge
   Street, St James's Piccadilly,
   Westminster Pollbook, silversmith
   (WAC: CDRom)
1754 Alice Montgomery, witness in an
   Old Bailey trial, I am a goldsmith
   (OBP: t17541023-4)

Moran (Watchmaker*)
118 WEATHERHEAD, P63
Vere Street by Oxford Chapel
1728 Andrew Morran, two Old Bailey trials concerning gold and silver watches stolen from his shop, some taken from a shew-glass (*OBP: t17280501-8, t17280605-48*)
1731–60 Andrew Mooran, St Marylebone; after 1740 at the Crown, Harlesden (*Britten*)
1734 possibly Barth Moran, Princes Street, registered for Poor Rate (*WAC: MF655 D39 item1, Gt Marlboro division*)
1738 Mr Moran, Vere Street by Oxford Chapel, advertised in *The London Daily Post & General Advertiser* for the return of a watch by Josephson, watchmaker (*BL: Burney 333B, 09 Nov 1738*)

Morris (Broker)
54 WEATHERHEAD, P55
near Midle Row, Holborn
1732 Benjamin Morris, Holborn, St Andrew Holborn, St George the Martyr, registered for Poor Rate (*CLS: UTAH MF29 item6*)

Morris (Broker)
116 WEATHERHEAD, P63
Mattox Street
1734 David Morris, Maddox Street, registered for Poor Rate (*WAC: MF435 C38 item32*)

Morris (Goldsmith)
14 WEATHERHEAD, P53
Smithfield
1720 Henry Morris, Wood Street; 1739 Smithfield, Goldsmith; 1744 Fleet Street; 1731 Goldsmiths' Company Livery, largeworker (*Grimwade*)
1734 Henry Morris, Barts the Less precinct, Farringdon Without ward, registered for Land Tax (*GLMS: MF11316 vol 104*)
1739 Henry Morris, Smithfield, plateworker (*Heal*)
1753 Henry Morris, the younger, Fleet Street, listed as inhabitant of St Bride's parish (*GLMS: 6561*)

Myne (Broker)
26 BULSTRODE, P71
Long Alley
1729 possibly Widow Maine (Man),

Moorfields precinct, St Leonard's Shoreditch, registered for Poor Rate; also 1729 Jane Man, Holywell Street, St Leonard's Shoreditch, registered for Poor Rate (*LMA: P91/LEN/47*)

N

Nangle (Jeweller)
121 HOLTOM, P47
Russel Street
Not found

Needham (Watchmaker)
11 WEATHERHEAD, P53
Little Britain
1709 possibly Benjamin Needham; free of the Clockmakers' Company (*Britten*)

Nelme (Goldsmith)
12 HOLTOM, P41; FIG 40
Amen Corner
1721 Francis Nelme at Gold Bottle, Ave Mary Lane; 1722–27 Ave Mary Lane; 1736 St Martin's Ludgate, goldsmith (*Heal*)
1733 Francis Nelme St Martin's Ludgate precinct, Farringdon Within ward registered for Land Tax (*GLMS: MF11316 vol 103*)
1734 Francis Nelme St Martin's Ludgate registered for Poor Rate (*GLMS: 1315, vol 1*)
1739 Francis Nelme of Ave Mary Lane; 1741 bankrupt (*Grimwade*)

Neve (Watchmaker)
160 HOLTOM, P47
Corner of Fountain Court, Strand
1680–1740 Jonathan Nene, Strand; 1740 Jno, Henry and Henry Neve (*Britten*)
1727 Henry Neve, tenant of a house in the Strand owned as Trustee for children by Daniel Gell(?) of St John, Westminster; insured by Neve for £300, one of five houses, watchmaker (*GLMS: 11936 vol 24 [SI 43317]*)
1734 Henry Neve, Strand, registered for Poor Rate (*WAC: MF183 B38 item2*)
1735 Neve listed in Clockmakers' Company South West Walk (*GLMS: 2715 vol 4*)
1736 Henry Neve, Strand, advertised in *The Daily Post* for the return of a lost watch, watchmaker (*BL: Burney 319B, 30 Apr 1736*)

Newingham (Broker)
21 WEATHERHEAD, P53
Charterhouse Lane
1734 Richard Newenham, Charterhouse Lane, registered for Poor Rate (*GLMS: 9110 vol 1*)

Nicholls (Goldsmith)
49 WEATHERHEAD, P55
Bell Court, Brooks Market
Not found

Nichols (Goldsmith)
6 BULSTRODE, P69
Barbicon
1718 Christopher Nicholle, in Barbican, free joyner, smallworker (*Grimwade*)
1733 Christopher Nichols, Barbican, Cripplegate Without ward, registered for Land Tax (*GLMS: MF11316 vol 103*)

Norwood (Broker/pawnbroker)
137 HOLTOM, P47
Hart St
1734 John Norwood, Hart Street, registered for Poor Rate (*WAC: MF1595 H43 item14*)
1743 possibly Mr Norwood, Old Bailey trial concerning a stolen spoon, property of Peter Hales, goldsmith, pawned with him, pawnbroker (*OBP: t17431012-24*)

O

Oliver (Jeweller)
94 WEATHERHEAD, P59
St Andrews Street, 7 Dials
1733 possibly George Oliver, Old Bailey trial concerning a gold watch chain stolen from his house (*OBP: t17331205-50*)
1734 possibly Jonathan Oliver, St Andrews Street North side, St Giles and St George Bloomsbury, registered for Poor Rate (*CLS: UTAH MF99 item1*)

Oman (Broker)
78 WEATHERHEAD, P59
at ye X Keys, & in ye Cole Yard, Drury Lane
1734 possibly Aaron Orme, Coal Yard, St Giles and St George Bloomsbury, registered for Poor Rate (*CLS: UTAH MF99 item1*)

Osborn (Broker)
77 WEATHERHEAD, P59
Plumbtree Street, Bloomsbury
1734 Josiah Osborne, Plumbtree Street,
St Giles and St George Bloomsbury,
registered for Poor Rate (*CLS: UTAH
MF99 item1*)

P

Pack (Goldsmith)
40 HOLTOM, P43
Flower-de-Luces Court, Fleet St
1732 Nathaniel Pack, Flower-de-Luces,
Fleet Street, smallworker (*Grimwade*)
1733 Nathl Pack, Flower de luce Court, St
Dunstan-in-the-West precinct,
Farringdon Without ward, registered
for Land Tax (*GLMS: MF11316, vol 104*)

Page (Goldsmith)
68 WEATHERHEAD, P57
Orange Street
1729–39 Francis Pages, Golden Cup,
Orange Street, near Red Lion Square,
plateworker (*Heal*)
1732 Francis Page, Orange Street, St
Andrew Holborn, St George the
Martyr, registered for Poor Rate (*CLS:
UTAH MF29 item6*)
1739 Francis Pages, Golden Cup, Orange
Street, nr Red Lion Square; 1737
Goldsmiths' Company Livery, gold-
smith (*Grimwade*)
1739, Francis Pages, Orange Street nr Red
Lion Square, insured six houses nr the
Crown in Huminerton (Homerton?),
parish of St John, Hackney, for £450,
goldsmith (*GLMS: 11936 vol 54
[SI.82253]*)
1744 Mr Page, Orange Street, Red Lion
Square, advertised in *The Daily
Advertiser* for the return of a lost large
table spoon marked I.S, goldsmith (*BL:
Burney 381B, 08 May 1744*)

Paradise (Goldsmith*)
52 HOLTOM, P43; FIG 36
by Fleet Bridge
1720 William Paradise, London, possibly
Lad Lane, largeworker (*Grimwade*)
1724–51 William Paradise, London,
possibly Lad Lane, plateworker (*Heal*)
1731 William Paradise appeared in an Old
Bailey trial concerning a cane stolen
from his shop (*OBP: t17310908-22*)

1732 William Parradice, Fleet Street,
listed as inhabitant of St Bride's parish,
goldsmith (*GLMS: 6561*)
1733 Wm Paradise, Fleet Street precinct,
Ludgate Hill, Farringdon Without
ward registered for Land Tax (*GLMS:
MF11316 vol 104*)

Parks & King (Watchmakers)
4 HOLTOM, P41
Rose Street, Newgate St
1728–35 possibly Benjamin Parkes,
watchmaker (*Britten*)
1733 Parkes and 1734 Parkes & King
listed in Clockmakers' Company New
Walk (*GLMS: 2715 vol 4*)
1734 possibly Jeremiah King, St
Leonard's precinct, Aldersgate Within
ward, registered for Land Tax (*GLMS:
MF11316 vol 102*)
1737 John Parks at the Dial over against
Salutation Tavern in Newgate Street
insured his stock in trade as an iron-
monger for £500 and, as a watchmaker,
manufactured and wrought plate for
£300 watchmaker/ironmonger (*GLMS:
11936 vol 48 [SI.76175]*)

Parr (Broker/pawnbroker)
84 HOLTOM, P45
St Clements Lane
1734 Jno Parr, Clements Lane, registered
for Poor Rate (*WAC: MF183 B38 item2*)
1734 John Par, Old Bailey trial concerning
apparel and goods stolen from his
house, pawnbroker (*OBP: t17341016-4*)

Parry (Goldsmith and jeweller)
176 WEATHERHEAD, P67
Hemmingss Row
Not found

Parsons (Broker/pawnbroker)
52 WEATHERHEAD, P55
Fox Court, Brooks Market
1730 Arthur Parsons, Old Bailey trial
concerning £3 worth of silver plate
which he had given to Thomas Mann
to work up, he being a casting silversmith (*OBP: t17300704-31*)
1732 Eleanor Parsons, Fox Court, St
Andrew Holborn, St George the
Martyr, registered for Poor Rate (*CLS:
UTAH MF29 item6*)
1744 Mrs Parsons, Old Bailey trial
concerning a stolen silver spoon

pawned with her, pawnbroker (*OBP:
t17440113-8*)

Pattison (Jeweller)
8 HOLTOM, P41
Warwick Court, Warwick Lane
1733 Jms Pattison St Sepulchre's precinct,
Farringdon Within ward registered for
Land Tax (*GLMS: MF11316 vol 103*)

Payne (Watchmaker)
45 BULSTRODE, P71
Spittle Fields
1721 David Paine, Spitalfield Market,
watchmaker (*Britten*)
1733 possibly Wm Payne, listed in
Clockmakers' Company East Walk
(*GLMS: 2715 vol 4*)
1735–40 circa, David Pain, watchmaker
(*Britten*)

Payne (Broker)
112 BULSTRODE, P77
New Gravell Lane
1733 Nathanell Paine, New Gravell Lane,
St Paul Shadwell, registered for Land
Tax (*GLMS: MF6009 vol 3*)

Pearce (Goldsmith)
6 HOLTOM, P41
Rose St, Newgate St
1742–60 John Pearce, Golden Bellows,
Newgate Street, goldsmith (*Heal*)
1742–43 Mr Pearce advertised twice in
The Daily Advertiser seeking the return
of stolen goods, goldsmith (*BL: Burney
381B, 27 Nov 1742; 379B, 16 Apr 1743*)
1745–67 John Pearce, Newgate Street,
goldsmith (*Britten*)

Pearce (Watchmaker*)
75 HOLTOM, P43
Fleet St
1725 Thomas Pearce's Shop, under St
Dunstan's Church, Tithe assessment,
watchmaker (*GLMS: 3011*)
1730 and 1736 Thomas Pearce, over against
ye hors Shu ale house in Westhardin
Street Fetter Lane, smallworker (*Grimwade*)
1733 Thos Pearce, Chancery Lane, St
Dunstan in the West precinct,
Farringdon Without ward, registered
for Land Tax (*GLMS: MF11316 vol 104*)
1735 —Pearce, listed in Clockmakers'
Company South West Walk (*GLMS:
2715 vol 4*)

    Concordance of variant spellings of tradesmen's names pp132–36; index of streets p138; bibliography pp140–41

1740 Thomas Pearce, London, watchmaker (*Britten*)

1742 Thomas Pierce, under St Dunstan's
Church, Fleet Street, advertised in *The
Daily Advertiser* for the return of a lost
silver watch, watchmaker (*BL: Burney
379B, 21 Dec 1742*)

Peart (Goldsmith)
2 HOLTOM, P41
Crispin Court, Bagnio Passage, St
Martins Le Grand

1734 Thomas Peart, St Mary Staining
precinct, Aldersgate Within ward,
registered for Land Tax (*GLMS:
MF11316 vol 102*)

Pelletier (Goldsmith)
192 WEATHERHEAD, P67
Leicester Fields

1734 possibly Peter Pallairett,
Cranbourne Street, registered for Poor
Rate (*WAC: MF32 A134*)

Pepys (Watchmaker)
47 HOLTOM, P43; FIG 61
Fleet Street

1708–44 John Pepys; 1744 Crown &
Sceptre, Fleet Street (*Britten*)

1715–49 John Pepys, Crown & Sceptre, Fleet
Street, watchmaker and jeweller (*Heal*)

1725 John Pepys, Fleet Street, between
Bolt and 3 Kings Courts, Tithe assessment (*GLMS: 3011*)

1733 John Pepys, Fleet Street, St Dunstan-
in-the-West precinct, Farringdon
Without ward (*GLMS: MF11316 vol 104*)

1734 John Pepys in Clockmakers'
Company South West Walk (*GLMS:
2715 vol 4*)

1734–44 Mr John Pepys, Crown &
Sceptre, Fleet Street advertised seven
times in *The Daily Journal, London Daily
Post & General Advertiser* and *The Daily
Advertiser* for the return of watches
made by him (*BL: Burney 303B, 01 Jan
1734; 341B, 17 Jul 1739; 379B, 10 Jan
1743, 07 May 1743, 04 Aug 1743; 381B,
10 Apr 1744, 04 May 1744*)

Perkins (Broker)
78 BULSTRODE, P72
Little Minories

1730 Tho Perkins, Trinity Minories,
Tower Hill, registered for Sewer Rate
(*LMA: THCS 143*)

Perry (Broker)
130 BULSTRODE, P72
Hounds Ditch

1734 John Perry, Houndsditch,
Houndsditch precinct, Portsoken ward
(*GLMS: MF11316 vol 107*)

Peters (Broker / pawnbroker)
103 HOLTOM, P45
Horton Street, Clare Market

1724–44 Simon Peter, Golden Ball &
Cross Keys, Horton Street, Clare
Market, pawnbroker (*Heal*)

1734 Symon Peter, New Inn Back Gate,
registered for Poor Rate (*WAC: MF183
B38 item2*)

1744 Mr Peters, Golden Ball and Cross-
Keys, Horton Street, Clare Market,
announced his retirement in *The Daily
Advertiser* (*BL: Burney 397B, 15 Dec
1744*)

Mrs Pickard (Broker / pawnbroker)
60 BULSTRODE, P72
Smock Alley

1729 Sarah Pickard, Old Bailey trial
concerning theft from her house of 36
rings, watches and plate of considerable value (*OBP: t17290709-51*)

1729 Mrs (and Mr) Pickard, Old Bailey
trial concerning a stolen watch
pawned with her, pawnbroker (*OBP:
t17291015-79*)

1733 Widow Pickard, Petticoat Lane,
Covent Garden [*sic*] precinct,
Portsoken ward, registered for Land
Tax (*GLMS: MF11316 vol 104*)

1739 Mrs Pickard, Seven Stars, Petticoat
Lane, near Whitechapel, advertised in
The Daily Post & General Advertiser for
customers to redeem their pledged
items; cessation of business (*BL: Burney
347B, 18 Feb 1739-40*)

Pilleau (Goldsmith)
174 WEATHERHEAD, P67; FIG 53
Chandois Street

1719–55 Pezé Pilleau Jnr, Golden Cup on
the Paved Stones, Chandos Street,
goldsmith and maker of artificial teeth
(*Heal*)

1719–55 Pezé Pilleau, at the Sign of the
Golden Cup in Shandois Street (*no342
Quiet Conquest*)

1724–39 Pezé Pilleau, Chandois Street; Free
Goldsmith, largeworker (*Grimwade*)

1734 Peze Pilleau, Shandois Street, registered for Poor Rate (*WAC: MF1577
F488 item3*)

1749 Beze [*sic*] Pilleau, Chandois Street
(St Martins), silversmith (*WPB*)

Pinchbeck (Watchmaker)
44 HOLTOM, P43
Fleet St

1725 Charles Pinchbeck, Fleet Street,
Tithe assessment on two premises
(*GLMS: 3011*)

1733 Charles Pinchbeck, Fleet Street, St
Dunstan-in-the-West precinct,
Farringdon Without ward registered
for Land Tax (*GLMS: MF11316 vol 104*)

Pinchbeck (Watchmaker)
46 HOLTOM, P43
Fleet St

1732–66 Edward Pinchbeck, Fleet Street,
previously of St George Street,
Clerkenwell (son of Christopher
Pinchbeck) (*Britten*)

1733 Edwd Pinchbeck, Fleet Street, St
Dunstan-in-the-West precinct,
Farringdon Without ward, registered
for Land Tax (*GLMS: MF11316 vol 104*)

1736 Edward Pinchbeck, at the Musical
Clock within two Doors of the Leg
Tavern in Fleet Street warned in *The
London Daily Post* of replica goods
similar to his own (*BLCol: Burney 90B,
08 Jan 1736*)

1741 Mr Edward Pinchbeck advertised in
*The London Daily Post & General
Advertiser* his 'Curious Piece of
Machinery exactly representing the
Siege of Carthegena' to be exhibited at
Bartholomews Fair (*BLCol: Burney
356B, 03 Aug 1741*)

1755 Edward Pinchbeck at the Musical
Clock in Fleet Street insured his household goods, stock, plate excepted, in
his house for £300, watchmaker and
toyman (*GLMS: 11936 vol 109 [SI
144592]*)

Pons (Goldsmith*)
153 HOLTOM, P47
Tavistock St

1730 Peter Pons, Old Bailey trial
concerning gold and silver plate stolen
from his shop (*OBP: t17300828-42*)

1734 Peter Pons Co, Tavistock Street
South, registered for Poor Rate (*WAC:

MF1959 H43 item14)

1740–41 auction notice in *The London Daily Post & General Advertiser* of Peter Pons stock in trade from his house in the Haymarket, goldsmith and jeweller *(BL: Burney 355B, 12 Mar 1740-41)*

Pope (Goldsmith)
5 HOLTOM, P41
Rose St, Newgate St
1733 Abra Pope registered for Land Tax in St Sepulchre's precinct, Farringdon Within ward *(GLMS: MF11316 vol 103)*
1739 Mr Pope, Queen's Head, Newgate Street, Old Bailey trial concerning the purchase of stolen plate *(OBP: t17391205–68)*

Praunock (Goldsmith)
53 WEATHERHEAD, P55
near Midle Row, Holborn
1732 possibly Benjamin Braddock, Gray's Inn Lane, St Andrew Holborn, St George the Martyr, registered for Poor Rate *(CLS: UTAH MF29 item6)*

Pretty (Broker/pawnbroker)
109 HOLTOM, P45
Vere St
1734 Richd Pretty, Vere Steet, registered for Poor Rate *(WAC: MF183 B38 item2)*
1749 Richard Pretty, Old Bailey coining trial concerning the exchange of stolen gold for coin, pawnbroker *(OBP: t17490113-28)*

Price (Goldsmith)
41 HOLTOM, P43
Flower-de-Luces Court, Fleet St
1725 —Price, Flower-de-Luce Court Tithe assessment *(GLMS: 3011)*
1727 Harvey Price, sometime in Flower de Luce Court in Fleet Street, largeworker *(Grimwade)*
1737 Harvey Price of London, ex Flowerde-Luce Court, plateworker *(Heal)*

Price (Jeweller)
63 HOLTOM, P43
at a Fan Shop
1725 possibly Mr Price, Fleet Street, Tithe assessment *(GLMS: 3011)*
1733 William Price, Fleet Street, St Dunstan-in-the-West precinct, Farringdon Without ward, registered for Land Tax *(GLMS: MF11316 vol 104)*

1743 Mr William Price, Fleet Street advertised in *The Daily Advertiser* for return of a stolen Silver Tip for a Mug or Jack, goldsmith *(BL: Burney 379B, 19 Feb 1743)*

Priswell (Broker)
123 BULSTRODE, P75
St Catherines
1734 Saml Priswell, St Katherines by the Tower, Tower division, registered for Land Tax *(GLMS: MF6010 vol 3)*

Pupin (Watchmaker)
171 WEATHERHEAD, P67
St Martins Lane
Not found

Purden (Watchmaker)
170 WEATHERHEAD, P67
St Martins Court
1734 John Purdon, St Martin's Court, registered for Poor Rate *(WAC: MF1577 F488 item3)*
1743 Purden, St Martin's Court, London *(Baillie)*
1749 John Purden, Dean Street, parish of St Anne, Soho, Westminster Pollbook, clockmaker *(WAC: CDRom)*
1752 John Purden; circa 1790 Dean Street *(Baillie)*
1753 John Purden, near Meard Street, west side of Dean Street, parish of St Anne, Westminster, insured household goods and stock, clock and watchmaker *(GLMS: 11936 vol 102 [SI.136697])*
–Jonathan Purdin, and his son, John (1777–1820) *(Britten)*

Q

Quelch (Watchmaker)
63 BULSTRODE, P72
Red Lyon Street
1732 possibly Hannah Quelch, Petticoat Lane, Wellclose and other places, registered for Sewer Rate *(LMA: THCS 146)*
1735–54 Jeremiah Quelch, London, watchmaker *(Britten)*

Quillet (Goldsmith and jeweller)
182 HOLTOM, P49
Charing Cross
1734 ffrancis Quillet, Exchange, registered for Poor Rate *(WAC: MF1577*

F488 item3)
[1741–49 Stephen Quillet, possibly son of above, variations on his Charing Cross address, features in many newspaper advertisements and Old Bailey trials, jeweller, goldsmith and possibly pawnbroker]

R

Radford (Goldsmith and toyman)
92 HOLTOM, P45
angle Temple Barr, Clements Church
1734 Jno Radford, Strand Side, registered for Poor Rate *(WAC: MF183 B38 item2)*

Rainaud (Goldsmith)
197 WEATHERHEAD, P67
Suffolk Street
1710 Philip Rainaud, Suffolk Street, St Martin-in-the-Fields, Middx, for his goods (French policy) *(GLMS: 11936 vol 1 [SI.802])*
1720 Philip Rainaud, corner of Suffolk Street; 1721 Goldsmiths' Company Livery, plateworker *(Grimwade)*
1726 Philip Rainaud, corner of Suffolk Street, St Martin-in-the-Fields, insured household goods, plate, stock, etc in house for £500, goldsmith *(GLMS: 11936 vol 21 [SI.38856])*
1728 Philip Rainaud, Suffolk Street, bankruptcy, plateworker *(Heal)*
1729 Philip Rainaud, Old Bailey trial concerning 24 silver salt shovels, stamped with his Mark P.R, stolen from him *(OBP: t17291205-12)*
1734 Philip Rainaud, Suffolk Street, registered for Poor Rate *(WAC: MF1577 F488 item3)*

Rawlings (Broker/pawnbroker)
128 HOLTOM, P47
Drury Lane by Long Acre
1731 Mr Rawlings, Four Balls, Drury Lane, nr Long Acre, advertised in *The Country Journal or The Craftsman* seeking the owner of a stop watch *(BL: Burney 289B (reel 2), 28 Aug 1731)*
1734 Mr Rawlins, Old Bailey trial concerning a snuff box left with him *(OBP: t17341204-28)*
1734 Robert Rawlins, Drury Lane, registered for Poor Rate *(WAC: MF1577 F488, item 3)*
1743 and 1745 Mr Rawlins, Long Acre,

Old Bailey trial concerning two aprons a large quantity of jewellery and a watch pawned with him, the latter stolen from and advertised in Bath, pawnbroker *(OBP: t17430413-42: t17450116-16)*

1749 Robert Rawlins, Long Acre, parish of St Martins-in-the-Fields,Westminster Pollbook, broker *(WAC, CDRom)*

Ray (Broker)
32 HOLTOM, P43
Long Entry
1737 possibly Clifford Ray, at Mrs Male at Cow Lane, Smithfield, smallworker *(Grimwade)*

Ray (Broker/pawnbroker)
25 HOLTOM, P43
Holborn Bridge
1733 Peter Rayes, Ditch Side, nr Shoe Lane, Farringdon Without ward registered for Land Tax *(GLMS: MF11316 vol 104)*

Read (Broker)
112 WEATHERHEAD, P61
Carnaby Street
1734 Jer Read, Carnaby Street, St James's Piccadilly, registered for Poor Rate *(WAC: MF655 D39 item1, Gt Marlboro division)*

Reeve (Goldsmith)
73 BULSTRODE, P72
Minories
1731 William Reeve at the Blackmoors Head in the Minories, largeworker *(Grimwade)*
1731 William Reeve, Blackmoors Head, Minories; 1735–53, Lombard Street, plateworker *(Heal)*
1735 Reeves, listed in Clockmakers' Company New Walk *(GLMS: 2715 vol 4)*
1735 William Reeve, late of Lombard Street, goldsmith; bankruptcy notice (second Notice in 1736) *(Hart)*

Reynolds (Broker/pawnbroker)
138 HOLTOM, P47
Hart St
1732 Christopher Reynolds, Hart Street, Covent Garden, pawnbroker *(Heal)*
1734 Christopher Reynolds, Hart Street South, registered for Poor Rate *(WAC: MF1959, H43, item 14)*

1735 Mr Reynold, Hart Street, Covent Garden, Old Bailey trial concerning the theft of a silver tankard and spoons, pawnbroker *(OBP: t17350116-47)*

Reynolds (Broker)
30 BULSTRODE, P71
Hare Alley, holywell Lane, Shor
1729 possibly Thomas Reynolds, Moorfields precinct, St Leonard's Shoreditch *(LMA: P91/LEN/47)*

Rickman (Broker)
105 BULSTRODE, P77
Ratcliffe highway
Not found

Rigly (Goldsmith*)
22 WEATHERHEAD, P53
Hick's Hall
1729 Mr Ridgley, Old Bailey trial where he stated that, having bought a stolen diamond and gold ring, he was able to recognise it because he had been sent a Notice from Goldsmiths' Hall, goldsmith *(OBP: t17291213-11)*
1735 Richard Ridgly, The Golden Ball, St John Street, Old Bailey trial concerning a shew-glass containing items stolen from his shop, goldsmith *(OBP: t17350226-47)*

Rivers (Broker)
49 BULSTRODE, P72
Old George Street, Spittle Fields
1724 possibly Jno Rivers, Hamlett of Spitalfields, registered for Sewer Rate *(LMA: THCS 132)*

Road (Goldsmith)
142 BULSTRODE, P69
Golden Lane
1733 John Read, Kings Head Court, White Cross precinct, Cripplegate Without ward, registered for Land Tax *(GLMS: MF11316 vol 105)*

Roaker (Watchmaker)
13 WEATHERHEAD, P53
in the Passage
1733 Rooker, Snr and Rooker, jnr; 1734 Richd Rooker and Richd Rooker; 1735 —Rooker and Richd Rooker, junior, listed in the Clockmakers' Company North Walk *(GLMS: 2715 vol 4)*
1733 Richard Rooker, Broomstick Alley,

Barts the Less precinct, Farringdon Without ward, registered for Land Tax *(GLMS: MF11316 vol 104)*

Roberts (Goldsmith)
109 BULSTRODE, P79
Ratcliffe highway
1734 ffrans Roberts, Broad Street, St Dunstan Stepney, registered for Land Tax *(GLMS: MF 6014 vol 4)*
1741 Philip Roberts at the Pewter Dish, Bell dock, Wapping, St George-in-the-East, insured stock, wrought and manufactured plate £200, etc in his house for £500, pewterer and silver-smith *(GLMS: 11936 vol 61 [SI.89625])*
1751 Philip Roberts, Bell dock, Wapping; 1753, near the Hermitage, goldsmith *(Heal)*
1756 Mary Roberts, the Pewterers Dish in Bell Dock, Wapping, St George-in-the-East, insured household goods, stock, wrought and manufactured plate £200, etc £400, pewterer and silversmith *(GLMS: 11936 vol 115 [SI.150765])*

Robinson (Broker)
86 BULSTRODE, P75
Starr Ally
Not found

Robinson (Jeweller)
9 HOLTOM, P41
Warwick Court, Warwick Lane
1716 possibly Edward Robinson, Warwick Lane, near Newgate, gold-smith *(Grimwade)*

Robinson (Watchmaker)
76 HOLTOM, P43
Middle Temple Gate
1685 Francis Robinson, London, Inner Temple, apprenticed and free 1707; Master to the Clockmakers' Company; 1725–47 Watchmaker to the Prince of Wales *(Baillie)*
1685–1726 Francis Robinson, in the Temple, Inner Temple Lane, 'Servant to his Royal Highness' *(Britten)*
1731 Mr Robinson, Inner Temple Lane, advertised twice in *The Daily Advertiser* for the return of a lost watch, watch-maker *(BL: Burney 289B, 23 Jul 1731, 19 Nov 1731)*

Robinson (Broker)
31 WEATHERHEAD, P55
Cow Cross
1734 possibly John Robinson, near
Sharps Alley, Cow Cross, registered for
Poor Rate (*GLMS: 9110 vol 1*)

Robinson (Watchmaker)
49 HOLTOM, P43
Fleet St
1720 Oliver Robinson; 1727 free of the
Clockmakers' Company, London
(*Baillie*)
1733 Oliver Robinson, Fleet Street, Fleet
Street precinct, Ludgate Hill,
Farringdon Without ward registered
for Land Tax (*GLMS: MF11316 vol 104*)
1733 Olr Robinson and 1734, Oliver
Robinson listed in the Clockmakers'
Company South West Walk (*GLMS:
2715 vol 4*)

Robinson (Goldsmith)
59 HOLTOM, P43
Corner of Salisbury Court
1713–28 Philip Robinson, corner of
Salisbury Court, Fleet Street; 1734–44
(died), Fleet Street, goldsmith (*Heal*)
1723 Philip Robinson, Fleet Street; 1732
Goldsmiths' Company Court; 1744
died, largeworker (*Grimwade*)
1727 Philip Robinson, Fleet Street served
as Questman;** and Church Warden,
goldsmith (*GLMS: 6561*)
1733 Philip Robinson, Fleet Street, Fleet
Street precinct, Ludgate Hill,
Farringdon Without ward registered
for Land Tax (*GLMS: MF11316 vol 104*)
1735 Philip Robinson, Fleet Street,
insured his goods in pledge, plate &
jewels excepted, in North dwelling
house of Arthur Baden, Pawnbroker at
the Roses in the Passages in the West
side of St Bride's Churchyard for
£1,000, goldsmith and pawnbroker
(*GLMS: 111936 vol 42 [SI.68430]*)
1737–45 Philip Robinson, Fleet Street,
goldsmith (*Britten*)
1740 Philip Robinson, at the Golden Ball
& Crown, Salisbury Court, Fleet Street,
insured tenanted property in Bishops
Stortford, Herts for £200 (*GLMS: 11936
vol 57 [SI.86308]*)
1743 Mr Philip Robinson, Fleet Street,
advertised in *The Daily Advertiser* for
the return of a lost Motto ring, gold-

smith (*BL: Burney 379B, 04 Feb 1743*)
1743 Mr Philip Robinson, Corner of
Salisbury Court, Fleet Street auction
notice in *The Daily Advertiser* for his
stock in trade, late Goldsmith, deceasd
(*BL: Burney 381B, 27 Feb 1744*)
**Note*: Questman – *see* Bristow, p87.
Robinson paid a £14 fine in 1732 to be
exempt from three parish offices. Fines
levied were generally: Constable £9,
Parish Rate Collector £5, Vollunteer
[*sic*] £7.

Robinson (Watchmaker)
73 WEATHERHEAD, P59
Plumbtree Street, Bloomsbury
1709 William Robinson, apprenticed;
1720, free; 1720–45 London (*Baillie*)
1735 Wm Robinson, listed in the
Clockmakers' Company North Walk
(*GLMS: 2715 vol 4*)

Roger (Goldsmith)
148 HOLTOM, P47
Round Court
1734 Richard Rogers, Strand, registered
for Poor Rate (*WAC: MF1577 F488
item3*)

Rogers (Broker)
84 WEATHERHEAD, P59
Shorts Gardens
1728 Mrs Rogers in Shorts Gardens, Old
Bailey trial concerning items she had
stopt, pawnbroker (*OBP: t17280605-33*)
1734 Ann Rogers, Coal Yard, St Giles and
St George Bloomsbury, registered for
Poor Rate (*CLS: UTAH MF99 item1*)
1734 Ann Rogers and Thomas Rogers,
Castle Street, St Giles and St George
Bloomsbury, registered for Poor Rate
(*CLS: UTAH MF99 item1*)

Rollins (Broker/pawnbroker)
38 HOLTOM, P43
Fetter Lane
1733 possibly John Collins, Fetter Lane,
St Dunstan-in-the-West precinct,
Farringdon Without ward registered
for Land Tax (*GLMS: MF11316 vol 104*)

Rous (Broker/pawnbroker)
96 WEATHERHEAD, P59
St Andrews Street, 7 Dials
1734 possibly Nicholas Rouse, Queen
Street South, registered for Poor Rate

(*WAC: MF655 D39 item1, Golden Sq
division*)
1744 Mr Rowse, Little St Andrew's Street,
Corner of Lumber Court, near the
Seven-Dials, advertised in *The Daily
Advertiser* that he had 'stopt a large
Table-Spoon' (*BL: Burney 381B, 31 Mar
1744*)

Rousseau (Watchmaker)
178 WEATHERHEAD, P67
Hemmingss Row
1743–61 possibly James Rousseau,
London, watchmaker (*Baillie*)
1743 possibly Mr James Rousseau, Greek
Street, Soho, advertised in *The Daily
Advertiser* for the return of a lost
watch, watchmaker (*BL: Burney 387B,
02 Sep 1743*)

Rudge (Broker/pawnbroker)
133 BULSTRODE, P72
Hounds Ditch
1731 Thomas Rudge, Three Golden Balls,
Houndsditch, pawnbroker (*Heal*)

S

Sadler (Broker)
33 BULSTRODE, P71
Goddards Rents
1733 Benjamin Sadler, Goddards Rents,
St Leonard's Shoreditch, registered for
Poor Rate (*LMA: P91/LEN/1374*)

Salt (Jeweller)
88 HOLTOM, P45
New Castle Court
1734 Henry Saule, New Castle Court,
registered for Poor Rate (*WAC: MF 183,
B34, item 2*)
1749 Henry Saul, Newcastle Court,
Westminster Pollbook (*WPB*)

Mrs Saunders (Toyman*)
73 HOLTOM, P43
Fleet St
1725 John Saunders, under St Dunstan's
Church and at his Toyshop, two Tithe
assessments, mathematical instrument
maker (*GLMS: 3011*)
1733 John Saunders, Ludgate Hill, Fleet
Street precinct, Farringdon Without
ward, registered for Land Tax (*GLMS:
MF11316 vol 104*)
1733 Captn Saml Saunders, shops under

the Church, St Dunstan-in-the-West, Farringdon Without ward, registered for Land Tax (*GLMS: MF11316 vol 104*)

1734 Saml Saunders and 1735 Samuel Saunders, listed in Clockmakers' Company North Walk (*GLMS: 2715 vol 4*)

1743 Mr Samuel Saunders, Half Moon & Seven Stars, South-side of St Paul's, auction notice in *The Daily Advertiser* of his entire stock, toyman, mathematical instrument maker (*BL: Burney 387B, 08 Jan 1743*)

Scalf (Broker/pawnbroker)
29 WEATHERHEAD, P55
Cow Cross
1734 Wm Scafe listed in the Clockmakers' Company North Walk (*GLMS: 2715 vol 4*)
1734 William Scafe, Cow Cross, registered for Poor Rate (*GLMS: 9110 vol 1*)
1743 Mrs Margaret Scaffe, King David and Harp, Cow Cross, advertised in *The Daily Advertiser* requesting customers to redeem their pledged items, she leaving off Trade (*BL: Burney 387B, 28 Sep 1743*)

Mrs Scarlett (Broker)
100 BULSTRODE, P77
Ratcliffe highway
1733 Mary Scarlett, Upper Shadwell South Side, St Paul Shadwell, registered for Land Tax (*GLMS: MF6009 vol 3*)

Seamor (Goldsmith/banker)
67 HOLTOM, P43; FIG 31
Fleet St
1701–39 (died) James Seamer (Seamour, Seymour), Three Flower-de-Luces, cnr Mitre Court, Fleet Street, goldsmith (*Heal*)
1728 James Seamer at the Flower-de-luce in Fleet Street, goldsmiths' Warning Notice no11697 for the return of a gold snuffbox lost in Tunbridge Wells, goldsmiths (see below, Private Collection)
1733 Coll James Seamer, Fleet Street, Farringdon Without ward, registered for Land Tax (*GLMS: MF11316 vol 104*)
1736 Mr James Seamer, at the Flower de Luce, Fleet Street, bankruptcy notice in *The London Daily Post & General Advertiser*, goldsmith and banker and Auction Notice of his Jewels and Plate; bankrupt, late goldsmith (*BL: Burney*

320B, 30 Jun 1736, 03 Sept 1736*)
1736 James Seamer, Fleet Street, London, Notice of Creditors meeting (*Hart*)
1739 James Seamer, formerly living near Mitre Court, Fleet Street, advertisement in *The London Evening Post* by The Corporation of the Amicable Society concerning a claim due by his death (*BLCol: Burney 345B, 30 Jun-03 Jul 1739*)
1743 James Seamer deceased, late of Fleet Street, notice in *The Daily Advertiser* re payment of second dividend to creditors, goldsmith and banker (*BL: Burney 387B, 20 Jul 1743*)

Numb. 11697.

October 19. 1728.
LOST on Friday the 30th of August last, at Tunbridge Wells, a Four Square Gold Snuff-Box, Weight 2 Oz. 12 Pennywt. Whoever brings it to Mr. James Seamer, Goldsmith, at the Flower-de-luce in Fleet-street, shall have Ten Guineas Reward; or if already pawn'd or sold, their Money again with Content.

BENJAMIN PYNE, *Beadle*, at *Goldsmiths-Hall.*

31

Sears (Broker)
24 WEATHERHEAD, P53
St Johns Court
Not found
Also: **Sears** (Broker)
25 WEATHERHEAD, P53
St Johns Court
Not found

Sedon (Watchmaker*)
128 WEATHERHEAD, P65
by St James's House
1691–1739 (died) Nathan Seddon in St James's, a noted watchmaker (*Britten*)
18th century–1740 (died), John Seddon, St James's Street, Quaker, watchmaker (*Britten*)
1735–43 John Seddon, Pall Mall, advertised four times in *The Daily Post* and *The Daily Advertiser* for the return of watches by John Seddon, and Quenovault, watchmaker (*BLCol: Burney 90B, 10 Feb 1735; BL: Burney 319B, 12 Feb 1736; 387B, 11 Aug 1743, 06 Dec 1743*)
1743 John Seddon, Old Bailey trial concerning the theft of The Rt Hon Lord Viscount St John's gold watch stolen from Seddon's shop (*OBP: t17431207-61*)

Shaw (Goldsmith)
149 WEATHERHEAD, P67
Jarrot [Gerrard] Street by St Anns Church
1725, 1727, 1743–45 William Shaw, Golden Ball, Gerrard Street, Soho, goldsmith (*Heal*)
1729 William Shaw I, Gerrard Street, Soho; 1745 bankrupt, largeworker (*Grimwade*)
1734 William Shaw, Gerrard Street, registered for Poor Rate (*WAC: MF32 A134*)
1738 William Shaw, parish of St Anne's, Westminster, insured household goods, stock and wrought and manufactured plate, etc in house at corner of Maxfield Street, Gerrard Street for £600, goldsmith (*GLMS: 11936 vol 50 [SI.77483]*)
1742–44 Mr Shaw, Golden Ball, Gerrard-Street, Soho, advertised four times in *The Daily Advertiser* for the return of various items, goldsmith (*BL: Burney 381B, 29 Nov 1742; BLCol: Burney 689B, 14 Jan 1743; BL: Burney 379B, 05 Jan 1743; 397B, 23 Oct 1744*)

Sheldon (Broker)
33 HOLTOM, P43
Long Entry
1728 possibly Wm Sheldon, Bangor Court, parish of St Andrews registered for Poor Rate (*GLMS: 9975, vol 1*)
1733 possibly Wm Sheldon, Bangor Court, Farringdon Without ward registered for Land Tax (*GLMS: MF11316 vol 104*)

Shelley (Broker)
80 WEATHERHEAD, P59
in ye Cole Yard, Drury Lane
1734 John Shelley, Coal Yard, Drury Lane, St Giles and St George Bloomsbury, registered for Poor Rate (*CLS: UTAH MF99 item1*)

Shelty (Goldsmith)
145 WEATHERHEAD, P67
Jarrot [Gerrard] Street by St Ann's Church
1734 possibly Gilbert Sheldon, Gerrard Street, registered for Poor Rate (*WAC: MF32 A134*)

Shipton (Broker)
69 BULSTRODE, P75
Abells Buildings
1734 William Shipton, Abells Buildings,
6th division, St Mary Whitechapel,
Middx, registered for Land Tax
(GLMS: MF6015 vol 2)

Shoppo (Jeweller)
133 HOLTOM, P47
Hannover Street, Long Acre
1734 John Shapeau, Hanover Street,
registered for Poor Rate *(WAC: MF1577
F488 item3)*

Sidey (Watchmaker)
30 HOLTOM, P43
Crabtree Court, Holborn Bridge
1701–61 Benjamin Sidley; 1710 Watling
Street *(Britten)*
1728 Benj Sidey, Plumbtree Court, registered for Poor Rate *(GLMS: 9975, vol 1)*
1733 Benjan Siday, Plumbtree Court,
Farringdon Without ward, registered
for Land Tax *(GLMS: MF11316 vol 104)*
1734 —Siday, listed in Clockmakers'
Company New Walk *(GLMS: 2715 vol 4)*

Simmons (Casemaker / watchmaker)
36 HOLTOM, P43
New St
1732 John Simmonds, New Street, listed
as inhabitant of St Bride's parish;
served as a Questman** *(GLMS: 6561)*
1733 possibly —Simons in Clockmakers'
Company New Walk *(GLMS: 2715 vol 4)*
**See Bristow p87 and Robinson p120

Simmons (Goldsmith)
100 WEATHERHEAD, P59
Earl Street, 7 Dials
1725 Peter Simon, Earl Street; possible
Huguenot origin, largeworker
(Grimwade)
1725 Peter Simon, Earl Street, plate-
worker *(Heal)*
1733 Peter Symon, Earl Street, West End
North Side, St Giles and St George
Bloomsbury, registered for Poor Rate
(CLS: UTAH MF98 item8)

Simons (Jeweller)
147 HOLTOM, P47
Round Court
1731 possibly Samuel Simmons, Golden
Ball, New Round Court, advertised in

The Daily Advertiser for the return of a
lost ring, goldsmith *(BL: Burney 289B,
03 Dec 1731)*
1734 possibly Henry Simmons, Sheltons
Court, registered for Poor Rate *(WAC:
MF1577 F488 item3)*

Simson (Watchmaker)
114 WEATHERHEAD, P63
Glasshouse Street
1710 possibly John Simson, free; 1723
possibly John Simson, free *(Britten)*
1732 John Simpson, Glasshouse Street,
later Brewer Street; 1715 apprenticed;
1723 free, died 1743 *(Baillie)*
1734 John Simpson and 1735 Simson,
listed in the Clockmakers' Company
South West Walk *(GLMS: 2715 vol 4)*
1734 Jno Simpson, Glasshouse Street
South, registered for Poor Rate *(WAC:
MF655 D39 item1 Church & Market Sq
division)*

Skinner (Watchmaker)
5 BULSTRODE, P69
Barbicon
1713–50 possibly Mathew Skinner,
watchmaker *(Britten)*
1733 possibly Abel Skinner, Barbican,
Cripplegate Without ward, registered
for Land Tax *(GLMS: 11316 vol 103)*

Smallman (Broker / pawnbroker)
129 BULSTRODE, P72
Hounds Ditch
1728 John Smallman, Old Bailey trial
concerning stolen clothing offered to
him for pawn, pawnbroker *(OBP:
t17280117-1)*
1734 John Smallman, Houndsditch,
Houndsditch precinct, Portsoken
ward, registered for Land Tax *(GLMS:
MF11316 vol 107)*
1736 John Smallman, Golden
Wheatsheaf, Houndsditch, ceased
trading, pawnbroker *(Heal and Hart)*

Smith (Broker)
11 HOLTOM, P41
Ye Wheat Sheaf, Warwick Ct,
Warwick Lane
1733 possibly Chas Smith, St Martin's
Ludgate precinct, Farringdon Without
ward, registered for Land Tax *(GLMS:
MF11316 vol 102)*

Smith (Broker / pawnbroker)
132 WEATHERHEAD, P65
St James's, Market Lane
1723–25 Mrs Hannah Smith, Old Golden
Hall, Charles Street, St James's market,
pawnbroker *(Heal)*
1730 Mrs Smith, Market Lane, near St
James's Market, Old Bailey trial
concerning a diamond ring stolen from
John Treble, pawnbroker (p125)
(OBP: t17300228-24)
1734 Widow Smith, Market Lane, Pall
Mall, registered for Poor Rate *(WAC:
MF655 D39 item1, Church & Market
division)*

Mrs Smith (Goldsmith)
15 BULSTRODE, P69
Red Cross Street
1733 possibly Henry and Robert Smith,
Crowthers Well Alley, Red Cross Street
precinct, Cripplegate Without ward,
registered for Land Tax *(GLMS:
MF11316 vol 103)*

Smith (Broker)
122 BULSTRODE, P75
St Catherines
1734 James Smith and Robert Smith, St
Katherine Lane, St Katherine by the
Tower, Tower division, registered for
Land Tax *(GLMS: MF6010 vol 3)*

Smith (Broker)
9 BULSTRODE, P69
Bridgewaters Gardens
1733 John Smith, Bridgewater Gardens,
Red Cross Street precinct, Cripplegate
Without ward, registered for Land Tax
(GLMS: MF11316 vol 103)

Smith (Watchmaker)
96 BULSTRODE, P77
Ratcliffe highway
1693–1730 possibly John Smith, clockmaker *(Britten)*
1734 possibly Joseph, Richd, Robt and
Thos Smith and tenants, Highway
North, Upper division, St George-in-
the -East, Middx, each registered for
Land Tax *(GLMS: MF6016 vol 5)*

Smithman (Broker / pawnbroker)
70 WEATHERHEAD, P57
King Street, Bloomsbury
1734 Richd Smithman, King Street West

Concordance of variant spellings of tradesmen's names pp132–36; index of streets p138; bibliography pp140–41

End, St Giles and St George, Bloomsbury, registered for Poor Rate (CLS: UTAH MF99 item1)

1738 Richard Smitherman, Old Bailey trial concerning a gown pawned with him (OBP: t17381011-12)

1738 Richard Smitherman, Old Bailey trial concerning a silver spoon bearing the mark of Thomas Gilbert TGM [sic], pawnbroker (OBP: t17381011-14)

1743 Mr Smitheman, The Three Balls/Three Blue Bowls, Eagle Street, two advertisements in The Daily Advertiser for customers to redeem their pledged items, pawnbroker deceased (BL: Burney 379B, 28 Jan 1743, 28 Jun 1743)

Also: **Smithman** (Broker)
71 WEATHERHEAD, P59
Litle Russell Street, Bloomsbury
Not found

Smiths (Broker/pawnbroker)
201 HOLTOM, P51
Pye street, Westminster

1734 Mr Smith, Old Pye Street North and South, registered twice for Poor Rate (WAC: MF 2364, E355)

1744 Mr Smith, Four Sugar-Loaves, Old Pye-Street, Westminster, advertised in The Daily Advertiser for customers to redeem their pledged items (BL: Burney 381B, 15 Feb 1744)

1744 Mrs Ann Smith, Golden Ball, cnr of Orchard and Chapel Streets, Westminster, advertisement in The Daily Advertiser for customers to redeem their pawned items, lately deceased (BL: Burney 381B, 08 May 1744)

Smithson (Broker/pawnbroker)
88 WEATHERHEAD, P59
Castle Street, Long Acre

1718 Mrs Smithson, Blackamoors Head, Castle Street, Long Acre, pawnbroker (Heal)

1738 Mrs Smithson of Holborn, Old Bailey trial concerning her purchase of a stolen watch, broker and pawnbroker (OBP: t17381206-12)

1744 possibly Mr George Smithson, Corner of Middle Row, Holborn Bars, advertised in The Daily Advertiser that he had stopt a watch by Herring (BL: Burney 381B, 21 Feb 1744)

Snow (Goldsmith/banker)
90 HOLTOM, P45
without Temple Barr

1734 Thomas Snow, low end of St Martin's Lane, registered for Poor Rate (WAC: MF1577 F488 item3)

1734-37 Mess Snow & Poltack, Golden Anchor without Temple Bar, advertised three times in The Daily Journal, The London Daily Post & General Advertiser and The Daily Post for the return of lost items, bankers (BL: Burney 304B, 18 Nov 1734; 308B, 30 Nov 1734; 325B(reel 1), 01 Jul 1737)

1742 Thomas Snow & Co, Fleet Street, Banker; 1729, Snow & Poltack, goldsmiths; 1754–circa 1768 Snow and Denne, goldsmiths and bankers; 1768 Snow, Denne, Deene & Sandby, booksellers (Hilton-Price)

1744–68 Thomas Snow & Co, without Temple Bar, goldsmiths and bankers; 1754–circa 1768 Thomas Snow & William Denne, without Temple Bar, goldsmiths and bankers (Heal)

1744 Mess Snow & Co, without Temple-Bar, advertised in The Daily Advertiser for the return of a lost banknote (BL: Burney 381B, 10 Apr 1744)

Southam (Goldsmith)
19 WEATHERHEAD, P53
Smithfield Bars

1733 Giles Southam, Christ Church 2 precinct, Farringdon Within ward, registered for Land Tax (GLMS: MF11316 vol 103)

1734 Giles Southam, near Smithfield Bars, smallworker (Grimwade)

1738–39 Giles Southam listed in a Notice in The London Daily Post & General Advertiser stating charity money collected at the Feast of the Sons of the Clergy enabled an apprentice to be placed with him (BL: Burney 340B, 19 Feb 1738-9)

1744 Giles Southam, Little Britain, London, advertised with Job Lilley (p111) and others in The Daily Advertiser for the creditors of the goldsmith, Joseph Pargiter, goldsmith (BL: Burney 397B, 20 Nov 1744)

1745 Giles Southam, Little Britain with Thomas Caldecott (Heal)

Spencer (Goldsmith)
65 WEATHERHEAD, P57
New turn Stile Passage, Holborn

1733 Wm Spencer, Turn Stile, St Giles and St George Bloomsbury, registered for Poor Rate (CLS: UTAH MF98 item8)

Spragg (Goldsmith)
117 WEATHERHEAD, P63
Vere Street by Oxford Chapel

1734 Charles Sprage, corner of Chapel Court nr Oxford Chapel, largeworker (Grimwade)

1734 Charles Sprage, Chapel Court, plateworker (Heal)

Spring (Goldsmith)
178 HOLTOM, P49
Hartshorne Lane in the Strand

1701 William Spring, Strand near Charing Cross, plateworker (Grimwade)

1701–27 William Spring, Golden Cup, nr Hungerford Market, Strand; 1734 Strand, plateworker (Heal)

1713 William Spring at the Golden Cup near Charing Cross, Strand in the parish of St Martin-in-the-Fields, Middx, insurance policy, no details (GLMS: 11936 vol 3 [SI.3550])

1734 William Spring, Strand, registered for Poor Rate (WAC: MF1577 F488 item3)

1738 Mr Spring 'on this Side Charing Cross', Old Bailey trial concerning a stolen cup and spoon he had bought (OBP: t17381011-9)

Mrs Stevens (Broker)
72 BULSTRODE, P75
Ship Alley
Not found

Stevens (Goldsmith*)
43 BULSTRODE, P71
Bishop Gate Street

1734 James Stevens, Hand Alley, 3rd division, Bishopsgate Without ward, registered for Land Tax (GLMS: MF11316 vol 105)

1736 James Stevens, Old Bailey trial concerning a watch taken from a glass case hanging in his shop (OBP: t17360908-10)

1755 possibly Nathaniel Stevens, without Bishopsgate, Old Bailey trial concerning a stolen tankard (OBP: t17550226-34)

Steventon (Goldsmith)
143 BULSTRODE, P69
Golden Lane
1740 Stevenson (who goes by the name of Penn) in Golden Lane, Old Bailey trial concerning a stolen silver spoon pawned with him (OBP: t17400903-19)
1744 Mrs Stevenson, Golden Lane, advertised in *The Daily Advertiser* for the return of a watch by John Rainsford, pawnbroker (BL: Burney 397B, 19 Aug 1744)
1745 Widow Stevenson, Golden Cup, Golden Lane, St Lukes, pawnbroker (Heal)

Stock (Watchmaker*)
62 BULSTRODE, P72
White Chaple
1700 circa, Jabez Stock, Whitechapel; a long case clock made by him bears the wording 'I labour here with all my might / To tell the time by day and night / In thy devotion copy me / And serve thy God as I serve thee', clockmaker (Britten)
1742 possibly Andrew Stock and Catherine his wife, Old Bailey trial concerning a shew glass containing many silver items stolen from his shop (OBP: t17420224-6)

Stone (Broker / pawnbroker)
104 HOLTOM, P45
Stanhope Street, Clare Market
1734 Thos Stone, Stanhope Street, registered for Poor Rate (WAC: MF183 B38 item2)
1758 Thomas Stone, Rose & Three Balls, Princes Street, Clare Market, pawnbroker (Heal)

Mrs Stone (Broker / pawnbroker)
1 BULSTRODE, P69
Barbicon
1722 Mrs Stone, Barbican, on receipt of a Goldsmiths' Hall Warning, she stopt a stolen watch; associated advertisement from Goldsmiths Beadle for the benefits of advertising through Goldsmiths' Hall Warnings system (OBP: t17220907-18; advert OBP: a17220907-1 (see p10))
1733 Widow Stone, 4th precinct,

Aldersgate Without ward, registered for Land Tax (GLMS: MF11316 vol 102)

Stone (Broker / pawnboker)
17 BULSTRODE, P69
White Cross Street
1727 possibly Mr Stone, two Old Bailey trials concerning a stolen silver watch belonging to Andrew Moran (p115) and other stolen silver items, pawnbroker (OBP: t17271206-35; t17330112-25)
1733 Edward Stone, Cock Alley, White Cross Street precinct, Cripplegate Without ward, registered for Land Tax (GLMS: MF11316 vol 103)

Stow (Broker)
82 HOLTOM, P45
Chichester Rents, Chancery Lane
Not found

Stringer (Broker / pawnbroker)
110 HOLTOM, P45
Drury Lane, angle Russell Court
1734 Geo Stringer, Drury Lane, registered for Poor Rate (WAC: MF183 B38 item2)
1735 George Stringer, Old Bailey trial concerning 'Cloaths' pawned with him in Drury Lane, pawnbroker (OBP: t17350226-14)
1739 George Stringer, acquitted at an Old Bailey trial of receiving a stolen gold watch in case, pawnbroker (OBP: t17390221-20)
1743–44 Mr George Stringer, Three Bowls, Drury-Lane, nr The Playhouse, advertised twice in *The Daily Advertiser*, announcing he had stopped a stolen silver mug and seeking the return of items valued at £140 stolen from his house (BL: Burney 379B, 25 Apr 1743; 387B, 14 Jan 1744)
1744 George Stringer, 'I am a Broker and live in Drury Lane', Old Bailey trial concerning various items pawned with him, pawnbroker (OBP: t17440223-19)
1745 George Stringer, Three Bowls, cnr Bennets Ct, Drury Lane, pawnbroker (Heal)
1748 —Stringer, Drury Lane, Old Bailey trial concerning stolen plate pawned with him, pawnbroker (OBP: t17480224-1)
1749 George Stringer, Drury Lane, parish of St Clement Danes and St Mary-le-

Strand, Westminster Pollbook, pawnbroker (WAC: CDRom)
1752 William Stringer, Three Blue Balls, Bennetts Ct, Drury Lane, pawnbroker (Heal)

Stroud (Broker / pawnbroker)
95 WEATHERHEAD, P59
St Andrews Street, 7 Dials
1734 Wdo Stroud, St Andrews Street North side, St Giles and St George Bloomsbury, registered for Poor Rate (CLS: UTAH MF99 item1)
1743 Mr Stroud, Golden Key, Great St Andrew Street, advertised in *The Daily Advertiser* for customers to redeem their pledged items he leaving off that business (BL: Burney 387B, 06 Oct 1743)

Stroud (Broker)
47 WEATHERHEAD, P55
Leather Lane
1733 Thos Strode, Leather Lane, Liberty of Saffron Hill, registered for Poor Rate (CLS: UTAH MF415 item4)

T

Taylor (Broker / pawnbroker)
155 HOLTOM, P47
Maiden Lane
1728 possibly Mr Taylor, Old Bailey trial concerning a stolen watch pawned with him (OBP: t17280501-8)
1732 possibly Mary Taylor, Old Bailey trial concerning three stolen spoons pawned with her, pawnbroker (OBP: t17320419-2)
1734 Mary Savill Taylor, Maiden Lane South, registered for Poor Rate (WAC: MF1959 H43 item14)

Tellers Office (No trade)
195 HOLTOM, P51
Westminster Hall

Thibauld (Jeweller)
39 HOLTOM, P43
Fetter Lane
1715 Mr Thibault, Hind Court, Tithe assessment (GLMS: 3011)
1733 Thos Teboe, Fetter Lane, Farringdon Without ward registered for Land Tax (GLMS: MF11316 vol 104)
1734 Thomas Thibault (Teboe), Fetter Lane, goldsmith (Heal)

Thornborough (Watchmaker)
172 HOLTOM, P49
York Buildings
1734 John Thornburgh, Villers Street, registered for Poor Rate (*WAC: MF1577 F488 item3*)
1734 John Thornburg, parish of St Martin-in-the-Fields, insured his household goods, and goods in house at the Dial on west side of Villars Street York Buildings for £300, watchmaker (*GLMS: 11936 vol 41 [SI.64205]*)
1740 John Thornburgh, London (*Britten*)
1743 Mr John Thornburgh, Villar's Street, York Buildings, advertised in *The Daily Advertiser* for the return of a lost watch, watchmaker (*BL: Burney 379B, 10 May 1743*)

Threlgale (Goldsmith and toyman)
111 HOLTOM, P45
in Russell Court
1734 William Threlkield, Russell Court, registered for Poor Rate (*WAC: MF1577 F488 item3*)
1743 Mr Threlkeld, Russell Court, Drury-Lane, advertised in *The Daily Advertiser* for the return of stolen silver spoons, silversmith (*BLCol: Burney 689B, 04 Jan 1743*)
1742–45 possibly William Threlkeld, Ring and Ball, the Bottom of the Minories, Tower Hill, who advertised four times in *The Daily Advertiser*, goldsmith (*BL: Burney, 381B, 20 Nov 1742; 379B, 30 Dec 1742; 387B, 12 Jul 1743, 21 Dec 1743*)
1745 William Threlkeld of London, Old Bailey trial concerning deception and forgery, goldsmith (*OBP: t17451016-16*)

Threlgle (Watchmaker)
163 HOLTOM, P47
in the Strand
1700–10 William Threlkeld, 'in ye Strand'; 'W Threlkeld London signed on an engraved silver watchcase with mark GK', watchmaker (*Britten*)
1733, 1734 Threlcold and 1735 Wm Threlkeld, listed in Clockmakers' Company South West Walk (*GLMS: 2715 vol 4*)
1734 William Threlkeld, Strand, registered for Poor Rate (*WAC: MF1577 F488 item3*)

Tidmarsh (Broker)
86 WEATHERHEAD, P59
Bromley Street
1734 John Tidmarsh, Brownlow Street, St Giles and St George Bloomsbury, registered for Poor Rate (*CLS: UTAH MF99 item1*)

Tollson (Watchmaker)
41 BULSTRODE, P71
Bishop Gate Street
1715 John Toleson, free of the Clockmakers' Company, watchmaker (*Britten*)
1734 Jno Tolson, Hand Alley, possible tenant of Eliz Priddy, 3rd division, Bishopsgate Without ward, registered for Land Tax (*GLMS: MF11316 vol 105*)

Tonlain (Watchmaker)
85 WEATHERHEAD, P59
Bromley Street
Before 1752 possibly T. Tomlin or Tomlyn (*Baillie*)

Tower (Broker)
30 WEATHERHEAD, P55
Cow Cross
1734 possibly Alexander Torey, Sharps Alley, Cow Cross, registered for Poor Rate (*GLMS: 9110 vol 1*)

Treble (Jeweller*)
157 WEATHERHEAD, P67
Litchfield Street
1725 John Trible, Coventry Court, upper end of Hay-Market, advertised in *The Daily Courant* for the return of stolen goods, jeweller (*BLCol: Burney 301B, 07 Apr 1725*)
1730 John Treble, Old Bailey trial concerning a ring stolen from his shop (*OBP: t17300228-24*)
1734 John Treble, Litchfield Street, registered for Poor Rate (*WAC: MF32 A134*)
1749 John Treble, Litchfield Street, parish of St Anns, Westminster Pollbook, jeweller (*WPB*)

Trip (Broker / pawnbroker)
79 WEATHERHEAD, P59
in ye Cole Yard, Drury Lane
1734 Job Tripp, Coal Yard, St Giles and St George Bloomsbury, registered for Poor Rate (*CLS: UTAH MF99 item1*)
1738 Job Trip, Old Bailey trial concerning silver spoons pawned with him at his house, pawnbroker (*OBP: t17380906-8*)
1754 —Trip, St Martin's Lane, large-worker (*Grimwade*)
1754 Job Trip, Golden Ball, St Martin's Lane, facing May's Buildings, plate-worker (*Heal*)
1755 Job Tripp, Old Bailey trial concerning theft from his house; he states: 'I advertised [the stolen items] at Goldsmiths' hall, from whence notice is given to all the pawnbrokers and such places in four hours time, by distributing bills, I am a Goldsmith' (*OBP: t17550409-25*)
1758 Job Tripp, the Golden Ball in Leadenhall Street, insured his household goods in brick house, stock in trade, wrought and manufactured plate £500, utensils in the workshop behind, etc for £800, silversmith (*GLMS: 11936 vol 125 [SI.165756]*) And other later policies not included here

Tropher (Broker)
32 WEATHERHEAD, P55
Peters Street, Cow Cross
Not found

Truclock (Broker / pawnbroker)
77 BULSTRODE, P72
Little Minories
1730 Tho Truclock, Trinity Minories, Tower Hill, registered for Sewer Rate (*LMA: THCS 143*)
1743 Mr Thomas Truclock, the Golden Ball in the Minories, advertisement in *The Daily Advertiser* for customers to redeem their pledged items, deceased (*BL: Burney 387B, 19 Sept 1743*)

Tucker (Watchmaker)
174 HOLTOM, P49
angle Hungerford Market
Before 1726 Christopher Tucker, probably London (*Baillie*)
1726 Christopher Tucker, next door to the King's Tavern in the Strand over against Hungerford Market, advertised in *Mist's Weekly Journal* for the return of a stolen watch by Christopher Tucker (*BLCol: Burney 885B, 24 Sept 1726*)
1733, 1734 and 1735 Chr Tucker, listed in Clockmakers' Company South West Walk (*GLMS: 2715 vol4*)

1739 Mr Tucker, at his house in the Strand, against Hungerford-Market, advertised in *The London Daily Post & General Advertiser* for the return of a lost watch by Tucker *(BL: Burney, 340B, 30 Apr 1739)*

Turmeau (Jeweller)
184 WEATHERHEAD, P67
Orange Street
1748–55 possibly Allain Turmeau, Golden Key, Grafton Street; Golden Key, Litchfield Street; 1762 died, goldsmith; 1762 Jane Turmeau, successor to Allain Turmeau, Golden Key Litchfield Street; 1790–96 Turmeau & Kettlewell, no123 Villiers Street, Strand, jewellers *(Heal)*

Turner (Watchmaker)
43 WEATHERHEAD, P55
Hatton Garden
1709–52 Joseph Turner, Fleet Street and Clerkenwell *(Britten)*
1714–45 possibly Thomas Turner, clockmaker *(Britten)*
1733 Joseph Turner, Hatton Garden East Side, Liberty of Saffron Hill, registered for Poor Rate *(CLS: UTAH MF415 item4)*
1733 Josh Turner and 1734 —Turner, listed in Clockmakers' Company North Walk *(GLMS: 2715 vol 4)*

Turquand (Jeweller)
180 HOLTOM, P49
Northumberland Court, in the Strand
1734 Samuel Turquand, Somerset Court, Strand, registered for Poor Rate *(WAC: MF1577 F488 item3)*
1743 Mr Isaac Turquand, Crown & Ring, Northumberland-Court, Strand, advertised twice in *The Daily Advertiser* for the return of lost rings, jeweller *(BL: Burney 379B, 03 Feb 1743, 22 Mar 1743)*
1747, —Turquand, Northumberland Court, Strand, jeweller *(Heal)*
Possible Huguenot origin

Turrel (Goldsmith)
124 HOLTOM, P47
Russel Street
Not found

V

Vaughan (Broker / pawnbroker)
132 HOLTOM, P47
Dirty Lane, Long Acre
1728 Mr Vaughn, Old Bailey trial concerning stolen plate brought to him for sale, pawnbroker *(OBP: t17280228-47)*
1734 Edward Vaughan, Dirty Lane, registered for Poor Rate; again in Russell Court *(WAC: MF1577 F488 item3)*

Vaughan (Goldsmith)
144 WEATHERHEAD, P67
Princes Street by St Anns Church
1724 George Vaughan, Princes Street over against Lisle Street, parish of St James, Westminster, insured goods and merchandise in his dwelling house for £500, goldsmith *(GLMS: 11936 vol 17 [SI.32409])*
1731 —Vaughan, Blackamoor's Head, Princes Street, Leicester Fields, goldsmith *(Heal)*
1734 Geo Vaughan, Princes Street, registered for Poor Rate *(WAC: MF655 D39 item1 Gt Marlboro division)*

Vedeau (Goldsmith*)
183 WEATHERHEAD, P67; FIG 47
Orange Street
1723 Aymé Videau, apprenticed; 1733/34? free; 1739 Green Street, Leicester Fields; 1746 Goldsmiths' Company Livery; … his output [chased] from the mid-thirties, plateworker *(Grimwade)*
1734 Amy Vedeau, Green Street South, registered for Poor Rate *(WAC: MF1577 F488 item3)*
1737 Amy Vedeau, Old Bailey trial concerning a silver watch stolen from his shop *(OBP: t17370216-34)*
1739–73 Aymé Videau, Green Street, Leicester Field, plateworker *(Heal)*
1742 Amey Vedeau, with others, voluntarily yielded up his freedom of the Goldsmiths' Company in order to become an unbiased witness for the Company against the Counterfeiters of the Hall Marks; at a later date his freedom was restored as if it had never been yielded up *(GCCB, vol 15, 1742–53, p2)*
1749 Ayme Vedeau, Green Street, St Martin's, Westminster Pollbook *(WPB)*

Vick (Watchmaker)
114 HOLTOM, P45
angle Catherine St in the Strand
1692–1750 Richard Vick, Strand, watchmaker to his Majesty *(Britten)*
1750 'Last Saturday died at his House in King Street, St Ann's, Mr de Vic, Watchmaker to his Royal Highness, the Prince of Wales' *The London Evening Post (BLCol: Burney 436B, 20-23 Jan 1750)*

W

Wallis (Jeweller)
62 HOLTOM, P43
at a Fan Shop
1721 Peter Wallis, Fleet Street, served as a Questman**, jeweller; 1731, listed as inhabitant of St Brides parish, goldsmith *(GLMS: 6561)*
1733 Peter Wallis, Hanging Sword Alley, Fleet Street precinct, Farringdon Without ward *(GLMS: MF11316, vol 104)*
**See Bristow p87 and Robinson p120

Ward (Broker)
94 BULSTRODE, P77
Ratcliffe highway
1734 Wm Ward, Highway South, Upper division, St George-in-the-East, Middx, registered for Land Tax *(GLMS: MF 6016, vol 5)*

Warner (Broker / pawnbroker)
81 BULSTRODE, P75
King Street
1734 Tho Warner, King Street, St Botolph-Without-Aldgate, registered for Land Tax *(GLMS: MF6011 vol 4)*
1737 Thomas Warner, Old Bailey trial concerning an attempt to pledge two silver salts with him *(OBP: t17371012-25)*
1743 Mr Thomas Warner, Three Blue Bowls in King-Street, near Tower-Hill, advertisement in *The Daily Advertiser* for customers to redeem their pledged items, deceased *(BL: Burney 387B, 28 Nov 1743)*
1744 Thomas Warner, Three Balls, King Street, Tower Hill, pawnbroker *(Heal)*
1744 Thomas Warner, late of King Street, Tower Hill, two advertisements in *The Daily Advertiser* calling creditors' meetings, pawnbroker deceased *(BL: Burney*

387B, 02 Feb 1744; 397B, 25 Jul 1744)
1744 Thomas Warner late of King-Street, Tower-Hill, near the Victualling Office, two announcements in *The Daily Advertiser* of the auction of his Jewels and Watches by Tho Leach, pawn-broker deceased *(BL: Burney 381B, 27 Feb 1744, 01 May 1744)*

Warters (Goldsmith)
23 HOLTOM, P43
Holborn Bridge
1697? Richard Warter in Barbican, small-worker: Goldsmiths' Company Warden 1745–47 died *(Grimwade)*
1708–47died, Richard Warter, Golden Lion, Holborn Bridge, silversmith *(Heal)*
1722 Richard Warter of Golden Lyon in Holbourn Bridge, parish of St Andrews Holbourn, insured his goods and merchandise, etc in his house for £500, goldsmith *(GLMS: 11936 vol 14 [SI.26669])*
1724 Richard Warter, Golden Lyon in Holbourn Bridge, parish of St Andrew's, Holbourn, insured various tenanted houses and workshop for £500, goldsmith *(GLMS: 11936 vol 16 [SI.31783])*
1726 Richard Warter, Golden Lyon in Holbourn Bridge, parish of St Andrew, Holbourn, insured two houses in Black & White Court, Old Bailey in several possessions; six houses in Boxford Court in New Street in several occupations for £500, goldsmith *(GLMS: 11936 vol 22 [SI.39717])*
1733 Richard Waters, Ditch Side, nr Shoe Lane, Farringdon Without ward, regis-tered for Land Tax *(GLMS: MF11316 vol 104)*

Waters (Broker / pawnbroker)
20 WEATHERHEAD, P53
Charterhouse Lane
1729 Thomas Waters and 1731 Jonathan Waters, Sun, Charterhouse Lane, West Smithfield, pawnbrokers *(Heal)*
1731 Jonathan Waters, The Sun, Charterhouse Lane, near West-Smithfield, advertised in *The Daily Advertiser* that he had stopt six silver tea-spoons, pawnbroker *(BL: Burney 289B, 30 Nov 1731)*
1734 Jonathan Waters, Charterhouse Lane, registered for Poor Rate *(GLMS: 9110 vol 1)*

Mrs Waters (Broker / pawnbroker)
125 BULSTRODE, P75
St Catherines
1734 William Waters, Flemish Church Yard, St Katherines by the Tower, Tower division, registered for Land Tax *(GLMS: MF6010 vol 3)*
1744 Mrs Elizabeth Waters, widow, Flemish-Church-Yard, St Katherines, advertised in *The Daily Advertiser* for customers to redeem their pledged items, she leaving off Business, pawn-broker *(BL: Burney 381B, 18 Apr 1744)*

Wessea (Jeweller)
19 HOLTOM, P41
Ye Old Bailey
1733 and 1735 possibly John Wellington, listed in Clockmakers' Company South West Walk *(GLMS: 2715 vol 4)*
1734 possibly John Wellington & partner, Old Bailey Corner, St Martin's Ludgate precinct, Farringdon Without ward, registered for Land Tax *(GLMS: MF11316 vol 107)*
1734 possibly John Wellington & Co. Without the Gate, St Martin's, Ludgate, registered for Poor Rate *(GLMS: 1315, vol 1)*

West (Goldsmith)
20 HOLTOM, P41
Ye Old Bailey
1705 Matthew West, Foster Lane; Goldsmiths' Company Livery, large-worker *(Grimwade)*
1731–35 Matthew West, Seven Stars, Sun Tavern over against the Old Bailey, goldsmith *(Heal)*
1734 Mathew West, Without the Gate St Martins Ludgate registered for Poor Rate *(GLMS: 1315, vol 1)*

White (Goldsmith)
186 WEATHERHEAD, P67
Orange Street
1734 possibly John White, corner of Greek Street [south cnr of Green St], registered for Poor Rate *(WAC: MF1577 F488 item3)*
1739 John White, Green Street, plate-worker *(Heal)*
1739 John White, corner of Green Street, Leicester Fields, plateworker *(Grimwade)*

White (Broker / pawnbroker)
44 WEATHERHEAD, P55
Baldwins Gardens
1725 —White, a pawnbroker in Baldwin's Gardens, Old Bailey trial reveals that a silver porringer and other items were pawned with him. The owner had distributed printed advertisements to goldsmiths and pawnbrokers to retrieve the goods and Mr White sent his servant to demand the reward promised in the advertise-ment *(OBP: t17250513-22)*
1729 Mr White, Baldwin's Gardens, advertised in *Fog's Weekly Journal* stating he had a lost cane in his posses-sion, pawnbroker *(BLCol: Burney 331B, 27 Sep 1729)*
1732 possibly Richard White, Baldwin's Gardens, St Andrew Holborn, St George the Martyr, registered for Poor Rate *(CLS: UTAH MF29 item6)*
Also: **White** (Watchmaker)
45 WEATHERHEAD, P55
Leather Lane
1683–1743 possibly Thomas White, clock-maker *(Baillie vol 2)*
1714–66 possibly Joseph White, London; also Joseph White, free 1714 *(Baillie and Baillie vol 2)*

Wichcott (Watchmaker)
42 HOLTOM, P43
Corner of Flower-de-Luces Court, Fleet St
1716–75 Samuel Whichcote, Crane Court, Fleet Street; 1754–65 Fleet Street *(Britten)*
1733, 1734 and 1735 Samuel Whichcote in Clockmakers' Company South West Walk *(GLMS: 2715 vol 4)*
1733 Samuel Whichcote, Fleet Street, St Dunstan-in-the-West precinct, Farringdon Without ward registered for Land Tax *(GLMS: MF11316 vol 104)*

Wike (Goldsmith)
55 WEATHERHEAD, P57
near Midle Row
1732 possibly Peter Wyke, Holborn, St Andrew Holborn, St George the Martyr, registered for Poor Rate *(CLS: UTAH MF29 item6)*
1757 died, possibly Francis Wyke, opp Grays Inn Gate, Holborn, goldsmith *(Heal)*

Wild (Broker / pawnbroker)
18 BULSTRODE, P69
White Cross Street
1734 Robert Wild, White Cross Street, White Cross Street precinct, Cripplegate Without ward, registered for Land Tax (GLMS: MF11316 vol 103)
1737 Mr Wild, White Cross Street, Old Bailey trial concerning seven pieces-of-eight from a total haul of £470 worth of coin – Goods of the Governor and Company of Merchants trading to the South-Sea, pawnbroker (OBP: t17370526-38)
1744 Mr Wild at three balls in Whitecross Street, Old Bailey trial concerning clothing pawned with him, pawnbroker (OBP: t17440912-35)

Mrs Wilder (Broker)
68 BULSTRODE, P72
Colchester Street, Goodmans Fields
1734 Possibly William Hilder, Liberty of Wells Close, Tower division, registered for Land Tax (GLMS: MF6004 no16)

Wildman (Goldsmith)
22 HOLTOM, P41
Snow Hill
1720 Thomas Wildman in the parish of St Pulcher [St Sepulchre] Snow Hill, smallworker (Grimwade)
1733 Thomas Wildman, Snow Hill, Holborn Cross, Farringdon Without ward, registered for Land Tax (GLMS: MF11316 vol 104)
1742–62 Thomas Wildman at Black-a-moors Head, Cheapside, goldsmith (Heal)

Wildy (Toyman*)
15 HOLTOM, P41
at the Corner of St Paul's Chyard
1733 Geo Wildey registered for Land Tax in West precinct, Castle Baynard ward (GLMS: MF11316 vol 103)
1736–37 Geo Wildey at Willdey's Great Toy-Shop, the Corner of Ludgate Street by St Paul's advertised three times in The Daily Post detailing his stock in trade including spectacles (BL: Burney 319B, 17 Feb 1736; 325B (reel 1), 10 Mar 1737; 332B, 21 Feb 1738)
1739–44 Mr Willdey, Ludgate Street, advertised three times in The Daily Post, The London Daily Post & General

Advertiser and The Daily Post for the return of lost items, toyman (BL: Burney 340B, 21 Jun 1739; 341B, 05 Dec 1739; 379B, 10 Jan 1744)
1740 'Yesterday died very rich, at her lodgings at Clapton in Hackney, Mrs Willdey, who kept the Great Toy Shop in St. Paul's Churchyard', The London Post & General Advertiser (BL: Burney 347B, 29 Mar 1740)
1748 Tuesday Morning died in an Apoplectick Fit, Mr Thomas Wildey, Master of the Great Toy Shop, the Corner of St. Paul's', The Penny London Post (BL: Burney 427B, 20-22 Jul 1748)

Wilkinson (Goldsmith)
36 BULSTRODE, P71
Bishop Gate Street
1734 Mr Richd Wilkinson, Bishopsgate Street, 3rd division, Bishopsgate Without ward, registered for Land Tax (GLMS: MF11316 vol 105)
1743 Mr Wilkinson, Bishopsgate Street, advertisement in The Daily Advertiser for customers to redeem their pledged items, silversmith deceased (BL: Burney 379B, 02 May 1743)

Willaume (Goldsmith)
124 WEATHERHEAD, P65; FIG 34
St James's Street
1706–46 David Willaume, junior, London; 1716–20 Golden Ball on the terrace in St James's Street; 1721 St Martin-in-the-Fields, goldsmith and banker (Heal)
1710 David Willaume, against St Albans Street in Pall Mall, parish of St James's Westminster, Middx insured his goods (French policy), goldsmith (GLMS: 11936 vol 1 [SI.792])
1714 David Willaume, 1707 account for a silver teapot; 1728 circa David Willaume Snr retired (no335 Quiet Conquest)
1728 David Willaume II, St James Street off St George Hanover Square, largeworker (Grimwade)
1734 David Willaume, St James's Street, registered for Poor Rate (WAC: MF476 C157 item13)
1737–43 Mess Willaume and Jordens, the Terras, St James's Street, advertised in The Daily Post and The Daily Advertiser for the return of a watch by Dutan and a silver tablespoon, goldsmith (BL:

Burney 325B (reel 1), ** Mar 1737; 379B, 02 Jun 1743)

Williams (Goldsmith)
193 HOLTOM, P51
King St, Westminster
1726 Robert Williams, Golden Unicorn, King St, Westminster, largeworker (Grimwade)
1726–62 died, Robert Williams, Golden Unicorn, King Street, Westminster, plateworker (Heal)
1734 Robt A Williams, King Street, registered for Poor Rate (WAC: MF2364 E355)
1737–38 and 1743 Mr Robert Williams, King-Street, Westminster, advertised twice in The Daily Post & General Advertiser and The Daily Advertiser for the return of lost items, respectively silversmith and goldsmith (BL: Burney 332B, 07 Feb 1737-8; 387B, 22 Nov 1743)
1749 Robert Williams, King Street, St Margaret, Westminster & St John the Evangelist, listed in Westminster Pollbook, goldsmith (WPB)
1749 'A few days since died at his house in King Street, Westminster, of a Cancer in her Breast, Mrs Williams, Wife of Mr Williams, an eminent and wealthy Silversmith' The General Advertiser (BLCol: Burney 431B, 02 Nov 1749)

Willmot (Broker / pawnbroker)
132 BULSTRODE, P72
Hounds Ditch
1731 John Willmot, Clothworkers Shears, Houndsditch, pawnbroker (Heal)
1733 John Willmot, Houndsditch, 1st division, Bishopsgate Without ward, registered for Land Tax (GLMS: MF11316 vol 102)

Willson (Watchmaker)
34 HOLTOM, P43
New Street
1707–14 possibly John Wilson, Kings Head Court, Holborn, watchmaker (Britten)
1726 onwards, possibly William Willson, New Street, smallworker (Grimwade)
1733 —Wilson, New Street, New Street precinct, Farringdon Without ward registered for Land Tax with Sarah (GLMS: MF11316 vol 104)

1734 John Willson, New Street South registered for Poor Rate (GLMS: MF1577 F488 item3)
1735 John Wilson in the Clockmakers' Company North Walk and 1735 in the New Walk (GLMS: 2175, vol 4)

Winch (Broker)
92 BULSTRODE, P77
Ratcliffe highway
Not found

Woodford (Broker)
196 HOLTOM, P51
by the Church
1734 Jn Woodford, Sanctuary, Westminster, registered for Poor Rate (WAC: MF 2364, E355)

Woodman (Broker)
36 WEATHERHEAD, P55
Saffron Hill
1733 possibly Eliz and Wm Woodland, Saffron Hill, Liberty of Saffron Hill, registered for Poor Rate (CLS: UTAH MF415 item4)
1733 possibly John Widman, Saffron Hill, Liberty of Saffron Hill, registered for Poor Rate (CLS: UTAH MF415 item4)

Woolley (Broker)
59 BULSTRODE, P72
Smock Alley
1734 Geo Woolley, Pettycoat Lane, 1st division, St Mary Whitechapel, registered for Land Tax (GLMS: MF6015 vol 2)

Wright (Watchmaker)
119 WEATHERHEAD, P65
new Bond Street near Piccadilly
1728–81 possibly John Wright (Britten)
1734, John Wright, Bond Street, registered for Poor Rate (WAC: MF476 C157 item13)
1735 –Wright, listed in Clockmakers' Company South West Walk (GLMS: 2715 vol 4)
1743 Mrs Frances Wright, late of Bond Street, advertised her creditors' meeting in The Daily Advertiser (BL: Burney 379B, 17 Mar 1743)
Also: **Wright** (Broker)
120 WEATHERHEAD, P65
Vine Street
Not found

Wyborn (Broker/pawnbroker)
34 WEATHERHEAD, P55
Saffron hill
1729 Mr Wyburn featured in an Old Bailey trial concerning various stolen items pawned with him, pawnbroker (OBP: t17290521-48)
1733 Thos Wyburn, Saffron Hill, Liberty of Saffron Hill, registered for Poor Rate (CLS: UTAH MF415 item4)
1736 Mr Wybourn's on Saffron Hill, Old Bailey trial concerning two shirts pawned with him, pawnbroker (OBP: t17360610-3)
1738 Thomas Wybourne, Shoe Lane, inhabitant of St Bride's Fleet Street, pawnbroker (GLMS: 6561)

Wynn (Goldsmith*)
75 BULSTRODE, P72
Minories
1720 William Winne, Minories; 1724–34, Minories; 1744 near Aldgate, goldsmith (Heal)
1730 William Wynn, Old Bailey trial concerning a ring stolen from his shop (OBP: t17300228-56)
1733 possibly Henry Winn, 6th precinct, Aldgate ward, registered for Land Tax (GLMS: MF11316 vol 102)
1735 possibly Winn, listed in the Clockmakers' Company New Walk (GLMS: 2715 vol 4)
1744–45 Mr Wm Winne, of Aldgate, two Old Bailey trials concerning stolen silver spoons offered to him, a Goldsmith without Aldgate (OBP: t17441017-12; t17451016-14)

Y

Yarp (Broker/pawnbroker)
134 BULSTRODE, P72
Moor Fields
1728 Mr Yarp, Old Bailey trial concerning stolen clothing brought to him to pawn (OBP: t17281016-31)
1733 Mr Henry Yarp, Houndsditch, 1st division, Bishopsgate Without, registered for Land Tax (GLMS: MF11316 vol 102)
1736 Mr Yarp in Houndsditch, Old Bailey trial concerning stolen clothing brought to him to pawn (OBP: t17360721-11)

York (Goldsmith*)
194 HOLTOM, P51
King St, Westminster
1717–32 Edward York(e), King Street, Westminster, plateworker (Heal)
1728 possibly Mr York in Old Bailey trial concerning a stolen silver tankard (OBP: t17280501-24)
1729 Edward York, Old Bailey trial concerning a shew-glass stolen from his shop window containing a considerable number of items (OBP: t17290416-65)
1730 Edward York(e), King Street, Westminster, largeworker (Grimwade)
1734 Edwd York, King Street, Westminster, registered for Poor Rate (WAC: MF2364 E355)

******* (Broker)
202 HOLTOM, P51
Broadway, Westminster
Not found

32 *Bartholomew Fair. A man tickles the ear of his victim to distract him while he is picking his pocket.*
The fair was a notorious venue for petty crime and for the disposal of stolen property.

4

Lists

Concordance of tradesmen's names

This concordance gives, in the left column, names as found in rate books, trials and published works (see bibliography p140). The reader should be aware that those who were newspaper compositors or who collected rates were very probably no better at spelling than the compiler of the notebook (given in the right-hand column).
If there is more than one person with the same name and the same trade listed in the notebook, that name has been given only once in this concordance, but each person is listed on pp83–129 under the name in the notebook.

Name as found in publications and archives	Name as written in notebook	Name as found in publications and archives	Name as written in notebook	Name as found in publications and archives	Name as written in notebook
Brokers/pawnbrokers		Farmer (P)	Farmer	Lefevre	Lefavor
		Not found	Fennery	Longland	Longland
Allen/Allyn (P)	Allin	Ferguson	Ferguson	Maine/Man	Myne
Allome	Allome	Fitzhall	Fitzhall	*Not found*	Makin
Aris	Adsit	*Not found*	Foster	Manus	Mannus
Armsted	Armsted	Foulkes	Fowls	Mappes	Mappson
Not found	Ashbourn	Fradin	Fraydon	Martin	Martin
Babb	Budd	Francis (P)	Francis	*Not found*	Meredith
Barret	Barret	Gallwith (P)	Gallwith	Messiter	Messiter
Bartlett	Bartlett	*Not found*	Ganderoon(P)	Mitchell	Mitchell
Bashley	Bashly	Garbutt	Garbert	Morris	Morris
Not found	Battle	Gardner/Gardener	Gardener	Newenham	Newingham
Baty/Batey	Batty	Gasford	Gossford	Norwood (P)	Norwood
Beighton	Boyghton	Gay	Gay	Orme	Oman
Bell	Bell	Goddard	Goddard	Osborne	Osborn
Benson	Benson	Goffe	Gough	Paine	Payne
Bentley	Bentley	Good	Good	Parr/Par (P)	Parr
Biddell	Biddle	Goodman (P)	Goodman	Parsons (P)	Parsons
Billings	Billings	Gosling	Gosling	Perkins	Perkins
Birchmore/Burchmore (P)	Burchmore	Grainger/Granger (P)	Grainger	Perry	Perry
Booth	Booth	Grub/Grubb (P)	Grub	Peter/Peters (P)	Peters
Not found	Bowditch	Gun/Gunn (P)	Gun	Pickard (P)	Pickard
Bower	Borer	Hall (P)	Hall	Pretty (P)	Pretty
Bowman	Bowman	*Not found*	Hally	Priswell	Priswell
Bradley	Bradley	Hamlin	Hamlin	Rawlins/Rawlings (P)	Rawlings
Brigham	Brigham	Harrison (P)	Harrison	Ray	Ray
Broadhurst	Broadhurst	Hartley	Hartley	Rayes (P)	Ray
Not found	Bubb	Harvey/Harvy (P)	Harvey	Read	Read
Not found	Butterfield (P)	Hayden/Hayton (P)	Haydon	Reynold/Reynolds (P)	Reynolds
Calcot/Colcot/ Calcott (P)	Calcott	Hern	Herne	*Not found*	Rickman
Carmalt	Cormal	Herring	Hering	Rivers	Rivers
Chambers	Chambers	*Not found*	Hewett	Robinson	Robinson
Not found	Church	Hewitt	Hewett	*Not found*	Robinson
Not found	Clark	Higgenson/Higginson	Higerson	Rogers	Rogers
Cockett/Crokat	Croket	Highmore	Heymore	Rouse/Rowse (P)	Rous
Cole	Cole	Highstreet	Highstreet	Rudge (P)	Rudge
Collet	Caley	Higs	Higgs	Sadler	Sadler
Collier (P)	Collier	Hilder	Wilder	Scafe/Scaffe (P)	Scalf
Collins (P)	Rollins	Hill	Hill	Scarlett	Scarlett
Not found	Cookson	Hodges (P)	Hodges	*Not found*	Sears
Cooper	Cooper	Holmes	Holmes	Sheldon (P)	Sheldon
Cross	Cross	*Not found*	Horne	Shelley	Shelley
Curtis/Curtoys (P)	Curtoys	Hoskins	Hoskins	Shipton	Shipton
Dakin	Dokins	Howard (P)	Howard	Smallman (P)	Smallman
Daniel (P)	Daniel	Hudart (P)	Hudard	Smith (P)	Smith
Dawson	Dawson	Humfries	Humfries	Smith (P)	Smiths
Dean	Dean	Jacobsen/Jacobson (P)	Jacobsen	Smithman/Smithe(r)man (P)	Smithman
Dockra	Docher	Jarvis (P)	Jarvis	Smithson	Smithson
Doughty	Doughty	*Not found*	Jarvis	*Not found*	Stevens
Dugan/Dogan (P)	Dugin	Jenings	Jennings	Stone (P)	Stone
Edwards	Edwards	Johnson (P)	Johnson	*Not found*	Stow
Erwin	Erwin	King	King	Stringer (P)	Stringer
Evans	Evans	Kirby	Kirby	Stroud/Strode (P)	Stroud
Everett	Everitt	Kitchin/Kitchen (P)	Kitchin	Taylor (P)	Taylor
Not found	Eysham	Lane	Lane	Thatcher	Fletcher

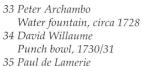

33 Peter Archambo
   Water fountain, circa 1728

34 David Willaume
   Punch bowl, 1730/31

35 Paul de Lamerie
   Ewer, 1736/37

36 William Paradise
   Teapot, 1728/29

37 John Farnell
   Tea caddies, 1716/17

38 Sarah Holaday (Halliday)
   Teapot, 1729/30

39 Thomas Folkingham
   Candlesticks, 1712/13

40 Anthony Nelme
   Dinner plates, 1719/20

41 William Lukin
   Chocolate pot, 1702/03

42 John Chartier
   Coffee pot, 1722/23

43 Charles Hatfield
   Waiter, 1731/32

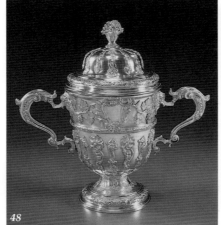

44 Louis Cuny
  Sauceboats, 1724/25
45 Ann Craig & John Neville
  Soup tureen, 1744/45
46 Isaac Davenport
  Forks, 1701/02
47 Aymé Vedeau
  Beakers, 1743/44
48 Edward Feline
  Cup and cover, 1746/47
49 Thomas Gilpin
  Salver, 1749/50
50 Paul Crespin
  Spice boxes, 1749/50
51 Augustine Courtauld
  Caster, 1726/27
52 Charles Kandler
  Candlestick, 1730/31
53 Pezé Pilleau
  Tea caddy, 1746/47
54 Samuel Wood (see p13)
  Tea caddy, 1764/65

Name as found in publications and archives	Name as written in notebook	Name as found in publications and archives	Name as written in notebook	Name as found in publications and archives	Name as written in notebook
Tidmarsh	Tidmarsh	*Not found*	Dearing	Morris	Morris
Torey	Tower	Demass	Duemas	Nelme	Nelme
Trip / Tripp (P)	Trip	*Not found*	Dovet	Nichols / Nicholle	Nichols
Not found	Tropher	Drummond (B)	Drummond	*Not found*	Nicholls
Truclock (P)	Truclock	Duge	Dugh	Pack	Pack
Vaughan / Vaughn (P)	Vaughan	Edlin / Edlen	Edlin	Page / Pages	Page
Ward	Ward	Edwards / Edmonds	Edwards	Pallairett	Pelletier
Warner (P)	Warner	England	England	Paradise / Parradice	Paradise
Waters (P)	Waters	Farnell / Fernhill	Farnel	*Not found*	Parry
White	White (P)	Feline	Feline	Pearce	Pearce
Wild (P)	Wild	Fellows	Fellows	Peart	Peart
Willmot (P)	Wilmot	Folkingham	Folkingham	Pilleau	Pilleau
Not found	Winch	Foot / Foote / ffoot	Foot	Pons	Pons
Woodford	Woodford	Fountain	Fountain	Pope	Pope
Woodland / Widman	Woodman	Fowler / ffowler	Fowler	Price	Price
Woolley	Woolley	George	George	Quillet	Quillet
Not found	Wright (P)	Gibbon	Gibbons	Radford	Radford
Wyburn / Wybourne (P)	Wyborn	Gibson	Gibson	Rainaud	Rainaud
Yarp	Yarp	Gilpin	Gilpin	Read	Road
		Godfrey / Godfry	Godfrey	Reeve / Reeves	Reeve
Goldsmiths/bankers		Gosling / Goslin / Gostling	Goslin	Ridgley / Ridgly	Rigly
		Gray / Grey	Gray	Roberts	Roberts
Admiral / Admirauld	Admiral	Green	Green	Robinson	Robinson
Alcock	Alcock	Hanet / Hannell	Hannell	Rogers	Roger
Amson	Almson	Hardy / Harding / Hardey	Hardy	Seamer / Seymour (B)	Seamo(u)r
Archambo	Archambo	Hart (B)	Hart	Shaw	Shaw
Ashly / Ashley	Ashly	Hastings	Haistings	Sheldon	Shelty
Askew	Askew	Hatfield	Hatfield	Simon / Symon	Simmons
Barbe	Barbott	Henry	Henry	Smith	Smith
Barbut / Barbot	Bartue	Hill	Hill	Snow (B)	Snow
Barnes	Barnes	Hoare / Hoar (B)	Hoare	Southam	Southam
Barthelemi / Barthelmy	Bartleme	Hodges	Hodges	Spencer	Spencer
Not found	Bartley	Hodsell	Hadsel	Sprage	Spragg
Beal / Beale	Beal	Holaday / Holiday / Holladay	Halliday	Spring	Spring
Beale / Beele	Beale	Holland	Holland	Stevens	Stevens
Birkhead / Burkitt	Burkitt	Hopkins	Hobkins	Stevenson	Steventon
Blisset / Bisset	Blisset	Horne (B)	Horne	Threlkield / Threlkeld	Threlgale
Boothby	Boothby	Housto(u)n / Howston	Houstown	*Not found*	Turrel
Not found	Boshad	How	How	Vaughan	Vaughan
Bracy / Brassey (B)	Brassay	Howard	Howard	Vedeau / Videau	Vedeau
Braddock	Praunock	Hutton	Hutton	Warter / Water	Warters
Bristow	Bristow	Jennings	Jennings	West	West
Brooks	Brooks	Jernegan / Journingham (B)	Jernegan	White	White
Browne	Brown	Jouet / Jowitt / Jovitt	Jovett	Wildman	Wildman
Carpender	Carpenter	Jourdain	Jourdaine	Wilkinson	Wilkinson
Carter	Carter	Kandler / Candler	Candler	Willaume	Willaume
Cartwright	Cartwright	Lamerie, de / Lemery *etc*	Delamarie	Williams	Williams
Cawthorne	Cawthorn	Laroch(e)	Laroch	Wyke	Wike
Chabbert / Chabbart	Chabert	Lepar / Lepper / Leaper	Leopard	Wynn / Winn / Winne	Wynn
Chambers (B)	Chambers	Lesage	Lesage	York(e)	York
Chartier	Chartier	Liger	Lieger		
Not found	Chenear	Lilley	Lilley	**Jewellers**	
Child (B)	Child	Loyd; Clark	Loyd & Clark		
Not found	Chirne	Ludlow	Ludlow	Admiral / Admirauld	Admiral
Clifton	Clifton	Luff(e)	Luff	*Not found*	Adrian
Cook(e)	Cook	Lukin(g)	Lukin	Arlaud / Arnoux	Arnaud
Cooper (B)	Cooper	Maitland / Martland	Makeland	Barker	Barcer
Courtauld / Courtaux	Courtould	Manners	Manners	Barron	Barrow
Cragg	Crag	Manning	Manning	Barry, du	Dubarry
Craig / Craige / Craggs	Cragg	Marlow(e)	Marlow	Bary, de / Debary	Debarry
Cranmer / Cranmore	Cranmore	Martin	Martin	*Not found*	Batut
Crespin / Crispin	Crispin	Merchant	Merchant	Brunet	Brunnett
Cuny / Cugny	Cuny	Merry	Merry	Chad	Chad
Curghey	Curghey	Middleton (B)	Midleton	Chardon	Chardon
Dailey / Dally	Dally	Montgomery	Montgomery	Chirac	Cherack
Davenport	Davenport			Cole	Cole

Name as found in publications and archives	Name as written in notebook
Corner / Connor	Corner
Corsier	Courtier
Cumbleford	Cumbleford
Dailey / Dally	Dally
Delafons / de la Fons	Delafonds
Demass	Duemas
Dubois	Du Bois
Duhamel	Duhamel
Not found	Dupain
Dutens / Dutems	Dutens
Eyemaker	Imacer
Fleureau / Floreau	Floreau
Not found	Flippo
Not found	Fountain
Not found	Fury
Gibson	Gibson
Not found	Gillard
Godfrey / Godfry	Godfrey
Gole	Gole
Green / Greene	Green
Hoosnell	Husnel
Hull	Hull
Jones	Jones
Jousselin / Jewslin	Joslin
Lacam	Lockan
Ladvocat / L'Advocat	Ladvocat
Lefeverie / Leafuber / Lefeaver	Lefavor
Not found	Lefong
Not found	Lockrum
Not found	Loyd
Manners	Manners
Not found	Marquar
Mayastre / Mayofara	M*****
Megault	Megault
Mesgret	Megrett
Not found	Nangle
Oliver	Oliver
Not found	Parry
Pattison	Pattison
Phillips	Flippo
Price	Price
Quillet	Quillet
Robinson	Robinson
Saule / Saul	Salt
Shapeau	Shoppo
Simmons	Simons
Thibault / Teboe	Thibauld
Treble / Trible	Treble
Turmeau	Turmeau
Turquand	Turquand
Wallis	Wallis
Wellington	Wessea

Toymen

Name as found in publications and archives	Name as written in notebook
Browne	Brown
Not found	Chenear
Deard(s)	Deard
Grimstead	Grimstead
Hurt	Hurt
Loyd; Clark	Loyd & Clark
Markham / Marcum	Marcum
Radford	Radford
Saunders	Saunders
Threlkield / Threlkeld	Threlgale
Wildey / Willdey	Wildy

Watchmakers

Name as found in publications and archives	Name as written in notebook
Abbott	Abbot
Alsop / Allsop	Alsop
Archambo / Archimbowe	Archambo
Badley	Bagley
Barrow	Barrow
Beauvais / Beauvau / Beavis	Beavois
Benn / Ben	Benn
Berry / Berrey	Berrey
Bilby	Bilby
Blanchard / Blainshard	Blanchard
Bradshaw	Bradshaw
Browne	Brown
Butterfeild / Butterfield	Butterfield
Camden / Campden	Cambden
Clark	Clark
Clay	Clay
Colly / Colley	Colly
Conyers / Conyars / Collier	Connier
Cooper	Cooper
Cox	Cox
Davis	Davis
Delander / Delaunder / De Lander	Delander
Deschamps / DeCharmes	Descharmes
Dudds	Dudds
Duhamel / du Hamel	Duhamel
Dunlop	Dunlop
Ellis	Ellis
Enderby	Endersby
Everall / Everell / Evereil	Everett
ffreeman / Furman	Freeman
Foot / Foote	Foot
Not found	Forterry
Not found	Fury
Ganneron / Ganero(o)n	Ganderoon
Gerrard / Guiraud / Jarrat / Garrard	Jeroet
Gibbs	Gibbs
Gibson / Gibbson	Gibson
Not found	Goodread
Graham / Grayham	Grayham
Gray	Gray
Gregg / Grigg	Grigg
Griffith	Griffiths
Grignion	Grigman
Hallifax	Hallifax
Hanet	Hannet
Harris	Harris
Not found	Harris
Harrison	Harrison
Not found	Harrison
Hatton	Hatton
Haydon / Hayden	Haydon
Hiccox / Hickox	Hiccox
Hilot / Hallett	Hillot
Hubert / Hubart	Hubbard
Jackson	Jackson
Jefferys / Jeffreys / Jefferies	Jeffries
Not found	Jourdaine
Kedden / Keddon / Keddin	Keddin
King	King
King	Parks & King
Kipling	Kipling
Lipscomb(e)	Lipscom
Lloyd / Loyd	Loyd
Lod(d)ington	Loddington

Name as found in publications and archives	Name as written in notebook
Long	Long
Martin	Martin
Martineau / Martin	Martineau
Massy / Massey	Massy
Molyns / Mullins	Molins
Morran / Mooran / Moran	Moran
Needham	Needham
Neve / Nene	Neve
Pain / Paine / Payne	Payne
Parks / Parkes	Parks & King
Pearce / Pierce	Pearce
Pepys	Pepys
Pinchbeck	Pinchbeck
Not found	Pupin
Purden / Purdon	Purden
Quelch	Quelch
Robinson	Robinson
Rooker	Roaker
Rousseau	Rousseau
Seddon	Sedon
Sidley / Sidey / Siday	Sidey
Simmonds / Simons	Simmons
Simson / Simpson	Simson
Skinner	Skinner
Smith	Smith
Stock	Stock
Thornburgh / Thornburg	Thornborough
Threlkeld / Threlcold	Threlgle
Toleson / Tolson	Tollson
Tomlin / Tomlyn	Tonlain
Tucker	Tucker
Turner	Turner
Vic, de / Vick	Vick
Whichcote	Wichcott
White	White
Wilson / Willson	Willson
Wright	Wright

Illustrations opposite:

55 *Thomas Colley, no962*
   Repeating watch, the case Stephen Goujon, 1755/56
56 *George Graham, no6460*
   Timepiece, the case John Ward, 1750/51
57 *Paul Beauvais, no593*
   Verge watch, the case 1708/09
58 *Henry Massy*
   Repeating watch, the case1710/11
59 *Daniel Delander, no567*
   Watch, the case William Jaques, 1729/30
60 *Joseph Martineau, no2767*
   Verge watch, the case 1754/55
61 *John Pepys, no3460*
   Watch, the case probably Ann Barugh, 1738/39, the chasing John Valentine Haidt
62 *George Graham, no570*
   Repeating watch, the case maker's mark WS, 1727/28, the chasing Ishmael Parbury

55

57

59

60

61

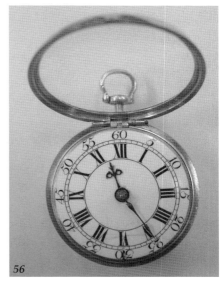

56

58

62

Streets

Notices

Notice	Beadle	Date	Names in notice	Trade	Address	Page
11503	Bodington	1726, 3 November	Ha(u)ll, Richard	Hertford carrier	Green Dragon, Bishopsgate	29
11528	Bodington	1726/7, 7 February	*Morris*		*Robin's coffee house*	29
11540	Bodington	1726/7, 8 March			*Robin's coffee house*	29
11581	Bodington	1727, 7 August	Benjamin Lambert Charron & Co Lambert, Sir John		*John Shipton's coffee house* Swithen's Alley, Royal Exchange	29
11582	Bodington	1727, 10 August	Brassey, Nath & Co Ray, Dan	Banker	*Baker's coffee house*	30
11585	Bodington	1727, 28 August	Twyford, William	Blacksmith	Blacksmiths Arms, Christchurch Surrey	21
			Barnet, Mr	Goldsmith	Tooly Street, Southwark	
11592	Bodington	1727, 22 September	Telles, Abraham Woodwards, Messrs Richard & Thomas	Bankers	*Robin's coffee house* Exchange Alley	29
11627	Bodington	1727, 21 December	Wentworth, Thomas Brown, Mr (jnr)	Watchmaker	Sarum *Palsgrave Head coffee house*	30
11639	Pyne	1727, 16 February	Telles, Abraham Woodwards, Messrs		*Robin's coffee house* Exchange Alley	30
11697	Pyne	1728, 9 October	Seamer, James	Goldsmith	Flower-de-Luce, Fleet Street	121
11736	Pyne	1728, 14 March	Randel, Christopher *goldsmith's shop advertised*	Gardener	nr Blue Anchor, Bermondsey *nr Cross Keys Tavern, Hatton Garden*	20
11711	Pyne	1728, 6 December	Levy, Jacob (jnr)	Jeweller	Upper end, Haymarket *Chadwell's coffee house*	20
11714	Pyne	1728, 18 December	Whitmore, William Pepys, William	Banker	*Jonathan's coffee house* Lombard Street	30
11746	Pyne	1729, 13 May	Stephen Wiggin		*Baker's coffee house*	20
11773	Pyne	1729, 11 September	Gines, Richard	Goldsmith	Rose & Crown, Lombard Street	14
11778	Pyne	1729, 6 October	William King	Watchmaker	*Baker's coffee house*	15
11787	Pyne	1729, 18 November	Elliot, William	Goldsmith	nr London Stone	24
11790	Pyne	1729, 24 November	Elliott, William	Goldsmith	nr London Stone	30
11863	Pyne	1730, 15 July	Hellier, Philip Cardigan, Earl of Brown, Mr		*Palsgrave's Head coffee house*	30
11874	Pyne	1730, 7 September	Bentley, Benjamin	Goldsmith	Ring, London Bridge	21
11908	Pyne	1730, 7 January	Telles, Abraham Woodward, Messrs Favre, Isaac	Jeweller	*Garraway's coffee house* Exchange Alley *Shadwell's coffee house* Golden Head, Fountain Court, Strand	31
11953	Pyne	1731, 24 June	Edwards, John Mustaphia, Benjamin		*Baker's coffee house*	30
12610	Jenkes	1737, 13 February	Deards, Mr	Toyman	St Dunstan's Church, Fleet Street	141
		1692	Hoar(e), Richard	Goldsmith	Golden Bottle, Fleet Street	106

Bibliography

Abbreviations for sources in section 3 (The Tradesmen) are given in bold at the end of each entry below.

Publications

Baillie, G.H., *Watchmakers and Clockmakers of the World*, NAG Press Ltd, London 1963. **Baillie**

Baillie, G.H. (ed), Loomes, Brian, *Watchmakers and Clockmakers of the World*, vol 2, 1976. **Baillie vol 2**

Baillie, G.H., Ilbert, C. & Chitton, C. (eds), *Britten's Old Clocks and Watches and their Makers*, 9th edn, 1982, Methuen, London 1982. **Britten**

Beattie, J.M., *Crime & the Courts in England, 1660-1800*, Clarendon Press, Oxford 1986.

Collins, A.J., *Jewels and Plate of Queen Elizabeth - the 1754 Inventory*, edited from Harley MS.1650 and Stowe MS.555 in British Museum, London 1955.

Collins *Concise Dictionary of the English Language*, 2nd edn, Glasgow 1988.

Edgcumbe, R., *The Art of the Gold Chaser in Eighteenth-Century London*, Oxford University Press in assn with Victoria & Albert Museum, London 2000.

Forbes, J.S., *Hallmark*, Unicorn Press, Redhill 1998.

Gentleman's Magazine, The

Glanville, P. & Goldsborough, J.F., *Women Silversmiths 1685-1845, Works from the Collection of The National Museum of Women in the Arts*, Washington DC, in assn with Thames and Hudson, 1990.

Grimwade, A.G., *London Goldsmiths 1697–1837, Their Marks & Lives*, 3rd edn, Redwood Press Ltd, London 1990. **Grimwade**

Hare, S. M., 'The History of the Goldsmiths' Company from their Records', *Proceedings of the Society of Silver Collectors*, vol II, nos 11-13, 1982.

Harris, M., *London Newspapers in the Age of Walpole - A Study of the Origins of the Modern English Press*, Associated University Presses, Cranbury, NJ; London and Mississanga, Ontario 1987

Heal, Sir Ambrose, *The London Goldsmiths 1200-1800*, reprint, David and Charles (Publishers) Ltd, Newton Abbot 1972. **Heal**

Hilton-Price, F.G., *A Handbook of London Bankers*, The Leadenhall Press, London 1876. **Hilton-Price**

Jefferson, L., *Wardens' Accounts and Court Minute Books of the Goldsmiths' Mistery of London 1334-1446*, The Boydell Press, Woodbridge 2003.

Lillywhite, B., *London Coffee Houses*, George Allen & Unwin Ltd, London 1963.

Murdoch, T., 'Early Warning System, Carriers; Walks in the 18th Century', *Country Life*, 2 November 1989.

Murdoch, T., *Proceedings of the Huguenot Society of Great Britain & Ireland*, vol XXVI, ch 8, pp241-57, 1994-97, Bigwood and Staple, Bridgwater. **Murdoch**

Museum of London, exh cat, *The Quiet Conquest - The Huguenots 1685-1985*, London 1985. **Quiet Conquest**

Prideaux, Sir W. S., *The Charities under the management of the Goldsmiths' Company being An Account of their Foundation and History*, Eyre & Spottiswoode 1899, private circulation.

Prideaux, Sir W.S., *Memorials of Goldsmiths' Company, being Gleanings from their Records Between the Years 1335 and 1815*, vols I & II, Eyre & Spottiswood, private circulation.

Rickards, M., *Encyclopaedia of Ephemera*, British Library, St Edmundsbury Press, Bury St Edmunds 2000.

Shoemaker, R., *The London Mob, Violence & Disorder in the 18th Century*, Hambledon & London 2004.

Spence, C., *London in the 1690s - A Social Atlas*, Centre for Metropolitan History, University of London 2000.

The majority of these publications are available at Guildhall Library.

Other Sources

Burney Collection of Early Newspapers, British Library, Euston Road, London. **BL**

Burney Collection of Early Newspapers, British Library Colindale, Greater London. **BLCol**

Camden Local Studies and Archives Centre, Holborn Library, Theobalds Road, London. **CLS**
   On microfilm: Poor Rate records: (St Andrew, Holborn; St George and St Giles, Bloomsbury; St Peter Saffron Hill)

Clothworkers, The Worshipful Company of, archives.

Corporation of London Record Office.

Goldsmiths, The Worshipful Company of, archives.

Guildhall Art Gallery, Corporation of London, Aldermanbury, London.

Guildhall Library, Corporation of London Libraries, Aldermanbury, London
   Printed Books: **GL**
   Prints, Maps and Drawings: **GLPrints**
   Manuscripts: **GLMS**

Hart, William, Extracts of entries of London Signs, 1649-1767, vols 19-25,MSS. **Hart**
Livery Company archives (The Worshipful Company of Fishmongers, The Worshipful Company of Clockmakers and The Worshipful Company of Clothworkers).
On microfilm: Land Tax Assessment Rates (parishes within the City of London and the surrounding parishes, including St Dunstan, Wapping; St George-in-the-East, Middx; St Paul, Shadwell).
Sun Insurance records.

Institute of Historical Research, University of London, Section BC25. **WPB**
   1749 Westminster Pollbook.

London Metropolitan Archives, 40 Northampton Road, London. **LMA**
   Poor Rate records (St Lukes, Shoreditch; Tower Hamlets).
   Sewer Rates for Spitalfields.

Mercers, The Worshipful Company of, archives .

Museum of London, London Wall, London.

National Archives, Kew, Richmond, Surrey.

Old Bailey Proceedings online, (www.oldbaileyonline.org.uk). **OBP**

St Bride Printing Library, Fleet Street, London.

Victoria & Albert Museum, Cromwell Road, and Blythe House (Hammersmith), London,
   Prints and Drawings dept. **V&A**

Westminster City Archives, St Anne's Street, Westminster, London. **WAC**
   On microfilm: Poor Rate records for St John's, Westminster; St Margaret's, (including St James's Piccadilly), Westminster; St George's, Hanover Square; St Martin-in-the-Fields; St Anne's Soho; St Paul's, Covent Garden; St Mary le Strand; St Clement Danes).
   On CD rom: 1749 Westminster Pollbook.

63 Notice no12610 dated 1737. Robert Jenkes became Beadle in 1732 following the death of Benjamin Pyne.

General index

This index does not include tradesmen listed in the Walks, for whom see Section 3 (pp81–129) and pp132–136; nor does it include every tradesman (mostly watchmakers) mentioned in the text of pp81–129.
See also p138 (streets) and p139 (people and addresses mentioned in notices).

Notes

THE SILVER SOCIETY

 Silver Studies is the journal of the Silver Society. It is recognised as the most valuable specialist publication for the study of silver. Much of the new research carried out in recent years has been published in the journal.

It is the intention of the Society occasionally to publish special issues of *Silver Studies*, in addition to the regular journal, focusing on a particular subject of research and funded by its research and endowment funds. In 2004 the Society published *Silver and the Church*, a catalogue of the exhibition held at Goldsmiths' Hall. *The Warning Carriers* is the first product of the Society's policy of actively promoting research projects that go beyond what can be published in its annual journal.

Silver Studies is published annually, in the autumn. It contains papers read to the Society at its meetings and other articles. Regular features include recently published books, objects which have appeared on the market, museum acquisitions and contemporary silver.

You can subscribe to *Silver Studies* without being a member of the Society. Annual subscription: £15 reduced to £12 if paid by standing order.

The Silver Society was founded in 1958 to advance the study of silver of all periods, places and forms. Its object is also to widen the appreciation and knowledge of work in silver and gold, as well as plated wares and other metals.

The Society welcomes research from authors on all aspects of the study of silver and related subjects. Please contact the Editor at the address below.

If you would like information about membership of the Society, subscription to *Silver Studies*, or the Society's funding of special projects, please contact the Secretary or see the Society's website.

The Society's website contains application forms, information about the Society's activities, a cumulative index and a list of contents of back issues of the journal, most of which are still available.

The Silver Society
Box 246
2 Lansdowne Row
London W1J 6HL

Email:
Secretary: secretary@thesilversociety.org
Editor: editor@thesilversociety.org

The Silver Society is a registered charity, no279352